Hate Speech against Women Online

SOCIAL
IMAGINARIES

Social Imaginaries

Series Editors: Suzi Adams, Paul Blokker, Natalie J. Doyle, Saulius Geniusas, John W. M. Krummel and Jeremy C. A. Smith

This groundbreaking series aims to investigate social imaginaries from theoretical, comparative, historical, and interdisciplinary perspectives. Its objective is to foster challenging research on the burgeoning but heterogeneous field of social imaginaries, on the one hand, and the related field of the creative imagination, on the other. The series seeks to publish rigorous and innovative research that reflects the international, multiregional and interdisciplinary scope across these fields.

Titles in the Series

Ricoeur and Castoriadis in Discussion
    Edited by Suzi Adams
Productive Imagination
    Edited by Saulius Geniusas and Dmitri Nikulin
Stretching the Limits of Productive Imagination
    Edited by Saulius Geniusas
Social Imaginaries: Critical Interventions
    Edited by Suzi Adams and Jeremy C. A. Smith
The Labyrinth of Modernity: Horizons, Pathways and Mutations
    Johann P. Arnason
The Creative Imagination: Indeterminacy and Embodiment in the Writings of Kant, Fichte, and Castoriadis
    Jodie Lee Heap
Hate Speech against Women Online: Concepts and Countermeasures
    Louise Richardson-Self

Hate Speech against Women Online

Concepts and Countermeasures

Louise Richardson-Self

ROWMAN & LITTLEFIELD
Lanham • Boulder • New York • London

Published by Rowman & Littlefield
An imprint of The Rowman & Littlefield Publishing Group, Inc.
4501 Forbes Boulevard, Suite 200, Lanham, Maryland 20706
www.rowman.com

86-90 Paul Street, London EC2A 4NE

British Library Cataloguing in Publication Information Available

Library of Congress Cataloging-in-Publication Data

Names: Richardson-Self, Louise, author.
Title: Hate speech against women online : concepts and countermeasures / Louise Richardson-Self.
Description: Lanham, Maryland : Rowman & Littlefield, [2021] | Series: Social imaginaries | Includes bibliographical references and index.
Identifiers: LCCN 2021034828 (print) | LCCN 2021034829 (ebook) | ISBN 9781538147795 (cloth) | ISBN 9781538147801 (epub)
Subjects: LCSH: Women—Social conditions. | Online hate speech—Prevention. | Sex discrimination against women.
Classification: LCC HQ1155 .R53 2021 (print) | LCC HQ1155 (ebook) | DDC 305.4—dc23
LC record available at https://lccn.loc.gov/2021034828
LC ebook record available at https://lccn.loc.gov/2021034829

ISBN 9781538147818 (paperback)

This book is dedicated in loving memory to my stepfather, Greg Self.
Greggy, you are sorely missed.

Contents

List of Figures and Tables

FIGURES

TABLES

Acknowledgments

I would like to begin by acknowledging that this book was written on lutru-wita (Tasmania) Aboriginal land. I pay my respects to elders past and present, to the many Aboriginal people that did not make elder status, and to the Tasmanian Aboriginal community that continue to care for the country.

The research and production of this book were primarily supported by an Australian Research Council Discovery Early Career Researcher Award (DE190100719). Some of the arguments elaborated in chapters 2, 3, 4 and 5 first appeared in Louise Richardson-Self, 'Woman-Hating: On Misogyny, Sexism, and Hate Speech', *Hypatia* 33 (2018), 256–272. Ethics approval for this study (Title: Hate Speech Against Women Online) was granted by the University of Tasmania, Reference number: H0018328. Special thanks to the editors of the Social Imaginaries series – Suzi Adams, Paul Blokker, Natalie Doyle, John Krummel and Jeremy Smith – for supporting this manuscript.

I would like to thank my colleagues at the University of Tasmania, whose support of my early research career has been invaluable. Special thanks in particular to Lucy Tatman, Dirk Baltzly, James Chase, Hannah Stark and Douglas Ezzy, as well as the many undergraduate and postgraduate students who have engaged with me and my research over the past few years. Were it not for UTAS' generous facilitation of external mentoring sessions with Katharine Gelber, my grant application may well have had a different outcome. I would like to thank Kath for her immense support as a mentor, which guided me in pursuing my early hate speech publications, and for her introduction to a broader community of hate speech scholars across the globe. I am particularly thankful for the invitation to participate in a panel with her, Anjalee de Silva, Alexander Brown, Erik Bleich and Matteo Bonotti at the International Political Science Association Annual Conference (2018). I am also grateful to her for the invitation to attend the Free Speech and its

Discontents research seminar at the Center for Human Values, Princeton University (2017). Additionally, I want to thank Sarah Sorial. Without her support immediately following my graduation, not to mention her guidance through the masses of scholarship on free speech and hate speech, I would not be where I am today. For her continuing mentorship, I must thank Moira Gatens. I am so grateful for her advice and feedback in all aspects of my career. Ours is a dynamic I hope to emulate for junior scholars, especially women and minorities in philosophy. I owe all of my success to her.

An institution greatly supportive of my early career is the University of Connecticut, in particular, the Humanities Institute directed by Michael Lynch. I was a residential fellow of the Humility and Conviction in Public Life Project in 2017, and have since returned a number of times to conduct and disseminate my research among the lively research community they have established. I would like to thank the staff and graduate students from the Humanities Institute, the Human Rights Institute, and the Philosophy Department who have generously engaged with my research. In addition, I would like to thank researchers at Monash University, University of Exeter, Universiteit Utrecht, University of Melbourne, University of Sydney, University of Queensland, University of Western Australia, Wuhan University and Yale University for inviting me to deliver my research at these institutions. In particular, I would like to thank Robert Simpson for organising the Philosophical Approaches to Hate Speech research workshop at University College London, and Lynne Tirrell for organising the politics and language research workshop at University of Connecticut. I would also like to thank audiences of the great many conferences I have presented at over the past few years, especially the Australasian Association of Philosophy, Australian Political Theory and Philosophy, Australasian Society for Continental Philosophy and Society for Applied Philosophy annual conferences. To those who have commented on earlier chapters of this manuscript – Millicent Churcher, Ben Cross, Moira Gatens, Casey Johnson, Suzy Killmister, Gabrielle Mardon, Claire McCarthy, Jenny Richardson – thank you. Your comments have immensely improved the final product, and I am so appreciative that you took the time to provide me with feedback.

And now, a strange sort of acknowledgement. Halfway through 2020 – after COVID-19 had already upset the routines of daily life – I suffered a dramatic pain flair and a general worsening of my overall chronic pain from which I still have not recovered (and may not ever recover, since no one really knows what's causing my pain to begin with). The last 9+ months have been a merry-go-round of medications and hospital admissions, and I am only now just settling into a 'new normal' (which I hope won't be my 'normal' forever). I want to acknowledge the limitations this liminal illness has placed upon my capacity to undertake research – it has affected me more dramatically than I could have imagined; I simply cannot work the way that I used to. My pain is invisible, but it is ever present, and it has made me very aware of who and what matters most to me. I am learning how to live an adjusted life which makes space to tend to this pain every day in every way: at work, socially and privately. Having my two fat and fuzzy companions, Mighty and Harlequin, has been a great comfort for the soul.

There are several people whose support has helped me through both the pain flair and the process of writing the manuscript. My parents, Ian and Jenny (especially my mumma bear, being one of only two people allowed to see me in hospital due to COVID-19 restrictions). My partner, Ilusha (my other hospital guest). My dear friends Libby, Bec, Kat, Fig, Calum, Jess, Danny, Anne, Daniel, Naomi, Andy and Stef. If not for these people – to talk to, play trivia with, cry with, joke with, dance with – I'm sure the process of healing and book writing would have been all the less achievable. To Ilusha, in particular. Thank you for your unending support of my health and career, and for ensuring that through both there will always be enough space for us to be able to enjoy a fun-filled and love-filled life. Thank you for choosing to be my family. Thank you for all the things you have sacrificed. There are no words to describe how much your presence in my life means to me. I love you deeply.

Introduction

Hate Speech against Women Online

Feminist maybe.feminine? no way. (Man)	*Who is this feminazi? Never heard of him. (Man)*
She's gotta be a lez. (Woman)	*she,s a female? Dam. (Man)*
Stupid Cow. (Man)	*A dim witted tart with slag tags [tattoos]. (Man)*
Stupid hypocritical imbecile. What a racist bitch. Eat shit scrag. (Man)	*She needs to spend her time more constructively by making me a sandwich. (Man)*

In 2018, I wrote an article entitled 'Offending White Men' and published it in the academic journal *Feminist Philosophy Quarterly*.[1] It was about the noticeable trend of white people, particularly men, making complaints to the Australian Human Rights Commission claiming to be victims of racist hate speech. To critique the logic motivating such acts, I drew from the blog posts of two men who had recently made complaints about a public state-ment made by Federal MP Linda Burney (an Aboriginal woman) regarding the *Racial Discrimination Act 1975* (Cth). In line with the view I defend in this book – that one can only be a victim of hate speech if they are a mem-ber of an oppressed group – I argued that these complainants were not only wrong to think they were truly harmed by perceived 'anti-white' and 'anti-male' speech, but that their complaints were doing a disservice to people of colour by trivialising the harm that hate speech foments. Not too long after its publication, I received a thoroughly condescending email from one of the men whose blog I had cited, 'to thank [me] so much for the laughter [I] provided to [his] wife and [him]', informing me that some unnamed person from my institution was responsible for forwarding him the piece. I didn't respond, though I was *very* tempted to follow through on his offer to draw a

1

cartoon to accompany my article. (He is a political cartoonist by profession, and I still wonder to this day what that depiction would have looked like.) Then, a few days later, I was tagged on Twitter. That Tweet, in turn, led me to a Facebook post by the other man (a failed Senate candidate) whose blog I cited. He had published a reply to my article on his blog, including a photo of me that he'd found online. Then he posted it on his public Facebook page. From there it was widely shared. Some of those shares were public, others private. The quotes you see above were all comments made of me on Facebook in response to that blog post. I have to admit, it *was* anxiety inducing. I wondered what might happen next. Would this get out of hand? Would people start targeting me directly? Would I be driven offline? I know of other feminists who have endured an onslaught of online hatred just because they have publicly advocated for marginalised groups' equality (i.e. they called out privileged groups for the ways they perpetuate, exploit and benefit from an unjust hierarchical status quo). So, naturally, I wondered whether this incident would blow over, or whether it would turn into a sustained campaign of harassment, leading to invasions of privacy (e.g. doxxing), or even threaten my job security.

Before this incident, I already had an interest in the problem of hate speech against women online – I had recently published my article 'Woman-Hating'[2] and had submitted a grant application to the Australian Research Council proposing to undertake further research on the issue (the result of such funding is this very book) – but this was my first time as the token subject of online misogyny. I was a nobody, until, for a weekend, I became a somebody – a *woman* deserving of public vitriol for my dim-witted (because stupid and hypocritical) views. And then, just like that, my article and I faded back into obscurity. It was a storm in a teacup after all. Weirdly, this event almost felt like a rite of passage. Since social media became a mainstay of daily life, I felt I could be hit with aggressive online misogyny at any time. This was 'always at the horizon of social imagination'.[3] After all, as Emma Jane remarks, 'If you're not being called ugly, fat, and slutty on the internet, odds are you're a man. Or a woman pretending to be a man'.[4] But what intrigued me most about this abuse, what made it seem distinct from the other accounts of online misogyny that I had read, was the fact that *I didn't really receive it.* While I was the *subject* of the speech, I wasn't *targeted* with online misogyny. I stumbled onto these comments. No one came after me (save that one condescending email and one Tweet, neither of which constituted hate speech). I was spoken *about*, I wasn't spoken *to*. Hence, I wondered, if this speech was not for me, then who was the speech for? Why say it at all? What does the speech do if the subject is not around to witness it? And who does it do it to?

In the hate speech literature, scholars frequently foreground first-personal harms to individual targets of hate speech to show why hate speech must be stopped. Effects like 'somatic responses, such as increased heart rate, elevated blood pressure, sweating, shaking, and, some time later, effects such as insomnia, anxiety, and lethargy', or 'PTSD symptoms'[5]; 'extreme emotional distress and even suicide'[6]; the 'pain, anguish, psychic harm, and related forms of distress' that occurs when one hears or reads insults[7]; even consequences rendering specific individuals 'undateable, unemployable, and unable to partake in online activities'.[8] 'Online abuse', says Mary Anne Franks, 'jeopardizes victims' physical safety, employment opportunities, educational achievement, personal relationships, and psychological health'.[9] Yet, while it is true that the comments about me could affect my 'ability to feel safe in "real" space, to make a living, and to engage publicly and politically',[10] and while it is true that I could have suffered tremendously from 'anxiety, depression, suicidal ideation, isolation, loss of employment prospects and relationship disintegration',[11] the fact of the matter is that I didn't suffer tremendously as an individual. But that, alone, doesn't mean the speech was harmless.

I believe that hate speech can do all of these things to its targets. Yet, I worry that this individuated, localised approach to detailing the harms of hate speech does not capture the effect hate speech has on social *groups*, namely, by maintaining unjust hierarchies of identity power.[12] Our image of group harm is woefully inadequate, and I agree with Margaret Thornton's assessment that it is impossible 'to compress a group interest [specifically, non-discrimination] within the constraints of the Nineteenth Century liberal conception of an individualised harm', and that objecting to discrimination too often creates an impossible situation wherein an individual complainant has to 'bear the entire onus of proof for what is effectively a classwide violation'.[13] This book is my attempt to meet 'this burden [that] is virtually insuperable'[14] – to show that such speech instantiates *group harm*, and to argue that we must urgently attend to the problematic social practice of hate speaking against women online. I show how hate speech, even when it is about specific women, affects women as a class. The claim I defend here is that hate speech is first and foremost a flex of social power, a *corrective action* which shows women users where lies the line of 'tolerable' behaviour. It does not matter whether an individual subject of such speech happens to bear witness to it, because the subject – as an individual – isn't really who the speech is intending (in the phenomenological sense).[15] Hate speech works to affect women (the target group) as a group via exposure.[16] Certain women become *tokens* insofar as they variously threaten the patriarchal status quo. That is, they are 'representative targets', meaning they are 'standing in imaginatively for a large swathe of others', and so the speech act must be understood as an assault on *women*.[17] Hate speech against a specific woman is, in fact, an expressive form of discrimination against women *per se*, and one that results in a hostile online environment. The creation and maintenance of hostile cyberspaces, in turn, constrains the way women are able to inhabit and to act in such spaces. This matters because, as Jessica Megarry summarises, 'equality online is dependent not only on the ability to *occupy* a space', an ability that is lessened when a hostile environment has been created, 'but to be able to *influence it* and *speak without fear* of threat or harassment'.[18] Hate speech against women online is a discriminatory act of subjugation; such treatment constitutes an injustice that must be rectified.

To anticipate an objection. While I take the primary harm of such general and token-targeting types of hate speech to be a status-based harm to women as a group, others may not be convinced that all the expressions I discuss herein are tantamount to a status-based harm against *all* women. A commentator may proclaim 'I don't have a problem with *women*, I only have a problem with women *like her*'. (This defence could be employed by the speakers I cite in the precis to this introduction, for instance.) But what exactly do women *like me* and like those targeted in my data set have in common? Our being women *and* also public influencers (as teachers, writers, politicians, etc.) whose social positions are backed by institutional power dynamics and norms that lend us a certain platform and degree of credibility; we are women who have the audacity to challenge the status quo. All women are affected by this intradivisional speech because the speech is really a warning to any and all other women who might dare to act like us. These comments *preemptively* 'put women in their place when they seem to have ideas beyond their station'.[19] They do this by identifying a specific Bad Woman or by castigating the figure of the Bad Woman more generally. By implicature, if some women are bad, then it must be possible to be seen as a Good Woman. (Note the capitalisation, which indicates I am referring to imaginal tropes applied to women, not to any actually existing persons.) This speech therefore forms part of a system of reward and punishment which captures all women, thereby strengthening a patriarchal status quo, making it quite clear to the woman-user reading the comments how she ought to act.[20]

This book proposes a social imaginaries framework to both understand what images of Woman (Good and Bad), Man, Individuals and Average Internet Users are reproduced through hate speech against women online, and to think through how we might imaginatively respond to this social practice. I argue that hate speech functions in a wider web of discriminating acts which subjugate women. This wider web involves institutional oversights (like inadequate organisational policies and procedures for removing harmful online content), the entrenchment of gender stereotypes in the Anglosphere today, power imbalances between men and women (as well as the imbalances produced through our intersectional identities), the behavioural and normative reproduction of patriarchal ideology in the context of the Anglosphere and other forms of violence against women. In this book, I acknowledge that hate speech is only a narrow subset of woman-subjugating speech, but it is a particularly egregious one (insofar as these speech acts constitute forms of systemic violence). Ultimately, while the specific issue of hate speech against women online will require tailored responses, I also believe that we need broader challenges to the central social imaginaries that make the social practice of hate speaking against women online not only possible, but ordinary, normal.

OUTLINE OF THE BOOK

Chapter 1 provides the theoretical framework for this investigation. It introduces the concepts 'social imaginaries' and 'imagined subjects', looking at the ways in which images, impressions and affects work together to motivate normative behaviours, establish social practices, generate specific narratives about the world as we know it and become institutionalised and normalised over time. For the purposes of this book, I am interested in the contours of the dominant Western social imaginary shared by the contemporary Anglosphere, and in particular, Australia, the United States and the United Kingdom. Importantly, one of the ways we can understand social imaginaries (i.e. one of the ways we can understand our world of experience) is by analysing images. This is a productive endeavour, since 'imagery may smooth over problems, close gaps, and/or cover a contradiction'.[21] Hence, images – of identities, harm, and cyberspace – are the central focus throughout this book. I interrogate them looking to stir up epistemic and affective friction,[22] which may, in turn, spark the production of new images that help us understand our worlds anew and suggest alternative courses of action and social practices that bring about just futures.

The purpose of chapter 2 is to elaborate on the nature of Women's subordination and Men's superordination under patriarchy using the social imaginaries framework articulated in chapter 1. This chapter starts by arguing that the central sexual imaginary is patriarchal. Next, it argues that Western patriarchy is *fraternal* patriarchy. Then it explicates sexism and two types of misogyny that together sustain the patriarchal status quo. Finally, it considers gendered relations of dominance and submission specifically in relation to sexual agency and the problem of sexual objectification. The aim of this chapter is thus to highlight the ways in which sex and gender continue to operate as a locus of oppression in the Western liberal democracies of the Anglosphere today, for only then is it possible to fully comprehend the nature and gravity of hate speech against women online.

In chapter 3, I turn directly to the issue of which expressions should be understood as acts of hate speech. Surprisingly, little academic attention has been paid to the scope of the concept 'hate speech'.[23] However, one recent, compelling attempt has been made by Katharine Gelber.[24] She calls it the *systemic discrimination approach* to identifying hate speech. Essentially, Gelber argues that speech is only an instance of systemic discrimination when it subordinates its target (a socially salient group, for example, a gender category), and its target is *already* an oppressed class of people (e.g. women or non-binary people, as opposed to men). I am largely in agreement with the constraints of this approach; however, I argue for a slightly narrower conception of 'hate speech', including only those expressions which systemically subordinate target through linguistic violence, for such violent speech represents attempts to shut down women's movement through and voice in public social spaces; they 'are not intended to facilitate or begin a dialogue' with the subjects affected.[25]

Having specified what constitutes hate speech, in chapter 4, I analyse the images of Woman (Good and Bad) conveyed in my dataset. Surprisingly, 'there is little empirical research, either qualitative or quantitative, on gendered-based hate speech in online environments'.[26] Hence, these data are also evidence for the claim that hate speech against women online is prolific, even in 'ordinary' cyberspaces. Mine is a qualitative analysis, though I do provide some basic statistics to give the reader a sense of scope. In the discussion, I argue the images of Woman (and, tacitly, Man) that are reproduced in hate speech work to maintain patriarchy as the central sexual imaginary, thereby not only subjugating women (through the violent speech act itself) but also through their constitution of cyberspaces hostile spaces for women. To navigate these hostile spaces, women are forced to undertake a kind of defensive bodywork to shield themselves from harm in these spaces as best they can. Since this bodywork is largely missed by prominent imag(in)ings of the harm of hate speech, I suggest re-imagining this harm in a way that better captures the constant threat of hostile attack and dangerous exposure.

Chapter 5 evaluates the countermeasures we might take to end hate speech against women online, while acknowledging that unfortunately none on its own, or even in concert, is likely to be a panacea. These include user-to-user strategies, such as utilising existing telecommunications laws or introducing legislation banning gendered hate speech. Others are state-to-platform strategies, such as legislating for the issuing of take-down notices, reclassifying platforms as publishers, or classifying some users of social media platforms (like legacy news media) as publishers on those platforms. Others still are platform-driven changes, like introducing or upholding community standards against hate speech, phasing out algorithms of 'personalisation' to avoid digital filter bubbles, considering evolving platforms into paid services in exchange for the removal of advertisements (akin, for example, to Spotify), continuing to develop algorithms that can identify hate speech, and hiring, training, compensating and caring for more moderators. Finally, I consider the popularly proposed remedy to hate speech: counterspeech. While counterspeech, in its basic formulation as 'speaking back', has significant problems, we can re-imagine what forms counterspeech might take. I then argue that *counter-imagining* is where we should invest our energies, since this underscores all efforts towards social change.

Chapter 6 furthers the proposed countermeasure of counter-imagining by elucidating what some of our central images of cyberspace are, and evaluating these to determine whether they, themselves, contribute to the proliferation of hate speech against women online. Specifically, I focus on four imagings of cyberspace: cyberspace as site of the public sphere; cyberspace as expansive and free, and, as such, home to free speech; cyberspace as a space with a dark side and cyberspace as home to the anonymous Troll. The former two of these images may be described as idyllic, the latter two realistic. Recall, however, that imagery can smooth over problems, hide gaps, and cover over contradictions. This is true for both sets. I demonstrate how these images work against women, demonstrating these must be either altered or rejected. Yet, the rejection and even alteration of meaning-generating images can leave us in a state of *meaning vertigo*, an 'unsettling emptiness at the level of social meaning' that triggers 'an urgent project of social meaning clarification'.[27] This can be problematic if it triggers a return to what is already known and understood – namely, the status quo one hopes to alter.

In the case of hate speech against women online, the project of imaginal (r)evolution will surely prove difficult. We need alternative resonant images of Women (and Men, and people with other genders), of 'hate speech', of the *harm* that hate speech generates, and alternate images of cyberspace(s) and the role of internet technologies in our social lives. Thus, to conclude this book, I elaborate on six necessary (but not sufficient) conditions that must be met for new or re-appropriated images to take on new life as central images that can spread throughout the dominant Western social imaginary: contradiction, desire, power, critique, resonance and time. While images that meet these criteria are not guaranteed to become a sedimented element in the dominant (Western) social imaginary, nonetheless these features offer some practical guidance for our necessary pursuit of gender justice.

NOTES

1. Louise Richardson-Self, 'Offending White Men: Racial Vilification, Misrecognition, and Epistemic Injustice', *Feminist Philosophy Quarterly* 4 (2018): 1–25.

2. Louise Richardson-Self, 'Woman-Hating: On Misogyny, Sexism, and Hate Speech', *Hypatia* 33 (2018): 256–272.

3. Iris Marion Young, *Justice and the Politics of Difference* (Princeton: Princeton University Press, 1990), 62.

4. Emma Jane, *Misogyny Online: A Short and Brutish History* (London: Sage Swifts, 2017), 17.

5. Susan Brison, 'Speech, Harm, and The Mind-Body Problem in First Amendment Jurisprudence', *Legal Theory* 4 (1998): 49, 45.

6. James Weinstein, 'Cyber Harassment and Free Speech: Drawing the Line Online', in *Free Speech in the Digital Age*, ed. Susan Brison and Katharine Gelber (Oxford: Oxford University Press, 2019), 53.

7. Frederick Schauer, 'Recipes, Plans, Instructions, and the Free Speech Implications of Words That Are Tools', in *Free Speech in the Digital Age*, ed. Susan Brison and Katharine Gelber (Oxford: Oxford University Press, 2019), 77.

8. Danielle Keats Citron, 'Restricting Speech To Protect It', in *Free Speech in the Digital Age*, ed. Susan Brison and Katharine Gelber (Oxford: Oxford University Press, 2019), 130.

9. Mary Anne Franks, '"Not Where Bodies Live": The Abstraction of Internet Expression', in *Free Speech in the Digital Age*, ed. Susan Brison and Katharine Gelber (Oxford: Oxford University Press, 2019), 140.

10. Soraya Chemaly, 'Demographics, Design, and Free Speech: How Demographics Have Produced Social Media Optimized for Abuse and The Silencing of Marginalized Voices', in *Free Speech in the Digital Age*, ed. Susan Brison and Katharine Gelber (Oxford: Oxford University Press, 2019), 150.

11. Anastasia Powell and Nicola Henry, *Sexual Violence in a Digital Age* (London: Palgrave Macmillan, 2017), 62.

12. Matthew Costello and James Hawdon, 'Hate Speech in Online Spaces', in *The Palgrave Handbook of Cybercrime and Cyberdeviance*, ed. Thomas Holt and Adam Bossler (Cham: Springer Nature, 2020), 1405.

13. Margaret Thornton, 'Affirmative Action, Merit, and the Liberal State', *Australian Journal of Law and Society* 2 (1985): 34.

14. Thornton, 'Affirmative Action', 34.

15. Specifically, this is a Merleau-Pontyan view of operative intentionality: 'intentionality is a practical directedness toward the world that is not necessarily present to reflective consciousness but is instead made manifest in the daily operations of a person's life'. See: Jennifer McWeeny, 'Operative Intentionality', in *50 Key Concepts for a Critical Phenomenology*, ed. Gail Weiss, Ann V. Murphy, and Gayle Salamon (Evanston: Northwestern University Press, 2020), 255. All speech acts have a certain 'directedness', deliberate *and* non-deliberate, even when one surprises oneself with what is said.

16. Costello and Hawdon, 'Hate Speech', 1401–1405.

17. Kate Manne, *Down Girl: The Logic of Misogyny* (Oxford: Oxford University Press, 2018), 58.

18. Jessica Megarry, 'Online Incivility or Sexual Harassment? Conceptualising Women's Experiences in the Digital Age', *Women's Studies International Forum* 47

(2014): 46, my emphasis. Bianca Fileborn makes the same point. See: Bianca Fileborn, 'Justice 2.0: Street Harassment Victims' Use of Social Media and Online Activism as Sites of Informal Justice', *British Journal of Criminology* 57 (2017): 1482.

19. Manne, *Down Girl*, 69.

20. Manne, *Down Girl*, 192; Millicent Churcher and Moira Gatens, 'Reframing Honour in Heterosexual Imaginaries', *Angelaki: Journal of the Theoretical Humanities* 24 (2019): 155.

21. Marguerite La Caze, *The Analytic Imaginary* (Ithaca: Cornell University Press, 2002), 25.

22. José Medina, 'Racial Violence, Emotional Friction, and Epistemic Activism', *Angelaki: Journal of the Theoretical Humanities* 24 (2019): 22–37.

23. Alexander Brown, 'What is hate speech? Part 1: The Myth of Hate', *Law and Philosophy* 35 (2017): 419–468, and 'What is Hate Speech? Part 2: Family Resemblances', *Law and Philosophy* 36 (2017): 561–613.

24. Katharine Gelber, 'Differentiating Hate Speech: A Systemic Discrimination Approach', *Critical review of International Social and Political Philosophy* (2019): 1–22. https://doi.org/10.1080/13698230.2019.1576006.

25. Megarry, 'Online Incivility', 52.

26. Powell and Henry, *Sexual Violence*, 171.

27. Filipa Melo Lopes, 'Perpetuating the Patriarchy: Misogyny and (Post-) Feminist Backlash', *Philosophical Studies* 176 (2019): 2531.

Chapter 1

Social Imaginaries and Imagined Subjects

We need to take account of the extent to which social life is a manifestation of . . . the social imaginary – the networks of interconnecting symbols that give meaning to our existence, together with our capacity to generate and modify such networks – and need at the same time to take the social imaginary itself as our most basic ontological category.

—Susan James[1]

I propose to analyse the problem of hate speech against women online through a social imaginaries framework. To do this, some exposition on this approach is necessary. In this chapter, I am going to provide a sketch of what social imaginaries are, how they operate and how they affect agents like you and me. I start with some basic concepts, namely 'imaginary', 'imagination' and 'images'. Second, I delve into the connection between feeling, or *affect*, and images. Third, I explain how social imaginaries fix borders around our interpretation of the world (what is and is not possible for me and for others in this environment). This is their structuring function. Fourth, I plot how dominant, central and marginal imaginaries interoperate. The dominant social imaginary of a particular milieu – understood as 'those common images, symbols, metaphors and narratives through which we make sense of social bodies'[2] – is in fact a conglomeration of central social imaginaries. Recognising this is important, since central imaginaries are by no means *necessarily* logically consistent. This, in turn, can generate moments of epistemic and affective 'friction' that can be the wellspring of social change.[3] Finally, I elaborate the claim that every social imaginary is populated by specific imagined subjects, such as Persons, Individuals, Men, Women, Trolls and Average Internet Users, among others. Focusing not only on the images that comprise imaginaries but also on the images of whom they apply to reveals dynamics of active, passive, agential and structural social power. In close, I briefly summarise these key insights on the architecture of human experience and sociability.

IMAGINARIES, IMAGINATION AND IMAGES

In this book, the terms 'imaginary' and 'image' are not used in their ordinary sense. When I talk about social imaginaries, I do not mean to say that their contents are a 'make believe' product of the imagination. The imaginary is not (necessarily) the opposite of the 'real'. Imaginaries can reflect truths about our worlds, and they can also reflect falsehoods. Thus, the imaginary does not stand in contrast to reality; rather, the two are (in)fused.[4] Imagining – exercising the imagination – should be understood as a particular *way of knowing* our world.[5] As Beth Lord explains, it is through engagement with the world around us – an engagement that is necessarily embodied – that we acquire 'images' of that world; that is, images derive 'from feelings and sensations' of the phenomena we encounter.[6] Said differently, 'through imagination we know ourselves and our world empirically',[7] and this is a knowledge driven by feeling, affect or the passions to use a more anachronistic term. These images that we develop of our worlds then 'become associated with others [that is, other images] according to experience and habit', and from this we make broader associations with other images and generalisations about how they hang together.[8] Without the application of the human imagination, the world of experience would not be available to us in the way that it is: as an environment full of possibility and meaning. Thus, far from its ordinary definition, '*imagination* describes all kinds of thinking from experience'.[9] The idea is that when we perceive the world around us, this is not simply a passive process of receiving sensory input. Rather, to see possibilities for living in the world around us *just is* to exercise the imagination.[10] Importantly, we do not undertake the work of imaginatively interpreting the world around us by ourselves. We are always engaged in a process of social (i.e. shared) production and sustainment of images (or imaginings).

Likewise, here an 'image' is not just a picture. I also mean to include the 'symbols, metaphors and representations' that are built and maintained by the human imagination across time.[11] So, for instance, it is possible to 'have an image' (alternatively, one might prefer the term 'impression') of 'universals like love, the state of the country, social difference, the pattern of a life, etc'.[12] We also share in spatio-temporal imaginings which are able to give our whole lives meaning: our imaginings 'weave together the sensory *present* with what is *past*, the projected *future*, and the spatial *elsewhere*'.[13] Our images of (aspects of) our worlds are both extensive and robust, and it is the linkage of our images to one another that is constitutive of our social imaginaries. In short, then, an 'imaginary' can simply be described as a certain 'stock of images'.[14] Importantly, these imaginings are not just shared impressions held 'in the mind'. They have a tangible presence in the material world; they structure all of our intersubjective engagements – that is, they are made manifest in our bodily behaviours, behaviours like shopping, driving, having a conversation, sex acts, work, dining out and on and on. Not only this, these stocks of images are also made manifest 'in institutions and in the social norms that constrain action and determine [social] meaning independently of the wishes of individuals'.[15] As Danielle Celermajer and others explain, 'by generating shared expectations for norms of behaviour, and by enabling [us] to predict how others will act, institutions release individuals from the cognitive burden of having to constantly engage in time-consuming deliberations in their encounters with the world'.[16] (Note here that a 'social norm is a collective expectation about what is to count as appropriate behaviour for a particular identity in a particular context'.[17]) Thus, it makes sense to say that 'the body as "lived" in particular contexts expresses a collective way of life'[18] – it is shaped by, but also simultaneously shapes, the institutional practices and norms of a given milieu.

The reason I am drawn to this theoretical framework, even though there is danger of misinterpreting its key terms due to their ordinary connotations, is precisely that the focus is squarely on what makes our collective lives *meaningful*. Here, I do not mean whatever one finds to be personally fulfilling in this world. Social imaginaries theory is instead concerned with how we have made and continue to make ourselves the centre of a meaning-full world, projecting and taking to heart images of 'who we are; how we stand in relation to others; what we owe them; what constitutes appropriate and inappropriate behaviour; and so forth'.[19] Thus, I am referring to the shared meanings that enable us to know 'how to behave, how to pursue one's projects without provoking enmity, and how best to preserve oneself, one's family, friends and goods' in the socio-historical context that constitutes one's world, for these engagements are always 'guided by both habitual and practical orientations toward the general business of living', and take place 'against culturally specific normative backgrounds that are largely taken for granted'.[20] Social imaginaries theories hold that there is no experience of the world as such that is unmediated by the human imagination (our own, but also that of those who came before us, and who exist in the present with us), and to understand these imaginaries and how they structure our lives we must critically examine their constitutive images.[21]

THE ROLE OF AFFECT

This explication of human existence and experience posits no hard dichotomy between reason and passion (or affect, feeling). Indeed, 'reason does not stop us from feeling or imagining. As long as we experience, we imagine, and imagining is our route to reasoning'.[22] Ours, writes Kathleen Lennon, 'is a world we strive to make not only cognitive but also affective sense of. The sense it makes for us is carried by the images that constitute its form'.[23] Millicent Churcher describes the place of affect in imaginaries thusly:

> Imaginaries do not furnish individuals with 'intellectual schemas' that enable them to comprehend aspects of their social experience 'in a disengaged mode'. The narratives, images, and symbols that comprise any given imaginary *appeal* to the imaginations of individuals, structuring perceptions of one's social environment that are shot through with affect, and which produce strong [visceral] attachments to particular social orders.[24]

We might even describe images as the vehicles of affect.[25] Here, I understand affect as involving emotions, desires, moods and 'other feeling states (e.g. a felt sense of salience, purposefulness, or concern)', which 'shape how we attend to and engage with the world'.[26] Investigating further, there are also two aspects to affect. 'One is the capacity of our bodies to *be affected*, to bear the marks of our interactions with the world and other bodies'[27] – marks like blushing, rigidity of the body, crossing one's arms, flared nostrils and so on, as well as, for instance, pregnancy, scars, goose bumps, donning a wedding ring or a hijab and so on. 'Another is our capacities to *respond*, expressively or purposively' to the world,[28] by, say, smiling, grasping, side-stepping or even storming out of a room, choosing to buy an advertised product, asking a friend whether they are receiving health care, writing a letter to the editor, maintaining a blog or vlog, throwing a party and so forth. Thus, we see that 'both receptivity and spontaneity are in play' through affect in our experience of the social world.[29] We are not passive, but (re)active creatures in this world we collectively imagine.

The connection of imagining to affect is therefore inescapable, and, importantly for my purposes here, as mentioned above, the affective texture of our imaginings generates strong, visceral attachments to particular social dynamics. As Churcher explains, 'affects serve a regulative function' (driving us to behave in certain ways and not others as well as expecting certain behaviours from other people) 'that can be particularly powerful'.[30] We might say, then, that images – in relation to which social narratives and norms are developed – bring to bear an 'affective logic' on those captivated by them.[31] We behave *this* way because we feel like it is the right/appropriate/only thing to do (and we expect specific others to feel the same way). We avoid behaving *that* way because we feel like it is bad/inappropriate/impossible *for me* and for *people like me* (and expect others to feel the same). The inextricable link between images and affect is what explains how imaginaries drive us to act in particular ways (namely, we are affectively captivated by them), but it is also by virtue of this dynamic that we can feel that our lives are in any way meaningful (*meaning-full*). The role of affect in sustaining imaginaries is not an unfortunate inevitability; affect functions to both positive and negative ends.

THE STRUCTURING FUNCTION
OF SOCIAL IMAGINARIES

I have said that imaginaries construct human sociability. Indeed, they act as 'the always present backdrop to meaningful social action'.[32] But, more than this, their constitutive images orient us towards a particular interpretation of some *thing* in the world (an object, person, landscape, etc.) and suggest certain actions which are *appropriate* in response to the meaning conveyed by that thing. This is their structuring function. The claim that social imaginaries have a structuring function is the claim that social imaginaries fix borders around our *interpretation* of the world, what is and is not possible for me and for others to do in this environment. Turning to Marguerite La Caze for explication of this statement, we find that imaginaries actually work in three structuring ways. First, imaginaries function to *express* ideas and affects, as we saw in the preceding section. Second, they *condition* our responses and function to *sway* our judgement. Third, they *enframe cognition*, setting borders around what can be thought in a certain context in the first place.[33] Importantly, in the words of Filipa Melo Lopes, social imaginaries 'constitute a necessary "cultural backdrop" to our activities *together*'.[34] These structuring functions are collective. So, the structuring function of social imaginaries provides a scope of acceptable interpretation on a particular 'scene' to a group; that scene can be a social interaction playing out right before one's eyes, or a fictional scene in a movie, or a static scene in a work of art, and so on. To *get by* in this world – which involves more than merely understanding one's world – we must take on (or take up) those pre-existing world-structuring meanings, those already-sedimented collective imaginings, until they settle into us as though they were truly organic, instinctual or self-originating.[35]

Let us here note explicitly encounter our dominant social imaginary as 'ready-made',[36] and because of this we tend not to notice its operation. The world we find ourselves born into is already structured by 'a matrix of social practices, institutions, media, culture and history', which seems to have some sort of a 'total' shape.[37] We absorb the norms, narratives and meanings attached to the images we commonly encounter in our milieu. The dominant social imaginary should therefore be understood as the 'interconnected web of meanings that constitute a "second nature"'.[38] Put another way, 'social imaginaries work to structure implicit background assumptions that lead individuals to judge, feel, and act in ways that evade their explicit awareness and that may be in tension with their avowed . . . beliefs'.[39] Per Churcher, note how, 'by distributing meaning and significance in this way, social imaginaries influence collective modes of interpretation, evaluation, judgement, and belief among members of a given culture, rendering certain possibilities visible or invisible, intelligible or unintelligible'.[40] The claim, then, is that we perceive our worlds through our imaginaries and we live by our imaginaries, even though we very rarely notice our imaginaries because we encounter them ready-made. Imaginaries will often tick along – for oneself as for others – below the level of conscious awareness precisely because *this is (what everyone takes to be) normal*; so, 'social imaginaries work to structure implicit background assumptions'.[41] Still, this does not mean we become passive subjects, automatons programmed by imaginal input. Our experience of being is much like developing the capacity to drive a car: once we have embodied the skills to operate a motor vehicle, it becomes possible to drive through ever-changing road conditions and for that complex activity to feel organic, easy, second nature and we retain the capacity even when we do not exercise it.[42] Consider another example. Our mother tongue is something we are not born with, it must be learned; language is a tool like any other that we become skilled at utilising. As Lucy Osler clarifies, 'tools can be incorporated into our lived body when they are used in a way that they become transparent, come to shape and mould our experience', and 'language and words are also part of our equipment . . . which we incorporate into our lived body'.[43] Once learned, communication in our mother tongue feels instinctual, like a natural capacity we always had. One does not need to concentrate on how to make certain (meaningful) strings of words come out of one's mouth or fingertips, we simply do it. The point: we can become aware of the fact that collective imaginings have a structuring function over our very experience of being and of social meaning only *after* we have already been immersed in these cognitive-affective systems. Things seem natural until we discover they are not.

THE INTERRELATIONSHIP OF IMAGINARIES

I've provided a sketch of our immersion into a dominant social imaginary and the affective investments this generates. So, at this stage it makes sense for me to explicitly flesh out the way I understand the interrelationship of dominant, central and marginal imaginaries. In any given milieu, there can only be *one* dominant social imaginary. Indeed, the phrase 'the dominant social imaginary' is intended to capture our *gestalt*-like (organised, schematic, singular) experience of our ready-made milieu, or 'world', an experience which is generally (but not always) both unified and cohesive.[44] However, one's experience of being oriented to '*the*' world is really a simultaneous experience of immersion in *multiple kinds of central imaginaries* (see figure 1.1). These 'include religious, political, economic, sexual, racial, ethnic, moral, national and international imaginaries', among others.[45] (As this book is concerned with online hate speech targeting women, I am particularly interested in the central sexual, ethico-political and digital imaginaries of the contemporary Anglosphere, as well as the various sorts of imagined subjects that populate these.) In fact, each central imaginary, which applies to its own particular domain of social life, has its own social scripts and sets of normative expectations that apply to specific sorts of subjects in those specific domains. However, these scripts and norms do 'link up' (represented by the adjoining lines in figure 1.1) – their images, narratives, norms and subjects permeate one another. This explains why what can be conceptualised as multiple is nonetheless usually experienced as singular: as one world that makes sense to us in a particular sort of way.

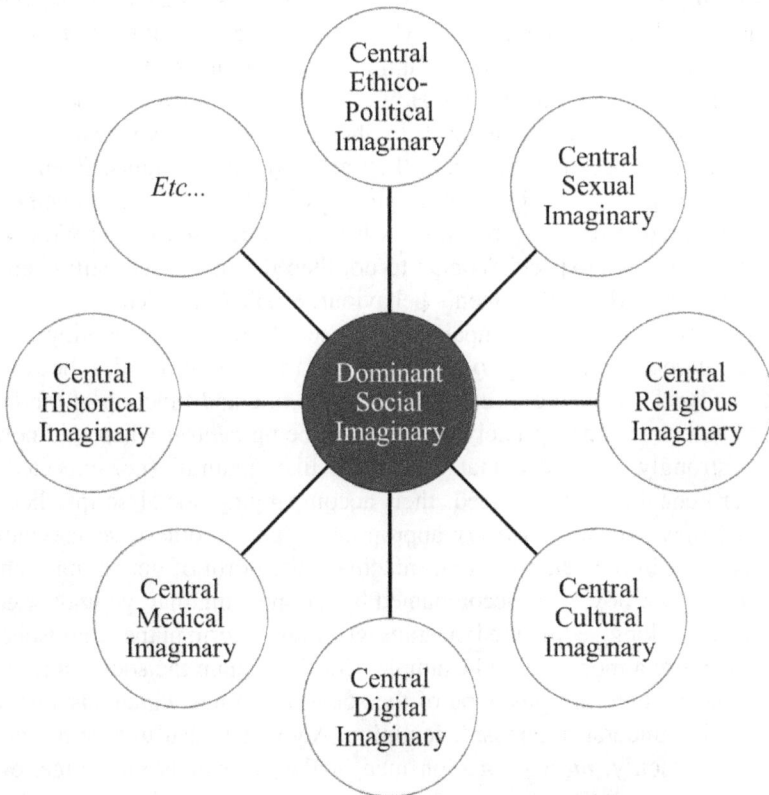

Figure 1.1   Central Social Imaginaries and the Dominant Social Imaginary.

Central imaginaries are what we collectively tap into when we determine how we should act, which, in turn, has an impact on the way we move in and through our world, and we do this quite independently of whether we ourselves genuinely endorse that imaginary's norms, narratives and images, and sometimes we do so even when we judge them to be somehow problematic. This speaks to the power of sedimented, collective expectations and meanings; they shape not only behaviour but also *world-orientation*, that is, how one relates to and sees specific possibilities (and impossibilities) for oneself and people like them, as well as people different to them in their same socio-historical context. But it is important to recognise that what makes an imaginary central, rather than marginal, is *not* the number of people who consciously and wholeheartedly endorse it. What makes an imaginary central is simply everyone's shared sense that *this stock of images* (which entails sets of norms and narratives) is the one in which *everyone else* is invested. We can imagine, for example, a girl – call her Shelley – growing up in a world where it seems like all girls and women have hairless armpits, both in real life and in, say, media and advertising. Then she hits puberty and suddenly hair appears. It would seem perfectly natural for her to want to start shaving given the image of Woman she is familiar with, the one that is conveyed by her family, society and the media. However, it could *in principle* be the case that the majority of women and girls in Shelley's world *do not want to shave*; they only do so because they think they must by others' lights. Even if the numerical majority of women would prefer not to shave, if they nonetheless hold the shared impression that this is what everyone else expects Women to look like, and thus expects Women to do, then the image will still exercise influence over girls' and women's behaviour, Shelley included.

Indeed, some image, accompanied by its set of meaning-generating norms and narratives – pertaining to, for example, the healthy or sick body; the sexed body; the structure of our economy; the role and function of the family and so on – is appropriately described as being *central* when said norms are so strongly embedded that they seem like 'natural' (i.e. expected or *normal*) behaviour, and, indeed, their accompanying social scripts license certain behaviours as *obviously* appropriate, right or otherwise inevitable. For instance, in the central sexual imaginary the norm of gendering a child at birth – 'It's a boy'! – is accompanied by the meaning that 'genitals = gender'. This is a long-sedimented meaning-generating norm in the Anglosphere. Let us explore a more detailed example. Consider again the social norm that women shave their armpits. One of the social meanings which sustains this norm is that underarm hair isn't feminine. Another is that underarm hair is disgusting (tacitly, *on women* – on men, underarm hair is masculine, even sometimes sexy).[46] We know that this normative practice belongs to a *central* imaginary because even though women naturally grow armpit hair, it is the vision of the hairy woman who stands out; her transgression is what draws focus (i.e. the hairy armpits of a woman are 'seen'; hairless armpits are not). Women's armpits are not a confronting sight *until* the norm is transgressed. We also know this image belongs to the central *sexual* imaginary because we only expect Women to modify the natural appearance of their armpits, and do not so expect this of Men (noting that only two subject types are commonly imagined here). For women, transgressions are viewed as both 'yucky' and unattractive, perhaps to the point of triggering outrage. (For men, removing their hair is viewed as feminine, and even queer, though the practice is accepted in some sporting cultures.)

So, we see how familiar, pre-established norms and narratives mutually reinforce one another to maintain certain social truths (e.g. that Women don't have hairy armpits), those 'truths' being signified in multiple ways. When a norm like shaving is questioned, the narrative can be drawn up into consciousness to justify it. Say Shelley asks her parents to buy her a razor so that she can shave her underarm hair. Her father might turn to her mother and ask, 'Isn't Shelley too young to shave'? to which her mother may, in turn, reply, 'Shelley needs to shave or else she'll get teased; girls aren't supposed to have hair'. When a narrative is questioned, one can point to the *ordinariness* of the practice to justify it. Say Shelley's older brother repeats the stereotype, 'You know, women don't shave their underarms in France', only to have her older sister reply, 'Yeah, but French chicks are weird! Nobody does that here', in turn, reinforcing the norm. And it is amidst all this – through interpersonal and mediated engagements with pre-existing, shared, interconnected images, norms and narratives – that Shelley (in fact, all of us) learns how to fit in and get by.

Interestingly, it is cases like Shelley's which also show us that imaginaries are neither fixed nor stagnant. They are (re)produced by us actively over the course of our engagements in day-to-day life. Every act is an iteration of some other act that has gone before, and iterations 'never simply produce a replica of the original . . . rather, every repetition . . . transforms meaning, adds to it, enriches it in ever-so-subtle ways'.[47] Sometimes, these changes might be described (from a particular analytic perspective, such as a feminist perspective, which is a mode of marginal imagining) as *good* for an imaginary's subjects, or as *bad*. For instance, beyond women's repeated acts of armpit hair removal, we find that it is becoming increasingly common for women to eliminate all hair from their arms, not just their armpits. This could be critiqued or celebrated depending on the point of view of analysis. My aim is not to do that here. This is just said to highlight that social norms organically change, and when they change, so too do their meaning-generating narratives. Likewise, if a meaning-generating narrative shifts (e.g. if 'genitals = gender' becomes 'genitals ≠ gender'), we may well see tweaks in normative and institutional practices (e.g. the practice of listing 'gender' on birth certificates).[48]

Changes to social imaginaries can be the result of a collective's conscious choices to go against the grain, but the affective pull of central imaginaries is strong, and this means they often continue to influence our day-to-day behaviour, sometimes without our noticing it, and even sometimes in spite of our conscious desires to act differently. Let's return to Shelley. She is now grown and has come to judge the practice of women's armpit hair removal to be problematic. She feels the tug of the double standard that the presence of such hair is interpreted as masculine and even attractive on men, yet unfeminine and disgusting on women, when both naturally grow armpit hair. She also feels indignant that she is subject to the male gaze, being assessed for her bodily beauty before any other talents or aptitudes, which includes the presence or absence of hair in certain places. Motivated by these affects, Shelley decides to stop shaving, an act she has seen a sparse amount of women do. We might say, then, that Shelley has invested in alternative meaning-generating narratives: that women's hair removal stems from an arbitrary standard of beauty; that it is natural for women to have underarm hair; that the social preoccupation with women's beauty (a beauty which is, implicitly, *for* men) is nothing but a patriarchy-enforcing world-orientation and so on. These alternate impressions of what women are 'really' like, and of how women 'should' be, are marginal imaginings that drive an alternate non-normative behaviour: Shelley's *not* shaving. And Shelley's choice to keep her hair – that is, to go against a sedimented social norm – can be described as an *instantiation* of the alternate image in which she invests; Shelley becomes visibly abnormal, unlike most other women.

Still, in her defiance, hers is an act sprung from a marginal imagining that is designed to normalise, and thus centralise, the image of body hair on women (see figure 1.2). But Shelley can't shift a central image, much less an entire imaginary, all on her own. Should Shelley inspire her friends to likewise quit shaving, which, in turn, inspires a local business to use hairy women in their advertising, which, in turn, inspires more women unknown to Shelley to quit shaving and so on, then this *may* sediment what was once a once marginal image (women with body hair) in the central sexual imaginary, evolving what is seen to be 'normal' for women to look like. Unfortunately for those of us who experience injustices due to the central imaginings that affect us, successful (r)evolution of the images sedimented in central social imaginaries is wildly unpredictable.[49] This alternate image Shelley conveys with her body may not become sedimented at all. After all, critique is one thing. Establishing new social norms is another. And going against the grain – even for very justified purposes – is easier said than done. Breaking social norms has costs (costs like derision, humiliation

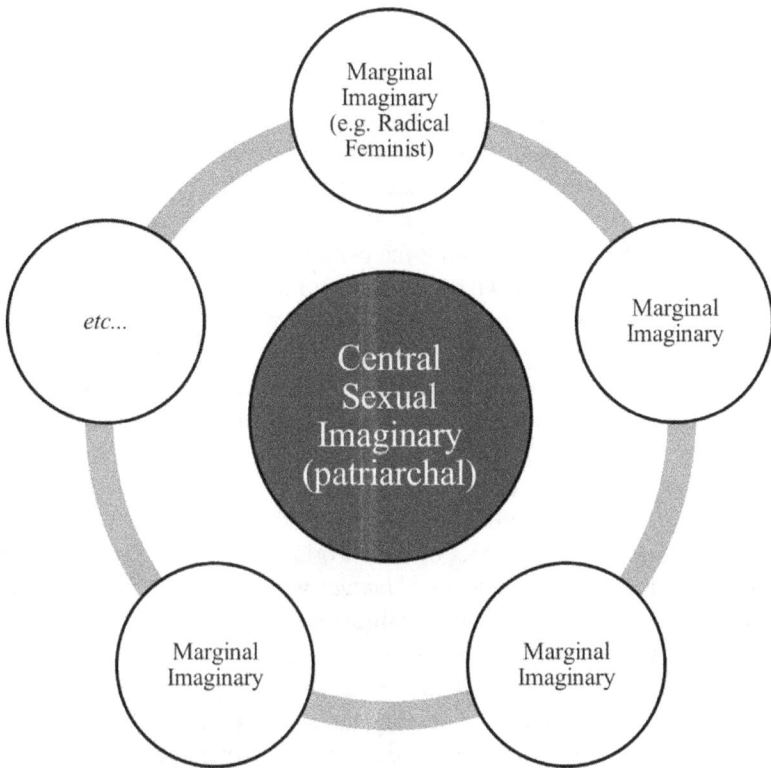

Figure 1.2 Central and Marginal Social Imaginaries.

and feelings of shame and insecurity), as does questioning any collective's received view of 'the way things are' (and the way things *ought* to be).[50] Some of Shelley's friends may endorse her decision not to shave, but feel too embarrassed to join her, for instance. So, while Shelley models an alternative image of Woman, it is not one that spreads with sufficient uptake. Others may laugh at Shelley behind her back, or talk about how bad she looks. Shelley may see the markers of revulsion on the faces of men (or women) she might hope to date. All of this may cause her to feel shame about her hairy faux pas. (Or this might cause a righteous rage – many affective responses are possible.)

Sometimes we even undermine our own efforts for change. As mentioned already, central images that we may wish to challenge, like women having hairless armpits, do not just sediment 'in the mind', they become manifest in and so orient our bodily behaviours. So, even though she has made the principled decision not to shave, Shelley may understandably find herself feeling anxious when she is out in public ('are people staring at me?'); the way she inhabits the social space – that is, the way she moves her body through that space – may even change (as she walks, she pins her arms firm against her sides, keeping her armpits hidden from view; online, she never posts any photos where her hair is visible). She does this because 'images can operate beneath the radar of our ordinary doxastic self-scrutiny, sometimes even despite beliefs to the contrary'.[51] What's more, the unease Shelley feels – the 'am I being stared at?' feeling – might even compel her to act in ways which, in fact, prevent her from disrupting the central image, social norms and narratives that she consciously wishes to disrupt. For example, she may find that she feels more at ease wearing shirts with sleeves in public, with the effect that her armpits are always hidden from strangers' (and friends') view. This behaviour, though affectively soothing, would undercut the possibility of spreading and thus sedimenting her consciously maintained alternative image of what Women are like.

Now, in figure 1.2, we see that central imaginaries are surrounded by marginal imaginaries, but it is possible – perhaps even more common – for people seeking to challenge some aspect of their world to invest in *specific marginal images* rather than *marginal stocks of images* wholesale. But marginal imaginaries do exist and are influential. For instance, in response to a central sexual imaginary that is patriarchal, feminists have developed specific yet robust counter-imaginaries that offer alternative ways of living in and making meaning of one's world. (Note that such imaginaries are not isolated but 'speak to', or seep into one another, as represented by the grey outer circle.) Yet, it is also the case that people can find certain marginal images appealing without investing wholly in a world-reorienting imaginary. Take another example. Consider the image of 'the tattooed woman'. Over the past few decades, women's tattoos have started to move from fringe to mainstream as part of an 'ordinary' feminine aesthetic.[52] As more and more women become tattooed with particular designs, in particular locations, and within a specific size range, the image of the tattooed woman becomes normalised. We can imagine, then, a woman (call her Tia) finding the image of the 'heavily-tattooed woman' a particularly appealing aesthetic because it 'stands out' from the generic image of the 'tattooed woman', and she may pursue this look for that reason alone (i.e. not because it can challenge norms of femininity and beauty).

Here, Tia is influenced by a marginal image – the 'heavily tattooed woman' – but is not invested in a marginal imaginary. She just wants to stand out from the crowd. However, we can easily imagine another similar scenario where Tamara is motivated to pursue the 'look' of the heavily tattooed woman because it distorts the newly accepted and now fetishised image of the 'tattooed woman', a look still considered 'unfeminine'. The 'heavily tattooed woman' image, she believes, glitches the central cis-hetero-patriarchal imaginary; it triggers moments of epistemic and affective friction in those who encounter her. It upsets taken-for-granted norms and narratives about how Women ought to look and why (and it tacitly acknowledges that the 'cleanskin' body cannot perform this same function.) Tamara knows this and pursues the look for that reason, being committed to a certain feminist marginal imaginary that decentres the importance of women's (conventional) beauty. As a consequence of humans' creative interplay with the world around them, as well as the sometimes subtle, sometimes substantial challenges to imaginaries (and their constitutive images) that (collectives of) people make, which occur through our iterations and our refusals of social norms and narratives, imaginaries are at every level insecure, though they may not seem like it experientially.

So, we have seen that what is marginal (whether a single image or a whole counter-imaginary) can become central, and vice versa, and that imaginaries are fluid, never fixed systems. We 'see that the system of linked social imaginaries is being constantly transformed and refigured', and therefore that social change – a different world – is possible.[53] What is less clear is what it takes to purposively, successfully shift an image or imaginary. Still, we can infer that it takes more than individual aspirations and acts. There must be collective change, not only at the level of behaviour, but also in one's sense of how things are, and how they ought to be. In sum, figure 1.3 represents this total architecture of our dominant, central and marginal imaginaries. It is important to recognise the multiplicity of social imaginaries, as well as the ways in which these imaginaries influence each other and 'link up'. Even if we usually experience our world as unified and whole, what drives us as social actors is our immersion across multiple meaning-generating imaginaries simultaneously, imaginaries in which others from my milieu are likewise invested. In fact, imaginaries – consisting of stocks of images, which are brought into being and sustained by the human imagination, as well as their literal manifestation in the societies we build – are 'a precondition of there being a real for us' to experience.[54] Since, consequently, there is no way to 'step outside the social imaginary and see the truth about the world, clearly and without distortion',[55] the task of theorists who find this social imaginaries model to have explanatory power with respect to human sociability and societies must be to (A) elucidate what shared imaginings exist, (B) what affective investments they elicit, (C) how they drive subjects to act and (D) how certain stocks of images (may) come to shift over time. We may also ask: (E) who benefits from the sedimentation of certain images and who is disadvantaged, (F) are our imaginings within and across imaginaries consistent and (G) to which sorts of subjects do certain norms and expectations apply?

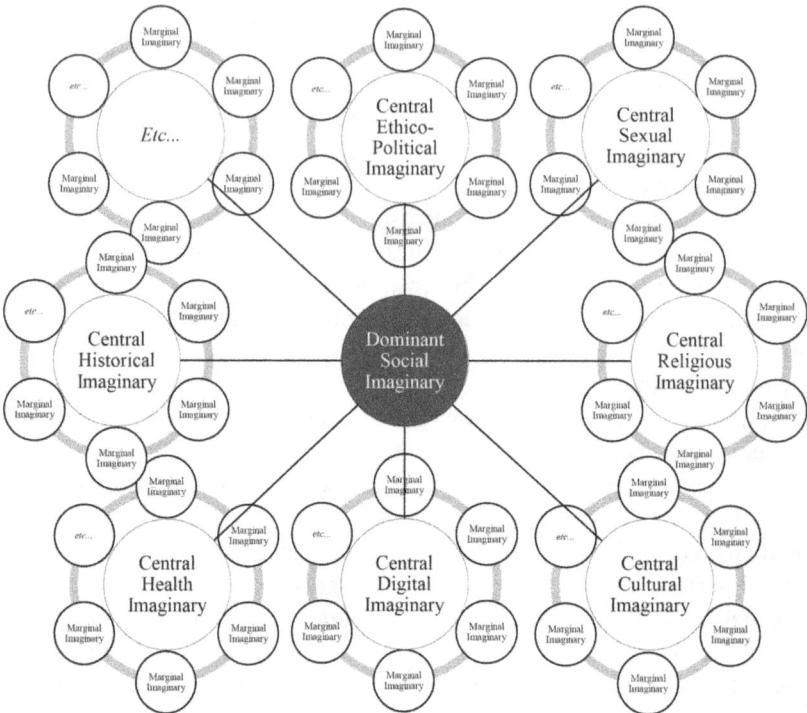

Figure 1.3   Social Imaginaries Architecture.

IMAGINED SUBJECTS AND
SOCIAL IDENTITY POWER

We have already seen that social imaginaries have a structuring function: they place a border around what can be imagined, they set expectations for which kinds of people will perform particular types of actions, they elicit affective responses (depending on whether our expectations are being met and on the goings on in the particular context), and they make sense of the total picture by providing us with some sense-making story of how things are. Imaginaries can only be said to have this structuring function because they help us to interpret *everything* in our environment, *including the presence of others*.

Every imaginary has its own imagined subjects, kinds of people that do and don't belong, who are or aren't one of 'us', those instantly recognisable types of human beings distinguished by modes of dress, skin pigmentation, physiological features, physical abilities and so forth. We can say, then, that 'social imaginaries work to assign differential meaning and value to *particular bodies* and help to legitimise social practices by grounding normative expectations and patterns of behaviour that vary for different social subjects'.[56] We have already seen this in the case of Shelley, who feels societal pressure to shave her armpits *because she is a woman*. Churcher explains further that 'imaginaries condition perceptions of *what* is owed to *whom* regarding fundamental rights, protections, and entitlements and underwrite people's sense of obligation to respect and promote these goods'; and 'the affective investments of esteem, mistrust, concern, or contempt that we have in others' bodies as they are collectively imagined (e.g. as fellow citizens or as outsiders; as criminal, vulnerable, or untrustworthy; etc.) play a key role in motivating the asymmetric treatment of different social groups'.[57] This will be important to keep in mind as we consider the ways women are mistreated in online social spaces where we often find that 'the body is the locus of abuse'.[58] Here, simply note the ways certain identities are readily applied to certain sorts of people with presumed bodily traits, while they are less readily applied to differently embodied persons, and these are (usually, not always) the subjects we become.

Other types of imagined subjectivities are not so obviously tied to bodily traits but are described in terms of capacities. For instance, in the central legal imaginary the paradigm subject is the Person.[59] This Person is understood to be an assertive, self-interested yet *also* (paradoxically) a disinterestedly objective agent; a unitary self-contained individual, and thus also a self-owner.[60] Then there is the image of the Individual – central in the West's ethico-political imaginary, and so, too, the dominant Western social imaginary – which supposedly applies to all human persons irrespective of any group-based identity traits they may bear. The Individual and the Person are often treated as one and the same. Note that there are subtle differences though. This legal conception of Personhood has allowed for non-human entities to count as Persons under the law (e.g. corporations), and has also allowed for human entities to *not* count as Persons (e.g. slaves).[61] In spite of this, such subjects are tacitly imagined with specific bodily traits. What's more, in an almost paradoxical way, these imaginaries – legal and ethico-political – *still presuppose sexed and gendered subjects as its inhabitants*: Men, Women and increasingly other gender identities and statuses.[62] These 'background' subjectivities move into and out of focus in the dominant Western social imaginary, and in these component central imaginaries, depending on the context at hand. Gendered and sexed subjects are, on the other hand, the explicitly central figures of *sexual* imaginaries. However, as we shall see in the next chapter, patriarchy – which functions as the central sexual imaginary, and which posits humanity as consisting of (cis-hetero) Men and Women bound in a natural, complementary hierarchy – is able to cloak its presence and influence in contemporary Western societies by shielding itself behind the figures Individual and Person, which are ostensibly neutral but in fact tacitly (cis-hetero-)androcentric subjectivities. In short, what one can and cannot do, how one can or cannot live, depends on who one is, on the imagined subjectivities available to specific persons *in relation to others*. Thus, imagined subjects are always bound up in power relations. When we examine social imaginaries as they affect, say, Men and Women (to name only two possibilities), rather than how they affect hypothetical subjects abstracted from their bodies, their context and its history, the nuances of the many and varied power dynamics between agents, and between agents and institutions, start to be revealed. They come to light whereas previously they were overshadowed by images of Persons and Individuals.

Power comes in many varieties, but essentially it involves a capacity to influence some state of affairs. For example, a teacher has the capacity to discipline a student's misbehaviour by giving them a detention. If the teacher exercises their capacity by issuing a detention, this is an active operation of power. If the mere capacity itself is influencing students' behaviour (i.e. they are behaving well because they don't want a detention), on the other hand, then the power is still operational, but it is operating passively.[63] When it is a person, a group of people, or even an institution that is influencing the behaviour of another person, group or institution, this should be described as agential power. However, sometimes our sedimented social norms, which are not clearly codified by any particular body, influence how things go for certain groups, too. Let us imagine a scenario where there is a tacit social norm that piloting is Men's work and not Women's work. If this norm operates to keep women from pursuing careers as pilots, then a *purely structural* operation of power has occurred (because nothing stands in the way of women becoming pilots, and women are not actively discouraged by other people from pursuing this line of work, but the tacit norm guides them away from this line of work anyway).[64] Now, while power can operate purely structurally, as we have just seen, note that agential power *always* entails the operations of structural power. It relies on practical coordination with other social agents, institutions and our normative expectations to be effective. As Miranda Fricker says, 'any operation of power is dependent upon the context of a functioning social world – shared institutions, shared meanings, shared expectations, and so on'.[65] In short, active or passive exercises of agential power, as well as structural power, always depend on the structure of interconnected central social imaginaries.

The kind of power that will interest me through the remainder of this book is *social identity power*: where the social imaginary in question inheres in the members of an identity-based group *power-over* another identity-based group,[66] irrespective of whether an individual actually *exercises* that power as an agent (i.e. it can be merely passive, or operate structurally without an agent), and where a plausible case can be made that this capacity to control such a group is unjust. Thus, in chapter 2, I will argue that the central sexual imaginary and ethico-political imaginary – which are all interlinked in the dominant Western social imaginary – are structured hierarchically by dynamics of unjustified social identity power between (cis-hetero-) Men and other genders. I want to emphasise that this type of power is not always exercised actively, intentionally or with malice. Identity power can *also* operate purely structurally once established (as we see in the example of piloting as Men's work). But even when no one is choosing to exercise social identity power, if relations of power contribute to situations of injustice – such as gender oppression – then this identity power must be recognised and reckoned with.

The complexities of power dynamics reveal themselves further when we note that actual embodied human beings are immersed in multiple central imaginaries simultaneously, where they have specific identities, and so are strung in networks of power with other agents in the same milieu. Said otherwise, different types of identities are stratified in more or less stringent hierarchies of power.[67] Thus, I am at once, for instance, a Person, a Woman, White, an Academic, an Individual, Queer, a Girlfriend and so forth. Although in theory I ought to have equivalent powers to all others because we are all Individuals living in a Western liberal democratic milieu, in practice, because of the identities I embody, this turns out not to be the case. In fact, I have power-over certain others in both limited and enduring contexts. For example, I have agential power-over Students as a Lecturer (a justifiable power). I also have informal, context-derived power-over people of colour due to the contours of an institutionalised racial imaginary functioning in my milieu (an unjust power). However, others also have power-over me insofar as I am Queer, insofar as I am a Woman, and because I am both. So, the *prima facie* equal power that Individuals have per our liberal humanist ethico-political imaginary is really a mirage; the figure(s) of the Individual Person veils our extensive and expansive social identity power dynamics.

Another reason it is important to reflect on imaginary subjects and our donning of multiple identities simultaneously is that, experientially, at least sometimes, in some scenarios, I will be confronted with clashing expectations about how I should act, and I will need to figure out how to navigate these tensions. The normative expectations of Individual behaviour may clash, say, with the normative expectations of Women's behaviour. Whereas Individuals are autonomous, self-sufficient, self-interested (and disinterested in others) and objective, Women are relational, nurturing, self-sacrificing, caring and other oriented. Thus, when a woman behaves like an Individual, her acts may be perceived as cold, narcissistic, selfish or otherwise wrong. Yet, when a man behaves as an Individual, he is seen as rational, fair, reasonable, competent and so forth. This, as we shall see in chapter 2, is because the Individual is tacitly androcentric, meaning this identity is a more organic 'fit' for men than for women. Thus, when analysing social imaginaries, it is important to always consider not just which norms and narratives structure one's milieu, but *to which sorts of subjects these norms and narratives are applied*, always remembering that every agent is an intersectional subject – a being of many social identities – and always remembering that social power dynamics structure all social relations. The good news is that those jarring moments when expectations conflict are the entry points to critically analysing what would have otherwise remained unnoticed: the tensions and contradictions of living multiple subjectivities in a particular milieu, and of facing fewer or greater constraints than distinctly dissimilar others. Because different central imaginaries imagine different subjects, and because central social imaginaries are constitutive of the dominant social imaginary, it is inevitable that the dominant social imaginary maintains incompatible (even paradoxical) standards for actual human beings to live up to. These enable moments of rupture in one's gestalt where imaginal (r)evolution can be pursued.

SOCIAL IMAGINARIES ARCHITECTURE

In closing, allow me to briefly summarise. What we see in figure 1.3 is the total social imaginaries architecture described above. Social imaginaries are shared impressions of 'our world' as conveyed to us by oft-repeated images (or impressions). We should understand social imaginaries 'in terms of the images and narratives that help construct meaning, belonging and identity for the members of a given community', and this must be understood to refer to the meanings of bodies in specific, historically inflected contemporary contexts.[68] These impressions are the result of the structuring function of social imaginaries, which is to say that they convey a meaning-generating narrative (which entails affective investment), and tell us which material practices are appropriate, establishing social norms. They are already-formed systems into which we are thrown at birth. Because they pre-date our own existence, we are immersed in them, and because of this immersion social imaginaries usually convey meaning and shape our actions below the level of conscious awareness. They are also that which establishes and maintains power dynamics institutionally and between social groups. This means social imaginaries determine social groups' 'value, their status and what will be deemed their appropriate treatment'.[69]

Social imaginaries also have an inextricable influence on our very identities. The self is always shaped by the social meanings of one's body(-as-perceived-by-others), and we are all also fashioned by features specific to our social context, such as the spaces we inhabit (homes, gyms, schools, etc.; being in a particular nation, state, city, etc.) and our moment in history (e.g. post-colonial Australia in the twenty-first century). One's sense of self is necessarily produced from the outside as well as the inside, and subjectivity *becomes over time* via a constant intertwining of internal-external perception/ reception of one's world which is mediated by these imaginaries. Importantly, we must here acknowledge that when others identify us, they often do so by assigning us into socially salient groups, that is, as *imagined subjects*, 'which are always already associated with specific attributes, stereotypes, and norms' that themselves have arisen out of pre-existing socio-cultural structures.[70] However, imaginaries are always plural, coming in central and marginal modes, and are always in a state of flux. This suggests that, although social imaginaries usually operate at the level of the preconscious, and though certain power dynamics may seem natural and inevitable, there is always the possibility of reforming harmful imaginaries and eliminating harmful images, including those which attach to imagined subjects.

Importantly, challenges to a particular central imaginary (or challenges to an image within a particular imaginary) can have flow-on effects in other central imaginaries. For example, when there is an attempt to shift current woman-centred norms of childcare labour to, say, a norm of equitable childcare labour between (cis-hetero-) parents – challenging the images that 'Women care' and 'Men work' – this necessarily implicates norms and narratives in other imaginaries, such as the economic imaginary with its particular vision of working hours, employer responsibilities, employee entitlements and so forth. Indeed, as Moira Gatens says, 'such challenges threaten not simply this or that particular cultural practice but, at least potentially, whole clusters of interconnected norms'.[71] It is precisely these 'frictions' which, once we are cognisant of them, can be exploited in the quest for cultural revolution. Now, it is time to pay closer attention to some of our prominent shared images in the central sexual imaginary.

NOTES

1. Susan James, 'Freedom and the Imaginary', in *Visible Women: Essays on Feminist Legal Theory and Political Philosophy*, ed. Susan James and Stephanie Palmer (Oxford: Hart Publishing, 2002), 181.

2. Millicent Churcher and Moira Gatens, 'Reframing Honour in Heterosexual Imaginaries', *Angelaki* 24 (2019): 154.

3. José Medina, 'Racial Violence, Emotional Friction, and Epistemic Activism', *Angelaki* 24 (2019): 22–37.

4. Kathleen Lennon, 'Imaginary Bodies and Worlds', *Inquiry* 47 (2004): 107.

5. This view is inspired by Baruch Spinoza's philosophy which underscores important feminist engagement with the notion of social imaginaries, most notable

of which are Moira Gatens' and Genevieve Lloyd's scholarship (See e.g.: Moira Gatens and Genevieve Lloyd, *Collective Imaginings: Spinoza, Past and Present* (London: Routledge, 1999) and Moira Gatens, *Imaginary Bodies: Ethics, Power, and Corporeality* (London: Routledge, 1996)). However, the imagination and the imaginary have been important to many canonical philosophers (and in both continental and analytic traditions), as Kathleen Lennon and Chiara Bottici show. (See: Kathleen Lennon, *Imagination and the Imaginary* (London: Routledge, 2015) and Chiara Bottici, *Imaginal Politics: Images Beyond Imagination and the Imaginary* (New York: Columbia University Press, 2014)).

6. Beth Lord, 'Spinoza on Thinking Substance and the Non-Substantial Mind', in *Philosophy of Mind in the Early Modern and Modern Ages: The History of The Philosophy of Mind*, vol. 4, ed. Rebecca Copenhaver (London: Routledge, 2018), 187.

7. Lord, 'Spinoza', 187.

8. Lord, 'Spinoza', 187.

9. Lord, 'Spinoza', 187, original emphasis.

10. Lennon, *Imagination*, 11.

11. Gatens, *Imaginary Bodies*, VIII.

12. Lennon, *Imagination*, 3.

13. Lennon, *Imagination*, 4, original emphasis.

14. I draw this terminology from Gatens, who in turn draws it from Michèle Le Dœuff. See: Moira Gatens, 'Polysemy, Atopia, and Feminist Thought', in *Michèle Le Dœuff: Operative Philosophy and Imaginary Practice*, ed. Max Deutscher (Amherst: Humanity Books, 2000), 50.

15. Moira Gatens, 'Can Human Rights Accommodate Women's Rights? Towards an Embodied Account of Social Norms, Social Meaning, and Cultural Change', *Contemporary Political Theory* 3 (2004): 279.

16. Danielle Celermajer, Millicent Churcher, Moira Gatens, and Anna Hush, 'Institutional Transformations: Imagination, Embodiment, and Affect', *Angelaki* 24 (2019): 4.

17. Gatens, 'Women's Rights', 284.

18. Gatens, 'Women's Rights', 286.

19. Millicent Churcher, *Reimagining Sympathy, Recognizing Difference: Insights from Adam Smith* (London: Rowman and Littlefield International: 2019), 2.

20. Gatens, 'Women's Rights', 282.

21. Marguerite La Caze, *The Analytic Imaginary* (Ithaca: Cornell University Press, 2002), 19.

22. Lord, 'Spinoza', 189.

23. Lennon, *Imagination*, 4.

24. Churcher, *Reimagining Sympathy*, 4, my emphasis.

25. Lennon, *Imagination*, 1.

26. Joel Krueger and Lucy Osler, 'Engineering Affect: Emotion Regulation, the Internet, and the Techno-Social Niche', *Philosophical Topics* 47 (2019): 208; see also: Lennon, *Imagination*, 1.

27. Lennon, *Imagination*, 52.

28. Lennon, *Imagination*, 52.

29. Lennon, *Imagination*, 52.

30. Churcher, *Reimagining Sympathy*, 4.

31. Lennon, *Imagination*, 52.

32. Gatens, 'Women's Rights', 277.

33. La Caze, *Analytic Imaginary*, 11.

34. Filipa Melo Lopes, 'Perpetuating the Patriarchy: Misogyny and (Post-) Feminist Backlash', *Philosophical Studies* 176 (2019): 2530, original emphasis.

35. Gatens, 'Women's Rights', 282.

36. Gatens, *Imaginary Bodies*, VIII. Note, though, that while we encounter imaginaries ready-made, they remain contingent and changing.

37. Anya Daly, 'The Declaration of Interdependence! Feminism, Grounding, and Enactivism', *Human Studies* 44 (2021): 49.

38. Moira Gatens, 'Conflicting Imaginaries in Australian Multiculturalism: Women's Rights, Group Rights, and Aboriginal Customary Law', in *Political Theory and Australian Multiculturalism*, ed. Geoffrey Brahm Levey (New York: Berghahn Books, 2008), 161.

39. Churcher, *Reimagining Sympathy*, 9.

40. Churcher, *Reimagining Sympathy*, 3.

41. Churcher, *Reimagining Sympathy*, 9.

42. Helen Ngo provides an excellent re-reading of both 'habit' and 'sedimentation' that allows us to acknowledge the active holding of an image versus the mere passive receipt of one. See: Helen Ngo, *The Habits of Racism: A Phenomenology of Racism and Racialized Embodiment* (Lanham: Lexington Books, 2017), 38–39.

43. Lucy Osler, 'Taking Empathy Online', *Inquiry* (2021): 18, https://doi.org/10.1080/0020174X.2021.1899045.

44. Lennon, 'Imaginary Bodies', 107, writes: 'The concept of the imaginary employed is not one in which imaginary worlds are contrasted with the real, but one in which imagination is a condition of there being a real for us'.

45. Gatens, 'Women's Rights', 282.

46. Breanne Fahs, 'Perilous Patches and Pitstaches: Imagined Versus Lived Experiences of Women's Body Hair Growth', *Psychology of Women Quarterly* 38 (2014): 167–180.

47. Seyla Benhabib, *Another Cosmopolitanism* (Oxford: Oxford University Press, 2006), 48.

48. Tasmania has recently made changes to the process of recording gender on birth certificates. See: Louise Richardson-Self, '"There are only two genders–male and female" An Analysis of Online Responses to Tasmania Removing "Gender" from Birth Certificates', *International Journal of Gender, Sexuality and Law* (2020): 295–322.

49. Susan James, 'Freedom and the Imaginary', 187, explains: 'While coming to understand the workings of social imaginaries is a vital condition of change, there is no recipe for success, no procedure for undermining or replacing particular images or their effects'.

50. Gatens, 'Women's Rights', 284.

51. Miranda Fricker, *Epistemic Injustice: Power and the Ethics of Knowing* (Oxford: Oxford University Press, 2007), 40.

52. A paradigm example of this can be found in a 1996 episode of *Friends* where Rachel gets a tattoo, a tiny love heart on her hip (that the audience never sees) – Ross is initially galled by her actions, but changes his mind when he sees the tattoo, dubbing it 'sexy'.

53. Gatens, *Imaginary Bodies*, IX.

54. Lennon, 'Imaginary Bodies', 111.

55. Gatens, *Imaginary Bodies*, 140.

56. Churcher, *Reimagining Sympathy*, 3, my emphasis.

57. Churcher, *Reimagining Sympathy*, 5, my emphasis.

58. Sarah Sobieraj, 'Bitch, Slut, Skank, Cunt: Patterned Resistance to Women's Visibility in Digital Publics', *Information, Communication and Society* 21 (2018): 1701.

59. Ngaire Naffine, 'Can Women Be Legal Persons'? in *Visible Women: Essays on Feminist Legal Theory and Political Philosophy*, ed. Susan James and Stephanie Palmer (Oxford: Hart Publishing, 2002), 69–90; Imani Perry, *Vexy Thing: On Gender and Liberation* (Durham: Duke University Press, 2018).

60. Gatens, *Imaginary Bodies*, IX.

61. Naffine, 'Legal Persons', 69; Perry, *Vexy Thing*, 19–21.

62. In Australia, for example, legal interpretations of sex, gender, and their relationship have transformed over time. Thus, the Australian legal imagination has moved from the view that gender is determined by 'physical characteristics present at birth' (*Corbett v Corbett*) to the view that gender identity is expressed "with or without regard to an individual's designated sex at birth"' (*Births, Deaths, and Marriages Registration Act 1999* (Tas), Section 2.2.13). This example demonstrates nicely the variability of central images within social imaginaries, even images of that which some take to be fixed and immutable, and how humans' constant, collective, creative interplay with the environment, bodies, meanings and norms of their milieu generates shifts in both social imaginaries. See: Tasmania Law Reform Institute (TLRI), *Legal Recognition of Sex and Gender*, Final Report No. 31 June 2020, accessed 11 April 2021, https://www.utas.edu.au/__data/assets/pdf_file/0018/1342080/tlri-legal-recognition-of-sex-final-report.pdf.

63. Fricker, *Epistemic Injustice*, 9.

64. Fricker, *Epistemic Injustice*, 10.

65. Fricker, *Epistemic Injustice*, 11–12.

66. Power-over can be distinguished from two other forms of power: *power-to*, which 'is the individual ability or capacity to act so as to attain some end', and *power-with*, 'which is the collective ability or capacity to act together so as to attain some common or shared end'. See Amy Allen, 'Rethinking Power', *Hypatia* 13 (1998): 36.

67. Allen, 'Rethinking Power', 29.

68. Gatens, 'Women's Rights', 286.

69. Gatens, *Imaginary Bodies*, VIII.

70. Iris Marion Young, *Justice and the Politics of Difference* (Princeton: Princeton University Press, 1990), 46.

71. Gatens, 'Women's Rights', 284.

Chapter 2

Sexual Imaginaries

> *Imaginaries establish tacit social assumptions that become so entrenched their truth value is taken for granted.*

—Millicent Churcher[1]

To analyse the central sexual imaginary – that is, 'the set of affective and imaginative resources that produce certain forms of sexual subjectivity'[2] – I begin with Catharine MacKinnon's statement that 'social supremacy is made, inside and between people, through making meanings'.[3] One form of social supremacy is gender supremacy. In the previous chapter, I discussed this phenomenon in terms of social identity power fitted to imagined subjects existing within and across multiple central social imaginaries. In brief, this chapter argues that the dominant Western social imaginary – which imbues our world with meaning – remains patriarchal in spite of various gains for women. The structure of this chapter is as follows: I first characterise key elements of patriarchy's ideology, highlighting the ways in which it employs a dimorphic biological essentialism to naturalise and hierarchise a gender binary, reinforcing stereotypes (i.e. images) about the aptitudes, talents, preferences, interests, roles and abilities of Men and Women, thereby subjugating women to men.[4] (Though it must be said that, in practice, few, if any, people perfectly embody our culture's imagining of the paradigm Man and Woman.[5]) Next, anticipating the objection that patriarchy, as I have characterised it, no longer exists, I show how patriarchy co-opts central images from the liberal humanist ethico-political imaginary to shield its contemporary presence and impact from recognition as such. Then I highlight the ways in which both sexism and misogyny function to maintain patriarchy over time. I also offer some reflections on the eroticisation of domination and subordination under patriarchy and its connection to the objectification of women, which is a central route of their subjugation in this milieu today.

THE CENTRAL SEXUAL
IMAGINARY IS PATRIARCHAL

The claim I am advancing in this chapter is that the central sexual imaginary is patriarchal. First, let us consider some of patriarchy's meaning-generating narratives, which happen to be *ideological*. Iris Marion Young clarifies that a meaning-generating narrative 'is ideological when belief in it helps to repro-duce relations of domination and oppression by justifying them or obscuring possible more emancipatory social relations'.[6] It can do this because ideolo-gies build into themselves 'an ontology and a set of norms, and it includes practices that make this ontology seem given',[7] so it is able to reproduce itself by appearing natural and necessary. Ideologies and normative practices sus-tain one another, too. When 'you *enact* a set of rituals that has this ideology as its precondition . . . you reinforce and reproduce the ideology . . . [and] *help constitute* the facts to which the ideology is committed'.[8] Ideology 'hides the contingent history of the social relations and identities that it reproduces' via this impression of *givenness*; this is its 'naturalizing effect' – it makes its own products seem 'natural, ahistorical, and not the kind of thing there is any point in critiquing'.[9] So, what does patriarchy try to convince us is given?

According to patriarchal logic, there are only two genders: Man and Woman. What's more, patriarchy figures Man and Woman as 'naturally dif-ferent' creatures.[10] Consequently, 'women and men cannot be equal in the sense of identical, for they are constrained both physically and socially by their biology. Women and men are bound to lead different sorts of lives with different sorts of preferences, activities, positions in the family and work-place, and so on'.[11] It just so happens to be the case that Men are naturally better at more public or civic social activities, while Women are naturally better suited to private affairs. Now, sometimes patriarchy figures the differ-ences between Man and Woman as oppositional – that is, patriarchy implies that 'whatever one sex is, the other simply is not'.[12] At other times, patriarchy figures Man and Woman as distinct but complementary halves that make one whole – though, importantly, the female position is 'necessarily subordinate within the pair'.[13] (Note: patriarchy happily accommodates *both* figurations, which is to say that 'every woman is normatively defined, in our culture, as the opposite *and* complement of man'.[14]) Either way, gender is binary.[15] It is natural differences of sex understood as dimorphic – that is, *there are two, and only two, genders*[16] – which (allegedly) explains or gives rise to the differences in the capacities, interests, preferences and talents of Men and

Women in society. This view is called 'biological essentialism', and it is cis-centric. That is, under patriarchy, being cisgender is taken for granted as 'natural' and thus 'normal'. The default imaging, in other words, is that 'we are all either male-man-masculine or female-woman-feminine'.[17] (The silent inference here is thus that being transgender is deviant, abnormal, foreign, wrong, fake, a delusion,[18] and that to be intersex is not to belong to a *different* (i.e. third, fourth or fifth) sex category, but to be a *pseudo*-Man or -Woman.[19])

Though it is biology which is imagined to separate humans into two distinct genders, *the body* figures much more prominently in patriarchy's image of Woman. She has been heavily associated with 'nature, corporeality, passion, emotion and domesticity',[20] and her being prone to said passions has been thought to stem from her 'disorderly' body[21] – a stereotype that hasn't yet budged. (Just think about how volatile women are said to be at *that* time of the month.) In the patriarchal sexual imaginary, Woman menstruates, gestates, births and lactates, whereas Man does not. These differences, in turn, demonstrate that Woman is naturally maternal, emotional and more caring, which stems from her hormones. Man is more level-headed, detached, rational.[22] (Apparently his hormones, bodily capacities and functions hardly affect him.) As such, Man has a natural authority over woman.[23]

There are other distinct differences between Man and Woman in our central sexual imaginary too, which likewise boil down to bodily difference. Because of his physique and 'innate' capabilities, Man is seen as superior in athleticism and physical strength.[24] That's not treated as a normative evaluation, of course. It's just a natural fact. Men are stronger, kick longer, jump higher and bowl faster than Women; that is, they are *more* athletic than Women. And, since at least as far back as Aristotle, Woman has been characterised as an inferior reasoner to Man – this, too, is apparently a biological inevitability,[25] and one that is most convenient for Man; this means that he is naturally suited to the level-headed tasks and roles that are characteristic of the civil sphere of public life.[26] Indeed:

> Women were incapable of controlling their bodies, they did not have the requisite power over their wills, to overcome the influence of the passions, sensations, and appetites. Hence they were less constant, less faithful, less intelligent, and so on. By contrast, on account of their different bodily temperament, men had greater moral and intellectual competence compared to women. Men were regarded as stronger, smarter, and capable of greater moral perfection.[27]

So, while Man's *body* in many ways explains his superiority to Woman, Woman is somehow figured as '*more* biological, *more* corporeal, and *more* natural' than Man, and this is a bad thing.[28] Inexplicably, Man is both corporeally superior and at the same time he is imagined to be incorporeal – a disinterested, rational, objective agent, one who transcends his physicality.[29] What's more, privileging 'abstract reason as a marker of humanhood' means that it is Man who is tacitly imagined when one speaks of the Individual.[30]

Alternatively, the alleged nurturing nature of Women suits them primarily to the private sphere where they are expected to be available for 'the service of men and men's interests as men define them'.[31] As Marilyn Frye details:

> Women's service work always includes *personal service* (the work of maids, butlers, cooks, personal secretaries), *sexual service* (including provision for his genital sexual needs and bearing his children, but also including 'being nice', 'being attractive for him', etc.) and *ego service* (encouragement, support, praise attention) . . . [But note:] The details of the subjective experience of this servitude are *local*. They vary with economic class and race and ethnic tradition as well as the personalities of the men in question.[32]

The presumption, in a sentence, is that 'women are born to please'.[33] This is 'the prison of biology' that patriarchy places real women within.[34] And note further still: insofar as patriarchy presumes the naturalness of Woman's service of Man,[35] and that Man and Woman naturally complete each other, patriarchy is hetero-centric in addition to being cis-centric. (Some feminists call this 'compulsory heterosexuality'.[36]) The image is that all 'normal/ordinary' Men and Women are heterosexual, and that all Men can expect to find wives who will fulfil said personal, sexual and ego service roles through their embodied labour. The image is that it is Woman's *destiny* to become a wife and mother, to serve others. The reason this matters is that powerful imaginary symbols sustain a range of normative judgements, social relationships and individual habits within a delimited central imaginary but also *across central imaginaries*.[37] These images of Woman and Man (and, as we will also see, the Individual) are powerful, enduring symbols which are not easily unstuck.

PATRIARCHY CAN BE SNEAKY

In Western liberal democratic English-speaking societies (specifically, the Anglosphere), there is a story that we members know well. It is a story about who we are, how we came to have a society like ours, and what it is we value dear.

> There was once a time of caste and class, when tradition decreed that each group had its place, and that some are born to rule and others to serve. In this time of darkness, law and social norms defined rights, privileges, and obligations

differently for different groups, distinguished by characteristics of sex, race, religion, class, or occupation. Social inequality was justified by church and state on the grounds that people have different natures, and some natures are better than others.

Then one-day Enlightenment dawned, heralding a revolutionary conception of humanity and society. All people are equal, the revolutionaries declared, inasmuch as all have a capacity for reason and moral sense. Law and politics should therefore grant to everyone equal political and civil rights. With these bold ideas, the battle lines of modern political struggle were drawn.

For over two hundred years since those voices of reason first rang out, the forces of light have struggled for liberty and political equality against the dark forces of irrational prejudice, arbitrary metaphysics and the crumbling towers of patriarchal church, state and family.

Today in our society very few vestiges of prejudice and discrimination remain, but we are working on them, and have nearly realized the dream those Enlightenment fathers dared to propound.[38]

This story is one of the core meaning-generating narratives of our central ethico-political imaginary, the liberal humanist imaginary. My ethico-political imaginary tells me that everyone is equal, that everyone should be treated the same way, with impartiality. My ethico-political imaginary tells me that it wasn't always this way; there were certain groups of people that we *used to* think of as irrational and overly emotional (Women), as savages (Indigenous people), as perverted (Queers), but not anymore. These were the dark times. But rejoice, for we are in the dark times no longer. We are enlightened now.

Unfortunately, this impression of our shared history as a long but steadily progressive march to justice obscures the fact that the core imagined subject of this imaginary was only tailored to fit a very specific type of subject. As Imani Perry reminds us, 'according to many Enlightenment thinkers, those who were not literally or potentially possessors of property generally stood outside political membership', as was the case for European women who, under the doctrine of femme coverture, generally had their legal existence – their Personhood (including any property they may have possessed) – incorporated into her husband's Person upon marriage.[39] In short, although there were sometimes exceptions, generally speaking women did not constitute the taken-for-granted subject to whom Enlightenment ideals and values applied. Although Enlightenment thinkers *did* imagine a political order that respected the so-called Natural Law and Rights of Man, and while it *is* true that these Enlightenment philosophers 'embraced a more abstract idea of who belonged as full members of the sovereign nation', it is *also* true that they 'developed taxonomies and presented an orderly set of social relations that idealized patriarchy'.[40] In Moira Gatens' words, theirs was 'a dream of equity, based on corporeal interchangeability'.[41] Indeed, the imagined subject standing at the centre of the central ethico-political imaginary is tacitly imagined a fraternal patriarch – specifically, a white, European, property-owning, reasonable Man who is a head of household.[42] This Individual is equal in dignity to his brothers – that is, to other white, European, property-owning, reasonable, adult Men – yet he retains a natural authority over Women. This was not an accident. Indeed, 'that some are left standing . . . outside *yet under the thumb of hegemonic power* is written into the idea of [the] liberal subject', says Perry.[43]

To be outside of, but nonetheless affected by the power of the liberal Individual, involved a separation of spheres: public and private. In the public sphere, the Individual is a 'brother', a Man among Men, equal to those with whom he is corporeally interchangeable. But in the private sphere he becomes, simultaneously, a little patriarch: his relationship with 'the other members of the household was analogous to a king or parliament's reign over the nation'.[44] Importantly, as Carole Pateman has argued, recognising the *fraternal* structure of patriarchy in our milieu reveals the tacit presumption of a prior, repressed *sexual* contract, one that enforced Men's natural authority in private affairs.[45] This 'contract' is both 'sexual in the [ordinary] sense of patriarchal – that is, the contract establishes men's political right over women – and also sexual in the sense of establishing *orderly* access by men to women's bodies'.[46] That is, it affirms 'male sex-right and female sexual submission'.[47] Out in the public sphere, the Individual is an equal among other Individuals (his brothers), but these brothers continued to think themselves entitled to the personal, sexual and ego services of Women just insofar as women were not-Men. (Churcher and Gatens describe this as 'an overblown sexual self regard and sense of entitlement' – it hasn't disappeared today.[48])

Of course, it's easy enough to argue that these Enlightenment writers just simply failed to appreciate their own biases of the day; because they were blinded by bias they were unable to follow the logic of their own arguments through to their proper conclusions. But, one may optimistically believe, we can still adopt their political individualism (extended to all humans for real this time) and we can adopt their central values, like liberty, autonomy and equality. In other words, while they only imagined some human beings to be Individuals, we can imagine all human beings as Individuals. So, let us gloss over the sexism in these Enlightenment texts, recast references to 'Man' and 'Persons' as applicable to us all. While they weren't truly neutral with respect to human differences, we can be. We can abide by the maxim that 'people should be treated as individuals, not as members of groups' because of the equal moral worth inhering in all humans.[49] Similarly, we can consistently follow a principle of non-discrimination: 'treat everyone according to the same principles, rules and standards'.[50] We truly *feel* that nowadays everyone is equal under the law, everyone gets to vote, everyone gets to work, everyone gets to learn. Everyone has dignity. Every Individual is free to forge his own path, to pursue what makes him happy, to live his life by his own lights. We *feel* that we are 'committed to principles of equal treatment'.[51] So, we can still affectively invest in the above-articulated meaning-generating narrative of human sociability. The dark times are indeed over.

Unsurprisingly, taking this story as gospel – believing that those revolutionary fathers *really did* declare that all people are equal, believing that we *really have* nearly realised the dream of a society devoid of prejudice and discrimination – leads us to the conclusion that, today, Western liberal democratic societies like Australia (and the United Kingdom and United States) are, as a matter of fact, *post-patriarchal* (among other things).[52] But feminists – myself included – aren't convinced by this evaluation. For, let us ask, how does Woman fit into this domain? In theory, at least, she ceases to be a Woman and becomes truly recognised as an Individual instead. But this still remains a dream of equity based on interchangeability, that is, *sameness*. In theory, Women can be recognised as bearing the traits of the Individual, but in practice women wear this identity like an ill-fitted suit. That's because women do not cease to be *recognised* as Women in both public and private spheres. Indeed, the fact that our ethico-political discourse centres on dynamics between Individuals (who are *prima facie* identical) simply obfuscates the fact that our gender identities are sedimented in the dominant Western social imaginary and so extend throughout all of our central imaginaries too. Gender is never *not* present.

Still, one may protest, women are not subjugated today. They are no longer excluded from the public sphere: they can vote, govern, work. There are laws which prohibit discrimination on the basis of gender. They have all of the same rights, entitlements and opportunities as men. But patriarchy, like all imaginaries, is not fixed. It is fluid. And patriarchy works sneakily through taken-for-granted impressions of what Men and Women are 'naturally' like. As Claire Chambers explains, nowadays 'in Western liberal orthodoxy patriarchy rarely presents women as *inferior*; instead it presents women as *differently-choosing*'.[53] Importantly, 'choice' is a tool borrowed from liberal humanism where it functions as 'a *normative transformer*: something that, by its mere presence, transforms an unjust (because unequal) situation into a just one' (because chosen).[54] So, take the gender gap in retirement savings as an example. This inequity, some might argue, is a consequence of women choosing to work in lower-paying professions, or part time, or not at all for periods of their lives (e.g. when raising children). Since they could have chosen differently, we must accept the consequence – that is, financial inequity – as *just*. Since this inequity was freely chosen, it is not evidence that women are subjugated. However, appeals to individual women's choices do not acknowledge that many of these types of 'choices' are not truly free; they 'are shaped by the social construction of appropriately gendered behaviour', which involves active and passive, agential and structural relations of power.[55] Even though these dynamics have evolved through successive iterations of gender in/appropriate behaviour (like a game of telephone), Men nonetheless remain primarily figured as civic subjects, as Individuals, and Women remain figured as carers, as 'guardians of the private realm of need, desire, and affectivity'.[56] Hence, we find, for instance, that patriarchy has adapted to this new normative dynamic of women's mass entry into the paid labour force by figuring certain professions as more desirable or naturally appealing for Women to choose.[57] These desirable, naturally appealing jobs – to absolutely no one's surprise – involve caring and service work: 'nurse, secretary, teacher', and the like.[58] Jobs that naturally appeal to Men, on the other hand, are found in fields such as finance, media and politics.[59]

So, patriarchy's story is that it just so happens to be the case that individual women *prefer* feminine roles and activities (both private and public), that they are *naturally* better at them, whereas individual men *prefer* masculine roles and activities, and are basically useless at domestic tasks. (We are all familiar with the stereotype of the dumb dad.) But, patriarchy says, there is nothing stopping a woman from pursuing more masculine activities if that is what she wants to do. Similarly, liberal humanism's story is that ensuring a formally equal playing field for men and women alike (via legislature and policies) is all that we have to do to create a just society. We are bound to ensure equality of opportunity, not equality of outcome,[60] for 'a situation can be unequal without being unjust, so long as those involved are able to make *choices* about their lives'.[61] The unstated inference is: if women *aren't* overwhelmingly present in socially significant fields and powerful institutions today, it's because they don't *want* to be there. The result is that any evidence of actual gender inequality, like the absence of women in a particular field, say, politics or evidence of lifetime financial disparities 'thus becomes the result of some combination of natural difference and free choice, and disrupting it becomes both unnatural and unjust'.[62] In short, patriarchy puts on a cloak of invisibility by working with the meaning-generating narratives and affect-laden values of the central ethico-political imaginary, and this allows it to retain its position as the central sexual imaginary, accommodating the advances of feminist activism (such as the right to work) into its structure.[63] Patriarchal ideology still essentialises differences between Men and Women when it can, and the actual inequities between Man and Woman are explained away through the framework of individual choices (which are therefore unproblematic, because chosen). *This* image has come to count as the taken-for-granted shape of things in my milieu today.[64]

SEXISM AND TWO TYPES OF MISOGYNY

In Western liberal democratic societies like mine, the narrative that 'times have changed for women' is a popular one. And it is true, times have changed. What is not true is the implicit premise that this statement projects. Namely, that women are no longer oppressed under patriarchy. The tools of patriarchy – sexism and misogyny – function all around us. Let us explore these now in more detail, starting with sexism.

As we saw above, patriarchal ideology provides a picture of Men's dominance and Women's submissiveness as natural and inevitable, and, importantly, 'the appearance of the naturalness of the dominance of men and the subordination of women is supported by anything which supports the appearance that men are very like other men and very unlike women, and that women are very like other women and very unlike men'.[65] People actively (but not necessarily deliberately) behave in sexist ways when they employ these aforementioned 'assumptions, beliefs, theories, stereotypes, and broader cultural narratives that represent men and women as importantly different', and thus play their part in maintaining the patriarchal status quo.[66] In Sara Ahmed's words, 'sexism is a set of attitudes that are institutionalized, a pattern that is established through use, such that it can be reproduced *almost* independently of individual will'.[67] For instance, when people believe that the overrepresentation of women in caring/service roles and overrepresentation of men in powerful, society-shaping roles is a consequence of Women's and Men's 'natural preferences', that is a belief shaped by sexism. But it doesn't mean the person who thinks this is *consciously* sexist. Basically, sexism works by trying to get us to fundamentally understand our world through the prism of Men's and Women's differences (even if we maintain that one's society is or ought to be formally equal); from there, it is easy to 'rationalize and naturalize patriarchal norms and expectations'.[68]

To this end, sexist speech is sometimes obvious, but other times it can be harder to spot. Consider a hard-to-spot example: a man exclusively calls women 'girls' without much conscious reflection on why he does it, and he does so without expressing any ill will. This nonetheless implies the inferior status of women to (implicitly) adult men, and as such (again, implicitly) justifies men's being given more credence and authority than women.[69] As Lynne Tirrell explains, 'calling a grown woman "girl" assigns a status-function that denies her adulthood and rationalizes male paternalistic behaviors'.[70] She adds, further, that 'its inappropriate use for an adult woman serves a purpose, to rationalize paying her less for her work, treating her as incapable of making serious decisions, and similar sorts of behaviors that undercut the full expression of her autonomy'.[71] This type of treatment might also compel or incline certain behaviour – for example, others (men or women) may be more inclined to take a man's word for something over the claims of 'some girl'. This is an example of sneaky sexism, or sexism that, by all appearances, seems so benign that to bother objecting to it would seem 'overly dramatic', and being overly dramatic is a sexist stereotype women typically try to avoid.

Then there are the more obvious examples. Consider former Prime Minister of Australia Tony Abbott's remark as he explained the economics of carbon pricing: 'What the women of Australia need to understand, as they do the ironing, is that if they get it done commercially it's going to go up in price and their own power bills when they switch the iron on are going to go up'.[72] Abbott's speech marks Women out as cognitively inferior, given their seeming inability to understand the nuances and implications of carbon pricing, needing it explained to them in very basic, feminised analogies. It is, furthermore, an instance of cultural imperialism, since Abbott's comment betrays the norm that Men's sphere is the civil public sphere by marking out Women with homely (private sphere) gendered stereotypes. Finally, Abbott's comment also naturalises the exploitation of Women – that is, makes their undertaking of household labour seem normal, mundane, innocuous – with the consequence that it frees Men up for more important worldly pursuits.

So, we see that sexism, broadly speaking, is in the business of normalising the subjugation of Women as a group to Men as a group, and via this naturalisation it inclines compliant behaviour in line with patriarchy's ideological expectations. This is achieved through the deployment of stereotypes and certain cultural narratives, which, through repetition, sediment and habituate our ways of being and seeing in the world, and being with and seeing one another. In turn, the narratives themselves come to have 'the overall function of *rationalizing* and *justifying* patriarchy' because patriarchy seems like the way things really are and can only ever be.[73] Sexism can be done through words, representations, actions and combinations of these. And as we can see from these examples, sexism need not be deliberate: 'No one needs to be *trying* to support the system; all it takes is behavior that coheres'.[74] Sexism can be perpetuated without reflection precisely *because* a patriarchal social world is our normality – that which informs guiding background presumptions and orients the way we act in and inhabit a variety of domains.

Misogyny, however, is quite a different beast. 'Misogyny is a dominant hegemonic force', the core kernel of which holds that 'it is right for men to command and women to obey'.[75] Thus, we should not think of misogyny strictly as woman-hating; rather, we should see misogyny 'as power. It is about punishing women who violate the norms of patriarchy'.[76] Hence, we see that misogyny is triggered by 'hierarchical insecurity'[77] (but note: it is not only Men who experience hierarchical insecurity) – misogyny is dished out when women are *felt* to be insubordinate, when they are *perceived* as behaving inappropriately, that is, when they fail (or seem like they might fail) to act in accordance with, or refuse to make themselves available for ego, sexual, and personal service work. This system restores order; it 'functions to police and enforce gendered norms and expectations, and involves girls and women facing disproportionately or distinctively hostile treatment'.[78] Still, it is important to note that misogyny is 'the hostility that women face, due to patriarchal forces, *rather than* the hostility that men feel, deep down in their hearts'.[79] To that end, anyone of any gender can act misogynistically. Kate Manne offers a nuanced definition of misogyny that is quite helpful here. Under patriarchy, 'women will tend to face hostility of various kinds because they are women in a man's world (i.e. a patriarchy), who are held to be failing to live up to men's standards (i.e. tenets of a patriarchal ideology which have some purchase in this environment)'.[80]

However, it is still worth emphasising the affective register of misogyny. Any act, including a speech act, is properly characterised as misogynistic when it displays 'moods and modes *in the general family* of hostility', which includes '"reactive attitudes" (e.g. blame, resentment, guilt); punishment; betrayal; mistrust; hierarchical jostling; and various forms of shaming, disgusted, and "ousting" behavior'.[81] This is one of the things distinguishing it from sexism. But misogyny is not just a display of hostility towards women. Misogyny is (and is about) power; it is corrective.[82] No longer are women 'encouraged' to behave according to patriarchal standards, no longer do the proponents of patriarchy try to cajole women and men alike into believing that this hierarchy of Men's superordinate and Women's subordinate status is inevitable, natural, good, right; misogyny is deployed to strong-arm women into compliance with patriarchal norms under threat of, or direct penalty. Misogyny is thus 'the "law enforcement" branch of a patriarchal order, which has the overall function of *policing* and *enforcing*' its governing ideology, norms, and expectations.[83] In short, then, the coercive enforcement of patriarchal norms is 'the functional essence of misogyny'.[84] And insofar as speech can be 'an expressive means of practicing inequality',[85] we can understand misogynistic speech as both a *threat* and a *penalty* itself. Said differently, 'misogyny is both a function and an expression of patriarchy'.[86] Let us see how this is so by examining gendered slurs like 'bitch', 'cunt', 'slut' and 'whore'.[87]

Slurs work by interpellating their targets; 'they call out to a subject, second-personally, and call upon her to recognize herself as (already) the self she is being recognized as being [a bitch, cunt, slut, whore], with the social identity [Woman] and position [subordinate to Man] she is recognized as having'.[88] The woman targeted with a misogynistic slur is being recognised, and is *viscerally pulled into recognising herself as being so-recognised*, as inferior to and worth less than Men, which is to say that the slur positions 'the interpellator above the one interpellated on some sort of hierarchy'.[89]

Through repeated interpellation, misogynistic slurs produce the types of subjects that are imagined to exist within patriarchy, and which are necessary under the logic of the central ideology through which the world is understood. That is to say, there 'are' sluts because women are interpellated, through (hate) speech, as 'sluts'.[90]

What is interesting about these misogynistic slurs is that, mostly, they refer to only *some* women rather than the whole group; that is, they appear to have no 'neutral' correlate.[91] Three out of the four slurs do this. ('Cunt' is the exception because it refers to – or, when directed at a woman, reduces a person to – a body part that all Women are imagined as having.) The subject positions in patriarchy, then, are not simply double: Man–Woman, but are, at least, triple: Man–Good Woman–Bad Woman. That women are divided into Good and Bad types under patriarchy is well documented among feminists.[92] Indeed, Andrea Dworkin argues that 'the politics of contempt for women as a class', (she calls it 'antifeminism') 'breaks down into contempt for particular kinds of women – as men envision the kinds of women there are'.[93] Here, she additionally lists the gendered insults 'dyke' and 'prude', among the others mentioned above. This class of Bad Women, she explains, coexists in the patriarchal imaginary with a 'woman-superior' ideological vision where Woman is wholly moral, good and right. Unfortunately for us, 'the morally superior nature of women is honored mostly in the abstract. The worship [of the Good Woman] is worship of a symbol – a symbol manipulated to justify the uses to which fallen women are put'.[94]

So, putting it plainly, misogyny comes in two forms: interdivisional and intradivisional. In short, interdivisional misogyny is that which manifests as a *universal* hostility towards women, as when one describes women as 'cunts', or when Eminem raps: 'They make it all up / There's no such thing / Like a female with good looks who cooks and cleans' (i.e. there are no Good Women at all). But such universal hostility is not misogyny's most common form. After all, 'why would any given man in a typical patriarchal setting have a problem with women universally, or even very generally, regardless of their relations? On the contrary, we would expect even the [least-] enlightened man to be well-pleased with some women, that is, those who amicably serve his interests'.[95] Indeed, as Manne queries, 'when it comes to the women who are not only dutifully but lovingly catering to his desires, what's to hate, exactly'?[96] The point is well taken. *Of course*, misogyny is not always universal – the very purpose of misogyny is to pull women into line with the norms of a patriarchal sexual imaginary and into the service of Men, under the command of Men, and some women do this all on their own. It is far more common, and indeed we should expect to encounter misogyny in its intradivisional form: separating the group Woman into two classes, Good and Bad. Patriarchy does not require hostility towards women who 'know their place' as givers, carers, and deputies. What's more, the very presumption that misogyny entails universal hatred of women is an assumption through which patriarchy can further efface itself. Consider this type of defence given by an internet troll who refuses to see his own behaviour as misogynistic: 'If someone had said to me, "Oh, you're a misogynist. You hate women" . . . I could say, "Nuh-uh, I love my mom. I love my sisters. I've loved . . . the girl-friends that I've had in my life"'.[97] This self-evaluation can be genuine. But if misogyny is primarily intradivisional, as I contend it is, the 'I love my mum/wife/daughter' defence doesn't prove that such acts target specific individuals over shared identity traits. Social imaginaries condition our behaviours and outlooks in all sorts of ways, and we don't always notice when we are affected by them. Separating a class into Good and Bad types makes it even less likely that we'll notice when we are being affected by deeply sedimented group-oriented stigmas.

DOMINANCE AND SUBMISSION, OBJECTIFICATION AND SEXUAL AGENCY

So far, this chapter has talked about patriarchy's constitution of Men and Women as natural opposites, around which a hierarchical complementarity has developed. What has been left unexplored is the nature of cisgender-heterosexual (cis-het) eroticism under patriarchy. Catharine MacKinnon once claimed: 'All women live in sexual objectification like fish live in water'.[98] Given the proliferation of online pornography, this statement rings especially true still today.[99] But this statement was not just about the literal projections of women's eroticised bodies in all kinds of places (not only in pornography but also advertising, film and television, in fashion magazines and so forth) to such an extent that we are effectively 'trained to oversexualise and objectify women's bodies'.[100] It was also indicative of the erotic dynamic that exists between Man and Woman under patriarchy. We must explore this, for the primary relationship of Woman to Man in the central sexual imaginary – and thus, so too in the dominant Western social imaginary – is a *sexual* one. This is one of her core fields of service work. Let us take a closer look at exactly how sexuality is figured in our central sexual imaginary and how it ties to gender identity, then.

As MacKinnon explains, 'the ruling norms of sexual attraction and expression are fused with gender identity formation and affirmation, such that sexuality equals heterosexuality equals the sexuality of (male) dominance and (female) submission'.[101] In short, dominance is both masculinised and eroticised, while submission is feminised and eroticised, and thus Men are expected to be (and are expected to *enjoy* being) sexually dominant; Women are expected to be (and are expected to *enjoy* being) sexually submissive. As MacKinnon explains, 'Women cope with objectification through trying to meet the male standard, and measure their self-worth by the degree to which they succeed'.[102] Women's purpose in this dynamic is to be the *object* of desire; she represents a *sexual potential* for Man, and he has the agency to pursue or reject her. Indeed, men and women alike come to share in an image wherein 'the bodies of women are there for male consumption and gratification'.[103] So it is that the patriarchal imaginary creates and sustains 'attitudes of sexual entitlement among men and encourage[s] a lack of sexual self-regard among women'.[104]

Now, cis-hetero-sexuality is (ideologically) compulsory under patriarchy. And, 'to the extent the gender of a sexual object is crucial to arousal' – which it is here: Men must only be attracted to Women and vice versa – 'the structure of social power that stands behind and defines gender' – namely, dominance for Men, submission for Women – 'is hardly irrelevant'.[105] Said differently, gender identity and sexuality are two aspects of the same inter-subjective social dynamic of gender dominance and submission; 'being this', that is, dominant/submissive 'as identity, acting it as role, inhabiting and pre-senting it as self, is the domain of gender. Enjoying it as the erotic . . . is the domain of sexuality'.[106] This dynamic is a social construct. However, under patriarchy, this type of 'sexual expression is implicitly seen [or, represented] as the expression of something that is to a significant extent *presocial*'.[107] This is significant because, insofar as patriarchy establishes an eroticised gender hierarchy as 'natural', the acts and relations it portrays seems at once inevitable and normal as well as erotic and desirable: Men are naturally dominant, Women are naturally submissive, and that's the way we (ought to) like it. This comes to be seen as an unchallengeable truth, rather than what it really is, namely, a product of social power.

So, Man is naturally dominant, Woman is naturally submissive. Note, then, that because of his dominance, Man pursues while Woman is pursued. In this way, Man is *a sexual agent*; he exercises his agency when he scores, hits it, nails, smashes, bangs, ploughs, drills, rams, destroys, screws or pounds her – after all, as they say, any hole is a goal. Woman, then, is not a sexual agent, but a *sexual object*. She is the thing that is ploughed, nailed, drilled, hit and smashed.[108] Note here, too, that the linguistic allusions describing Men's agential pursuit and attainment of cis-hetero-sex in our day-to-day slang are both violent and competitive. What does this reveal about the way we imag-ine the (cis-hetero-)sexual encounter? At least this: 'the correlation between sexuality and violence in patriarchal society . . . is uniquely constitutive of women's social reality', that 'love and affection are not what is sexualized in this society's actual sexual paradigm', and 'force' is 'power's expression'.[109] (Not all sexual euphemisms are violent or competitive, of course, and the violent ones are not exclusive to the cis-hetero-sexual encounter, but it is telling that so many of them are of this kind.) *If* Woman is ever imagined to have any agency in the sexual encounter – and the way we talk about (cis-hetero-)sex tells us that she often is not – her agency is imagined in only one of two ways, each of which is figured in terms of a commodity-exchange model: on the one hand, Good Women 'have no sexual desire, but are willing to have sex in exchange for a valuable reward such as financial stability, a baby, or marriage that will afford social respectability'; on the other hand, Bad Women 'give it away', and because they give it away, what is given *and the person who gives it* have no value.[110] Hence, unsurprisingly, as Emma Jane notes, 'gendered abuse and oppression' often 'reduces women to their sexual – or lack of sexual – value and then punishes them for this self-same characteristic'.[111]

Outside of this, Woman has no sexual agency. She is, rather, a sexual *object*, and is so in several senses. As we saw earlier, part of what being a Woman entails – sexual service – means 'being attractive for Men' – performing Womanhood correctly entails the pursuit of attractiveness in Men's eyes (i.e. being young, cisgender, fit, pretty). Women are expected to *want* to be the object of a Man's desire rather than to be a sexual agent herself. Woman is also objectified in the sense that her subjectivity is stripped away from her in the sexual encounter as imag(in)ed; as the above allusions indicate, Woman is figured as some *thing* that is acted upon: Man fucks, Woman gets fucked – which is to say, women's submission and passivity are rendered normative.[112] She is further objectified in the sense that Woman is treated as something objective, static, unchanging. Says Simone de Beauvoir, Woman is 'called "the sex", meaning that the male sees her essentially as a sexed being; for him she is sex, so she is it in the absolute'.[113] Woman, being sex to Man, is not a complex and unique individual to be respectfully engaged with. She is a body to be fucked. What we find here is that 'it is partly through projection that women are treated as objects, [and thus] denied autonomy'.[114] Men, on the other hand, 'are socially allowed selves hence identities with personalities', that is, they have complex subjectivities which men deny to actual women.[115] And, in any of these scenarios 'sexuality socially defines women'.[116]

CONTEMPORARY PATRIARCHY

In this chapter, I contended that our central sexual imaginary is patriarchal; that it imagines three subjects: Men, who are superordinate, Bad Women, who are subordinate, and Good Women, who are superordinate to Bad Women but nonetheless remain subordinate to Men. Under patriarchy, we retain 'the norm that women should give way to men's assertion of their authority'.[117]

Under this system, compliance with patriarchal normative expectations is achieved via the application of sexist reasoning, or else it is coerced through the deployment of misogyny. Some may believe that we, in the Anglosphere, now live in a post-patriarchal world. However, I have argued that while the world may sometimes appear to have achieved gender equality, this is only as a consequence of patriarchy's ability to use images from the androcentric liberal humanist imaginary (our central ethico-political imaginary) to efface itself. Yet, patriarchy still attaches very specific expectations of behaviour to Men and Women alike, values these hierarchically, and makes the structuring of our social world in these gendered ways affectively resonant through the elaboration of sexist meaning-generating narratives. It is clear that patriarchy primarily serves the interests of men, and rarely those of women. For, so long as the norm that there will be *some* Woman somewhere available to meet Man's service needs – to provide him with things like 'attention, affection, admiration, sympathy, sex, and children . . . safe haven, nurture, security, soothing, and comfort'[118] – men will generally benefit from patriarchy. Men's interest is, ultimately, to be able to command at least some women, where the characteristic form that such command takes is the demand for a particular set of personal, sexual and ego services.[119] They are, after all, members of the superordinate gender; each a little patriarch over his own private affairs (even if he prefers not to think of himself that way). Thus, we see that patriarchy effectuates men's social power to subjugate women.[120] I noted further the way that Men's dominance and Women's submission become *eroticised* under patriarchy, and the ways this positions Man as a sexual agent and Woman as a sexual object. This imaginal system elicits affective investments from men and women alike, which sediments and reinforces patriarchy's social identity power dynamics of dominance and submission in the present.

NOTES

    1. Millicent Churcher, *Reimagining Sympathy, Recognizing Difference: Insights from Adam Smith* (London: Rowman and Littlefield International: 2019), 5.

    2. Danielle Celermajer, Millicent Churcher, Moira Gatens, and Anna Hush, 'Institutional Transformations: Imagination, Embodiment, and Affect', *Angelaki* 24 (2019): 15.

    3. Catharine MacKinnon, *Only Words* (Cambridge: Harvard University Press, 1993), 31.

    4. I understand 'subjugation' as an act designed to bring some under domination or control; this is slightly different to 'subordination' which is to make some subservient or dependent. I suspect that to subjugate is necessarily to subordinate, but that there are more forms of subordination than just subjugation.

5. Marilyn Frye, *The Politics of Reality: Essays in Feminist Theory* (Freedom: The Crossing Press, 1983), xiii.

6. Iris Marion Young, *Justice and The Politics of Difference* (Princeton: Princeton University Press, 1990), 112.

7. Quill Kukla, 'Slurs, Interpellation, and Ideology', *The Southern Journal of Philosophy* 56 (2018): 18. An important difference between Kukla's take on ideology and my own is that I view ideologies as false representations of reality; Kukla's understanding of ideology is rather similar (but not identical) to my understanding of imaginaries.

8. Kukla, 'Slurs', 11.

9. Kukla, 'Slurs', 9. See also: Amy Allen, 'Rethinking Power', *Hypatia* 13 (1998): 22.

10. Young, *Justice*, 127.

11. Claire Chambers, 'Feminism', in *The Oxford Handbook of Political Ideologies*, ed. Michael Freeden, Lyman Tower Sargent, and Marc Stears (Oxford: Oxford University Press, 2013), 564.

12. Lisa Wade and Myra Marx Ferree, *Gender: Ideas, Interactions, Institutions*, 2nd ed. (New York: W. W. Norton and Company, 2019), 10.

13. Lorraine Code, 'Patriarchy', in *Encyclopedia of Feminist Theories*, ed. Lorraine Code (New York: Routledge, 2000), 378.

14. Moira Gatens, *Imaginary Bodies: Ethics, Power, and Corporeality* (London: Routledge, 1996), 37.

15. Wade and Ferree, *Gender*, 11.

16. Frye, *Politics of Reality*, 25.

17. Wade and Ferree, *Gender*, 23.

18. For a history of the many specifications of gender dysphoria in the *Diagnostic and Statistical Manual of Mental Disorders* and the *International Statistical Classification of Diseases and Related Health Problems*, see Jack Drescher, 'Queer Diagnoses Revisited: The Past and Future of Homosexuality and Gender', *International Review of Psychiatry* 27 (2015): 386–395.

19. Anne Fausto-Sterling, *Sexing the Body: Gender Politics and the Construction of Sexuality* (New York: Basic Books, 2020), 53–54.

20. Moira Gatens, *Feminism and Philosophy: Perspectives on Difference and Equality* (Cambridge: Polity Press, 1991), 4.

21. Gatens, *Feminism and Philosophy*, 5.

22. Young, *Justice*, 126; Churcher, *Reimagining Sympathy*, xiii.

23. Gatens, *Imaginary Bodies*, 21–24.

24. Kate Manne, *Down Girl: The Logic of Misogyny* (Oxford: Oxford University Press, 2018), 88; Wade and Ferree, *Gender*, 132.

25. Code, 'Patriarchy', 378. See also Genevieve Lloyd, *The Man of Reason: Male and Female in Western Philosophy* (New Yorkshire: Methuen, 1984).

26. Jessica Megarry, 'Online Incivility or Sexual Harassment? Conceptualising Women's Experiences in the Digital Age', *Women's Studies International Forum* 47 (2014): 48; Heather Savigny, *Cultural Sexism: The Politics of Feminist Rage in the #MeToo Era* (Bristol: Bristol University Press, 2020), 39.

27. Jacqueline Broad, 'The Early Modern Period: Dignity and the Foundation of Women's Rights', in *The Wollstonecraftian Mind*, ed. Eileen Hunt Botting, Sandrine Bergès, and Alan Coffee (London: Routledge, 2019), 29.

28. Elizabeth Grosz, *Volatile Bodies: Toward a Corporeal Feminism* (St Leonards: Allen and Unwin, 1994), 14, original emphasis; see also: Frye, *Politics of Reality*, 9.

29. Gatens, *Imaginary Bodies*, 24.

30. Churcher, *Reimagining Sympathy*, 6; Young, *Justice*, 109.

31. Frye, *Politics of Reality*, 9.

32. Frye, *Politics of Reality*, 9, my emphasis.

33. Savigny, *Cultural Sexism*, 44.

34. Chambers, 'Feminism', 566–567.

35. 'Even the most benevolent of men can avail themselves of this power if they so choose', though they can do so in relation to only some women (Allen, 'Rethinking Power', 24).

36. Adrienne Rich, 'Compulsory Heterosexuality and Lesbian Existence (1980)', *Journal of Women's History* 16 (2004): 10.

37. Susan James, 'Freedom and the Imaginary', in *Visible Women: Essays on Feminist Legal Theory and Political Philosophy,* ed. Susan James and Stephanie Palmer (Oxford: Hart Publishing, 2002), 187.

38. Young, *Justice*, 156–157.

39. Perry, *Vexy Thing*, 25. Note further: 'European women who were unmarried were *feme-sole* and had men who were relatives in charge of their affairs', ibid., 23.

40. Perry, *Vexy Thing*, 26, 16.

41. Gatens, *Imaginary Bodies*, 26.

42. Perry, *Vexy Thing*, 19. See also: Jane Dolkart, 'Hostile Environment Harassment: Equality, Objectivity, and the Shaping of Legal Standards', *Emory Law Journal* 43 (1994): 175.

43. Perry, *Vexy Thing*, 21, my emphasis.

44. Perry, *Vexy Thing*, 23.

45. Carole Pateman, *The Sexual Contract* (Stanford: Stanford University Press, 1988).

46. Pateman, *Sexual Contract*, 2, my emphasis.

47. Celermajer et al., 'Institutional Transformations', 14.

48. Millicent Churcher and Moira Gatens, 'Reframing Honour in Heterosexual Imaginaries,' *Angelaki* 24 (2019): 155.

49. Young, *Justice*, 157.

50. Young, *Justice*, 158.

51. Young, *Justice*, 134.

52. Manne, *Down Girl*, xii.

53. Chambers, 'Feminism', 578.

54. Chambers, 'Feminism', 574, original emphasis.

55. Chambers, 'Feminism', 565.

56. Young, *Justice*, 110.

57. I do not mean to imply that actual women had never been able to enter the workforce until recently. I only mean to say that this is patriarchy's new meaning-generating narrative around Women and work.

58. Wade and Ferree, *Gender*, 170.

59. Soraya Chemaly, 'Demographics, Design, and Free Speech: How Demographics Have Produced Social Media Optimized for Abuse and The Silencing of Marginalized Voices', in *Free Speech in the Digital Age*, ed. Susan Brison and Katharine Gelber (Oxford: Oxford University Press, 2019), 151; Manne, *Down Girl*, 88; Wade and Ferree, *Gender*, 132. Gendering of the blue-collar professions also occurs, with more physical professions including landscaper or mechanic gendered masculine, and appearance-centred professions including hairdresser and beautician gendered feminine.

60. This can be contrasted with 'equality in terms of outcome – equalising where people end up rather than where or how they begin' (Anne Phillips, 'Defending Equality of Outcome', *The Journal of Political Philosophy* 12 (2004): 1).

61. Chambers, 'Feminism', 565, my emphasis.

62. Chambers, 'Feminism', 565.

63. Savigny, *Cultural Sexism*, 36.

64. Churcher, *Recognising Difference*, 5.

65. Frye, *Politics of Reality*, 34.

66. Manne, *Down Girl*, 79.

67. Sara Ahmed, 'Introduction: Sexism – A Problem With A Name', *New Formations: A Journal of Culture/Theory/Politics* 86 (2015): 10.

68. Kate Manne, *Entitled* (New York: Crown, 2020), 8.

69. Lorraine Code, 'Sexism', in *Encyclopedia of Feminist Theories*, ed. Lorraine Code (New York: Routledge, 2000), 441.

70. Lynne Tirrell, 'Genocidal Language Games', in *Speech and Harm: Controversies Over Free Speech*, ed. Ishani Maitra and Mary Kate McGowan (Oxford: Oxford University Press, 2012), 193.

71. Tirrell, 'Genocidal Language Games', 193.

72. Connor O'Brien, 'A Look Back at Most Controversial Tony Abbott Moments, after Prime Minister Apologises for Winking', *News.com.au*, 23 May 2014, accessed 15 April 2020, https://www.news.com.au/national/a-look-back-at-most-controversia l-tony-abbott-moments-after-prime-minister-apologises-for-winking/news-story/8cf 978d61184346161ff48ec0099cb02. See also: Manne, *Down Girl*, 81.

73. Manne, *Down Girl*, 79, original emphasis.

74. Tirrell, 'Toxic Misogyny', 2440, original emphasis.

75. Tirrell, 'Toxic Misogyny', 2436; Code, 'Patriarchy', 378.

76. Tirrell, 'Toxic Misogyny', 2441.

77. Filipa Melo Lopes, 'Perpetuating the Patriarchy: Misogyny and (Post-) Feminist Backlash', *Philosophical Studies* 176 (2019): 2520.

78. Manne, *Entitled*, 7.

79. Manne, *Entitled*, 50, emphasis added.

80. Manne, *Down Girl*, 33–34; Tirrell, 'Toxic Misogyny', 2435.

81. Manne, *Down Girl*, 129, my emphasis.

82. Tirrell, 'Toxic Misogyny', 2441.

83. Manne, *Down Girl*, 63, 78. Note, Manne's definition at 63 uses the term 'ideology'; her definition at 78 uses the terms 'norms and expectations'.

84. Manne, *Down Girl*, 47.

85. Tirrell, 'Toxic Misogyny', 2436.

86. Savigny, *Cultural Sexism*, 43.

87. One recent study located the use of the insults in over 2.9 million tweets in just one week. They also found that 'words in a message that reinforce feminine stereotypes inflate the negative sentiment of tweets to a significant and sizeable degree. These terms include those insulting someone's appearance (e.g., "ugly"), intellect (e.g., "stupid"), sexual experience (e.g., "promiscuous"), mental stability (e.g., "crazy"), and age ("old"). Messages enforcing beauty norms tend to be particularly negative'. See: Diane Felmlee, Paulina Inara Rodis, and Amy Zhang, 'Sexist Slurs: Reinforcing Feminine Stereotypes Online', *Sex Roles* 83 (2019): 16–28.

88. Kukla, 'Slurs', 13.

89. Kukla, 'Slurs', 20.

90. Anastasia Powell and Nicola Henry, *Sexual Violence in a Digital Age*, (London: Palgrave Macmillan, 2017), 61.

91. Lauren Ashwell, 'Gendered Slurs', *Social Theory and Practice* 42 (2016): 236.

92. For example, Anne Summers highlighted Australia's ideological division of women into Damned Whores and God's Police. See: Anne Summers, *Damned Whores and God's Police*, 2nd ed. (Victoria: Penguin Books, 1994). This dimorphic vision extends to explanations for (threats of) violence against women, too. In her analysis of rape, Claudia Card argues that 'rape has two targets: "bad girls" and "good girls", those who are expendable ("throw-away women") and those to whom a message is sent by way of treatment of the former'. That message is: 'this is what will happen to you if you are not "good", if you fail to do as we say'. See: Claudia Card, 'Rape as a Terrorist Institution', in *Violence, Terrorism, and Justice*, ed. R. G. Frey and Christopher W. Morris (Cambridge: Cambridge University Press, 1991), 301, 303. Kukla, 'Slurs', 28, alternatively describes the pair as 'abject women' and 'good women'. Cheshire Calhoun explores the way 'bad women' became conflated with both the feminist movement and lesbianism during the 1880s–1920s. See: Cheshire Calhoun, *Feminism, the Family, and the Politics of the Closet: Lesbian and Gay Displacement* (Oxford: Oxford University Press, 2000), 142–143. Race also plays a role in determining who is included or excluded from the category 'good women'. For example, bell hooks notes that the predominant image of black women is as 'the "fallen" woman, the whore, the slut, the prostitute'. See: bell hooks, *Ain't I a Woman: Black Women and Feminism* (London: Pluto Press, 1982), 52.

93. Andrea Dworkin, *Right-Wing Women* (New York: Perigee Books, 1983), 197, 198.

94. Dworkin, *Right-Wing Women*, 205–206.

95. Manne, *Down Girl*, 47.

96. Manne, *Down Girl*, 47–48.

97. Cited in Manne, *Down Girl*, 52.

98. Catharine MacKinnon, 'Sexuality, Pornography, and Method: Pleasure Under Patriarchy', *Ethics* 99 (1989): 340.

99. Pornography is ubiquitous on the internet, so ubiquitous that one of the Rules of the Internet (Rule 34) is: 'There is porn of it. No exceptions'. See: Y. F. and Lolrus, 'Rules of the Internet', *Know Your Meme*, 2019, accessed 13 July 2020, https://knowyourmeme.com/memes/rules-of-the-internet. That the internet is full of pornographic content is not news to anyone half-way familiar with the world wide web. Even Trekkie Monster, of *Avenue Q* fame, sings: 'The internet is for porn! The internet is for porn! Why do you think the net was born? Porn! Porn! Porn'! See: Susanna Paasonen, *Carnal Resonance: Affect and Online Pornography* (Cambridge: The MIT Press, 2011), 31. A report into children's access and exposure to pornography is even titled 'Basically . . . Porn is Everywhere'. See: Miranda A.H. Horvath, Llian Alys, Kristina Massey, Afroditi Pina, Mia Scally and Joanna R. Adler, '"Basically . . . Porn is Everywhere": A Rapid Evidence Assessment on the Effects that Access and Exposure to Pornography has on Children and Young People', *The Office of the Children's Commissioner (England)*, 2013, accessed September 15, 2020, https://www.mdx.ac.uk/__data/assets/pdf_file/0026/48545/BasicallyporniseverywhereReport.pdf.

100. Lopes, 'Perpetuating the Patriarchy', 2525.

101. MacKinnon, 'Pleasure Under Patriarchy', 319.

102. MacKinnon, 'Pleasure Under Patriarchy', 340.

103. Powell and Henry, *Sexual Violence*, 136.

104. Churcher and Gatens, 'Reframing Honour', 152.

105. MacKinnon, 'Pleasure Under Patriarchy', 330.

106. MacKinnon, 'Pleasure Under Patriarchy', 332.

107. MacKinnon, 'Pleasure Under Patriarchy', 320. Elsewhere, MacKinnon (*Only Words*, 61) writes further: 'This is men's beloved "hard-wiring", giving them that exculpatory sense that the sexual desires so programmed [via their socialisation in a particular historical context] are natural and so operate before and beyond their minds – got there before they did, as it were'.

108. Churcher and Gatens, 'Reframing Honour', 156.

109. Megarry, 'Online Incivility', 50; MacKinnon, 'Pleasure Under Patriarchy', 327, 324.

110. Kukla, 'Slurs', 28. Dolkart ('Hostile Environment Harassment', 197) adds, 'This conveys to women the message that if they have not lived a saintly life, they are not entitled to complain about how they are treated'.

111. Emma Jane, *Misogyny Online: A Short and Brutish History* (London: Sage Swifts, 2017), 2.

112. Churcher and Gatens, 'Reframing Honour', 154; MacKinnon, 'Pleasure Under Patriarchy', 318; see also Rae Langton, *Sexual Solipsism: Philosophical essays on Pornography and Objectification* (Oxford, Oxford University Press, 2009), 2, 10.

113. Simone de Beauvoir, *The Second Sex*, trans. Constance Borde and Sheila Malovany-Chevallier (London: Vintage Books, 2010), 6.

114. Langton, *Sexual Solipsism*, 12.

115. MacKinnon, 'Pleasure Under Patriarchy', 316.

116. MacKinnon, *Only Words*, 36.

117. Celermajer et al., 'Institutional Transformations', 5.

118. Manne, *Down Girl*, 130.

119. The fact that there is an 'incel' movement – made up of men who are 'involuntarily celibate' and enraged that no women will have sex with them, an act they believe is their due – demonstrates this clearly (Tirrell, 'Toxic Misogyny', 2240; Savigny, *Cultural Sexism*, 43). It also tells us that *women* will be blamed when patriarchy does not accord to men the goods it has promised.

120. Recall that social power is 'a practically socially situated capacity to control others' actions, where this capacity may be exercised (actively or passively) by particular social agents, or alternatively, it may operate purely structurally'. See: Miranda Fricker, *Epistemic Injustice: Power and the Ethics of Knowing* (Oxford: Oxford University Press, 2007), 13, deemphasised.

Chapter 3

Conceptualising Hate Speech

I want to make clear what is being said when we say it. We need this word, this concept, and we need it to be sharp and sure.

—Marilyn Frye[1]

In the preceding chapter, I discussed gendered slurs and the way they function – namely, as one form of misogyny – to maintain the social condition of patriarchy in the present. Slurs, I contend, are a form of *hate speech* against women; however, they are not the only speech acts of this kind. Pivoting now from misogyny expressed through slurs to other means of expressing misogyny through speech, this chapter considers the precise scope of 'hate speech'. Interestingly, in the existing hate speech literature, there is little conceptual argument concerning what sorts of expression constitute 'hate speech'.[2] Instead, two interrelated debates take centre stage. The first is the debate over whether or not hate speech should be legally regulated and why. (I speak to this question in chapter 5.) The second is the debate over the degree to which hate speech is genuinely harmful and, relatedly, whether those harms are constitutive or causal. On this issue, there are two general positions. Either (A) one thinks that hate speech is merely offensive, that it cannot be shown to *cause* harm, and/or that the constitutive harm argument fails.[3] Or (B) one thinks that 'hate speech' is not synonymous with 'offensive speech', that there is good evidence of hate speech causing harm, and/or that there are compelling reasons to believe that hate speech can harm constitutively.[4] I speak to this issue herein, arguing for a functional account of hate speech that can be put to use as a normative category.[5]

Of the few scholars who have sought to argue explicitly for a particular definition of 'hate speech', Katharine Gelber does so with the aim of affirming that such speech constitutively harms its targets, while drawing a boundary around expressions that are validly regulable by law, thereby contributing to both of these key debates.[6] There is much to commend about Gelber's approach to identifying hate speech, which she calls the *systemic discrimination approach*. But, there are also elements worthy of further discussion. Gelber's view that hate speech can harm constitutively derives from scholarship that employs speech act theory. However, it is not clear that this is the only (or best) way to evidence the claim that hate speech harms. My own concern with speech act theory is not that it *fails* to explain how speech can be constitutively harmful. Rather, I think there is a simpler and more appealing way to make the argument that hate speech harms constitutively (i.e. *in the very saying of it*): by demonstrating that it is an act of oppression, and that expressions can oppress due to relations of social power, including social identity power. Ultimately this explication is consistent with Gelber's stance on what makes an expression 'hate speech', but it is (I think) more straightforward.

Additionally, I comment on Gelber's aim to provide a definition of hate speech that captures what is validly *legally* regulable (while simultaneously protecting all other speech acts that ought not to be so regulated) as a barometer for the concept's limits. A worry I want to address here is whether Gelber's systemic discrimination approach still captures too much. My concern here is pragmatic. In other words, I ask: if we follow Gelber's approach to the letter, might we still end up capturing expressions which it is *unhelpful* to describe as 'hate speech'? I think so. And for this reason I propose to describe the speech acts Gelber identifies as *oppressive speech*, leaving the locution 'hate speech' for speech acts that oppress in a particular way; namely, through the oppressive face of violence. Like Marilyn Frye (who wrote on the topic of oppression), I think that we *need* 'hate speech' – both the term and the concept – and that we need it to be sharp and sure.[7] It has work to do demarcating which speech acts should be subject to bans and punitive measures, whether legal or platform specific. The aim of this chapter is thus to represent Gelber's approach, evaluate it and provide an argument for my modifications, all in turn.

'HATE SPEECH' TARGETS GROUPS

Gelber's systemic discrimination approach consists of three key components, the first of which is that, for something to count as 'hate speech', it must 'be publicly directed at a member of a *group* that is identifiable as being subjected to systemic discrimination in the context within which the speech occurs'.[8] Hate speech is a *group injustice*. It is groups who are harmed by hate speech; individuals are harmed only secondarily and insofar as they are members of groups. So, the first thing to note is that what makes it appropriate to label an expression 'hate speech' is not the *form* the expression takes. For instance, if some person – call him Andy – were to insult another person – Brenda – by calling her an 'ostrich' (an epithet), conveying contempt for the fact that she 'sticks her head in the sand' rather than dealing with her problems, this is not rightfully called 'hate speech'.[9] Hate speech is not so-called *merely* in virtue of its semantic content, being vituperative or containing epithets or profanities. Rather, to be a candidate for 'hate speech', the statement must target a *shared trait* that is the basis of a socially salient identity-based group.

What I mean by 'social salience' is this: it is not sufficient for a collective to have some trait in common. Gelber's example is people with bushy eyebrows: though such people can be considered a group, the trait they share is of no relevance in day-to-day social life in our cultural milieu.[10] Likewise, though people who avoid their problems through active ignorance could also be considered a group, there is nothing that binds them together and makes them 'stand out' on this basis in day-to-day social life. So, the shared trait must have some stronger social meaning. To use the language of chapter 1, we may say that the expressions which are candidates for the label 'hate speech' track group-based identities that have a prominent place in the dominant shared (Western) social imaginary; that the expression *intends* (in the phenomenological sense, meaning that it is directed towards or is about) a type of *imagined subject*. Using Miranda Fricker's language, we may say that expressions that pick out people *qua social type* are candidates for the label 'hate speech'.[11] The social type (imagined subject) is already recognised in the milieu, and we are interested in language which homes in on traits imagined to belong to that collective.[12]

In Gelber's own words, only 'some people are systematically disadvantaged in forms of social oppression (such as people of colour, women and LGBTQI folk), whereas others (such as those with bushy eyebrows) are not'.[13] But, to be clear, it is not the case that people with bushy eyebrows are excluded simply insofar as they are not a socially salient group. Not only must the speech have as its referent a socially salient group, the salient group must also be subjected to *systemic discrimination* in the broader milieu. To discriminate is to perceive a difference between some set of things and to consequently treat differentially. This, in and of itself, is not an inherently problematic act. What makes discrimination problematic is when a perceived difference underscores differential, exclusionary treatment owing to what Fricker would call a 'tracker prejudice'[14] – however, I prefer the term tracker *stigma*, since a stigma implies a mark upon the (imagined) body, while prejudice implies the holding of a biased idea or belief. They are called *tracker* stigmas precisely because they follow and affect the group most everywhere, functioning both synchronically – presently affecting the group's members, or being applicable to any member of the group – as well as diachronically – applicable to and affecting the group's members over time, even over generations.[15] That is to say, we should consider discriminatory treatment *systemic* when exclusionary kinds of treatment occur against group members all throughout the various dimensions of social activity: 'economic, educational, professional, sexual, legal, political, religious, and so on'.[16] In this way, the stigma is persistent and its effects are systematic, thus it eventually becomes systemic.[17] So, we can see that what is distinctive about Gelber's definition is that it does not apply just to salient group *status* – for example, 'gender identity', 'race', 'sexual orientation' and so on; rather, certain groups which *are* salient – like men, heterosexuals, cisgender folk and white people – are likewise excluded because evidence that they face *systemic* discrimination (in the context of the contemporary Anglosphere) is lacking.[18] In other words, men and white people, among others, cannot be targeted by 'hate speech', even though they can be targeted with epithets, profanities or otherwise vituperative language.

To determine what types of acts are discriminatory in the relevant sense – that is, *when they are the result, but also an instance, of an identity-tracking stigma in one's milieu* – we should look for certain coherences (so judged by members of the collective whom the acts track).[19] The relevant coherences pertain to one's own personal history, shared group histories, direct and shared experiences, as well as awareness of and attentiveness to the hierarchies and power relations that are embedded throughout one's society.[20] Helen Ngo calls these *coherences of breadth*: where the same experience is shared by the same type of people in independent circumstances (e.g. say, intimate partner violence); *coherences of kind*: where the activity in question coheres with a bunch of other experiences that fall into the same type of activity (e.g. family violence, street harassment, image-based abuse, sexploitation, etc.); and, finally, *coherences of depth*: where the act coheres 'with the weight of historical practices' and 'systematization' of stigma, such that these practices and images become 'embedded in public life, discourse, and imagination' (e.g. the normalisation of men's violence against women in fiction and news media, ineffective laws for prosecuting sexual and family violence, cultural tolerance of demeaning behaviours, implicit acceptance of rape culture, etc.).[21] In short, acts which are discriminatory in the relevant sense will be recognisable – in the very least, from the target's situated social positionality – as part of a *pattern* of treatment, each evoking a history that is not declared but is, in a sense, already known.[22]

'HATE SPEECH' INVOLVES
CONTEXTUAL POWER DYNAMICS

The second key component of Gelber's systemic discrimination approach relates to the position of power the speaker holds in that context. Gelber posits that in order for the speech act to harm in the relevant way (i.e. constitute an act of systemic discrimination),

> the speaker needs to be *either* speaking from a position of relative authority that derives either formally or informally, *or in a capacity that enacts oppressive permissibility facts* in a rule-governed activity that perpetuates systemic discrimination against the group to whom the target of hate speech is perceived by the speaker to belong.[23]

Here is where Gelber turns to the work of speech act theorists to show how speech *does* rather than merely *says* something. A requirement is that the speaker has the 'authority' for their speech to count in such a way that the act is successfully performed. To use a familiar example, I may utter the words 'I now pronounce you married' in a wedding ceremony, but my speech won't actually marry the intending couple (that is, *do something*) because I am not a marriage celebrant. However, when a celebrant utters these words under the same conditions, their expression will *create* a marriage, since their speech is authorial by virtue of their assigned social role and the conditions of the social setting.

The necessity of speaker authority has led to what some call 'the authority problem',[24] for no formal relations of authority exist in a great many of our expressive interactions. For instance, men do not have formal authority over women (in my milieu) insofar as they are men. Cisgender people do not have formal authority over trans and non-binary people insofar as they are cisgender. Ditto for sexual orientation groups (etc.). But many believe that cis-het women, trans and non-binary people, and the rest of the queer community can be harmed by expressions. So, if no authority relation exists, the question is: how can the expression harm them? It seems there are only two possible responses. Either we conclude (A) that speech is not really harmful, that is, *those who think speech harms constitutively are mistaken,* or (B) that there must be other (informal) ways to obtain authority. If one opts for (B), one must specify what those informal ways to obtain authority are. Gelber argues that the latter is a viable approach to the authority problem, pointing to Ishani Maitra's work on conditions of authority to evidence the claim.[25] There is, however, a third option. Another way out of the authority problem is (C) to assert that it is, in fact, *social power dynamics* that modulate the capacities and impact of certain expressions. This is to argue that *power, not authority, has been the significant factor all along*, for authority is just a particular type of power.[26]

Moving from the language of formal 'authority' to informal 'power' is something Mary Kate McGowan – one of Gelber's interlocutors and a speech act theorist – does.[27] However, as elaborated in chapter 1, I take my understanding of the relevant type of power – *social power* – from Fricker. As discussed, social power can be both agential, active, passive and structural, and 'the point of any operation of social power is *to effect social control*, whether it is a matter of particular agents controlling what other agents do or of people's actions being controlled purely structurally'.[28] Effecting social control is only possible in, and hence all power depends on, 'the context of a functioning social world – shared institutions, shared meanings, shared expectations, and so on'.[29] In other words, *both agential and structural power depend upon the contours of our central social imaginaries*; these central social imaginaries (and the dominant social imaginary) set the parameters of what kind of control can be exerted and by whom, or as a consequence of what operations. And, as we saw in chapter 2, men, as Men, have both structural and (at least in certain circumstances) agential power over women (and other genders) due to the centrality of the patriarchal sexual imaginary and the permeation of its images throughout the dominant shared Western social imaginary.

Now, all of this is consistent with Gelber's own view of how speech can harm. (That is why we see the conjunctive 'or' in her articulation of the second key component of the systemic discrimination approach.) The point Gelber is making, in my terms, is just this: if you want to know whose speech can be harmful and to what extent, take a look at the power relations in the specific context (in light of its history), and pay attention to the contours of the dominant shared social imaginary governing it. Concentrating on social power dynamics, including (but not limited to) the dynamics of social identity power that pervade one's context, is one way of avoiding the authority problem altogether. By employing a social imaginaries framework we can easily make sense of the view that what is said can discriminate in and of itself. So, this approach to identifying 'hate speech', which may at first be mistaken as promoting double standards (i.e. men can't be victims but women can), turns out simply to be *context sensitive*.[30] And it is necessary to take a context-sensitive approach to identifying and responding to hate speech because 'some injustices can be detected only in temporally and socially extended contexts where patterns of communicative action unfold'.[31]

Thus, context and power dynamics determine both *what* constitutes 'hate speech' and *who* can be a target. To return to our earlier example, we can see that Andy's calling Brenda an 'ostrich' simply does not function in the same way as his calling her a 'cow' would. The reasons for this are that (A) the former does not target her as a woman, but the latter does (from historical, contextual usage); (B) in the contemporary Western world women face systemic discrimination (i.e., they suffer from mistreatment which exhibits coherences of breadth, depth, and kind; i.e., they are oppressed); (C) to describe as a 'cow' is to render her, as a woman, *subhuman*, which is to treat her with indignity; and, though one need not be a member of a privileged group to commit acts of 'hate speech'; (D) the fact that Andy is a man and Brenda is a woman is not insignificant, given that he has social identity power over her *ceteris paribus*. This is not to paint women as inevitable and perpetual victims, though.[32] Gender is but one axis of discrimination. Thus, I readily acknowledge that women 'can be both dominated and empowered at the same time and in the context of the same norm, institution, or practice', and that this is so because each subject lives an intersectional life.[33] I also acknowledge that the dynamics of social contexts are always in motion, and that there is a possible future where women are no longer oppressed as a class, and will at that time be invulnerable to hate speech.

In summary, Gelber and I are in agreement that 'because some speech perpetuates aspects of the oppression that obtains in the domain within which it is uttered' – more on which below – 'it does not require the same kind of authority' typically mandated by speech act theorists.[34] We agree that *who says what* and *in what context* makes a difference to the power of expression, including its capacity to harm.

'HATE SPEECH' IS OPPRESSIVE SPEECH

The speech acts Gelber wants to capture with the locution 'hate speech' are ones that harm in a particular way. They are the speech acts which 'harm by uttering words that cohere with, and thereby perpetuate an *oppressive rule-governed activity*'.[35] To clarify, the terminology 'rule-governed activity', which comes from McGowan's work on oppressive speech, just means 'any activity governed by norms'.[36] McGowan explains: 'The "rules" in question need not be explicit, formal, exceptionless or even consciously recognized. If at least some behaviours (as contributions to the activity in question) would count as out of bounds or otherwise inappropriate (as contributions to the activity in question) then that activity is rule-governed in the relevant sense'.[37] A clear parallel can be drawn from McGowan's vision of rule-governed activities and my account of societies as essentially networks of social imaginaries (developed in chapter 1): these are systems of norms and narratives that jointly make meaning of one's world, license in/appropriate behaviours for certain sorts of persons, give certain identities salience and project particular sorts of life trajectories for different sorts of people. To reframe Gelber's criterion more straightforwardly, then, we may say that one is able to oppress certain groups with their words just insofar as one's milieu is already shaped by hierarchical relations of social power, including but not limited to social identity power, where some groups are marked by tracker stigmas, and the expression perpetuates (because it is an instance of) the systemic discrimination already affecting that group. As to the matter of *who actually is oppressed* in specific times and places, we need only look for empirical verification.[38] Notably, Gelber writes, 'there is a wealth of evidence supporting the idea that discrimination against, as a symptom of oppression of, women is systemic in Western liberal democracies, as there is in relation to people of colour and LGBTQI+ folk'.[39] To be clear, then, I am claiming – *per* Gelber – that a speech act which perpetuates (because it is an instance of) systemic discrimination against women *just is* (one way) *to oppress women.* This is only possible because women, in my milieu, are in fact subjugated to (cis-hetero) men on the axes of gender and sex.

But what is oppression, exactly? In the most abstract sense, says Iris Marion Young, 'oppression refers to *structural phenomena* that immobilize or diminish a group'.[40] Not just this, it is a relational concept. Oppression refers to 'systemic constraints on groups' that need not be the result of the intentions (i.e. a deliberate action) of a tyrant or governing body, nor the result of some explicit policies or intentional choices, but rather are also systemic constraints that result just from our following and reproducing 'unquestioned norms, habits, and symbols' in our societies.[41] As Young summarises:

> In this extended structural sense *oppression* refers to the vast and deep injustices some groups suffer as a consequence of often unconscious assumptions an reactions of well-meaning people in ordinary interactions, media and cultural stereotypes, and structural features of bureaucratic hierarchies and market mechanisms – in short, the normal processes of everyday life. We cannot eliminate this structural oppression by getting rid of the rulers or making some new laws, because oppressions are systematically reproduced in our major economic, political, and cultural institutions.[42]

The good thing about focusing on structural and agential, individual, group, and institutional power (as discussed above) is that we can clearly see how it can be the case that some speech is powerful beyond what one would imagine (or had hoped) it would be. To emphasise the point using Marilyn Frye's words:

> It is clear that if one wants to determine whether a particular suffering, harm or limitation is part of someone's being oppressed, one has to look at it *in context* in order to tell whether it is an element in an oppressive structure: one has to see if it is part of an enclosing structure of forces and barriers which tends to

the immobilization and reduction of a group or category of people. One has to look at how the barrier or force fits with others and to whose benefit or detriment it works.[43]

Interestingly, those 'forces and barriers' come in several different modes. According to Young, there are five 'faces' of oppression. They are exploitation, marginalisation, powerlessness, cultural imperialism and violence (see figure 3.1). In brief, exploitation involves 'the transfer of energies from one group to another to produce unequal distributions'.[44] Marginalisation involves the expulsion of a whole category of people from useful participation in social life.[45] Rendering a group powerless involves situating members of that group so that 'they must take orders and rarely have the right to give them', inhibiting their agency.[46] Cultural imperialism involves the dominant group projecting its 'own experience as representative of humanity as such', rendering marginal groups invisible, while paradoxically marking them out as 'different' via prejudicial stereotypes.[47] Finally, the type of violence that is oppressive is systematic violence, violence that is wielded against some people *because of* their group status. This includes physical violence as well as systemic 'incidents of harassment, intimidation, or ridicule' that are 'degrading, humiliating, or stigmatizing [of] group members'.[48] This is significant because, as Anastasia Powell and Nicola Henry point out, our paradigm image of violence is constrained to physical violence, and so too often 'dominant conceptions of violence render other forms of violence . . . invisible or insignificant'.[49]

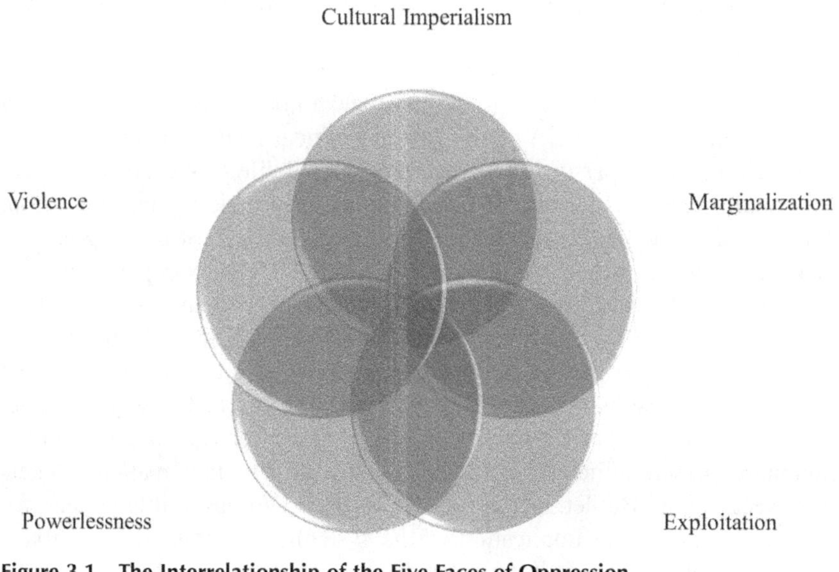

Figure 3.1   The Interrelationship of the Five Faces of Oppression.

What makes group-oriented violence – including non-physical violence (which is perhaps better termed 'abuse') – subordinating, is the weight of the risk of attack that the group members inevitably bear. Indeed, as Young clarifies, 'what makes violence a face of oppression is less the particular acts themselves . . . than *the social context surrounding them*, which makes them possible and even acceptable'.[50] She adds:

> The oppression of violence consists in not only direct victimization, but in the daily knowledge shared by all members of oppressed groups that they are *liable* to violation, solely on account of their group identity. Just living under such a threat of attack on oneself or family or friends deprives the oppressed of freedom and dignity.[51]

When a group is subjected to (the threat of) violence just because of their group identity, violence is used to discriminate. When this happens systematically, and shares coherences of breadth, depth, and kind with other acts that the group faces, violence discriminates systemically.[52]

BENEFITS AND IMPLICATIONS OF THE
SYSTEMIC DISCRIMINATION APPROACH

Gelber's systemic discrimination approach is formally neutral but practically partial. That is, in actual contexts, it only applies to certain imagined subjects and not others. If a group, even a socially salient one, is not subject to *systemic* discrimination owing to a tracker stigma (i.e. is not a member of an oppressed group), then expressions that are discriminatory (or rude, offensive, vituperative, etc.) towards them do not meet the threshold to count as 'hate speech'. Here, I want to explicitly take note of the intersectionality of our agential existence. As feminists and critical race theorists have long pointed out, every person lives an intersectional life.[53] We are all sexed, we are all gendered, we are all raced, we all have nationalities and so on. And, just as some people may be victimised on the basis of *one* stigmatised identity, so too can their other traits be targeted.[54] For example, I may be oppressed by gendered hate speech as a woman, by orientation-based hate speech as queer, or by gender-and-orientation-based hate speech (also known as *cis-hetero-misogyny*) as a queer woman. However, I cannot be oppressed by speech that insults my race (white) or my religion (technically Catholic, functionally Secular) because these groups do not suffer systemic discrimination in my present milieu.[55] I think the systemic discrimination approach gets this exactly right. But let us home in on privileged groups a little further, for there is an interesting implication of the systemic discrimination approach which has not yet been fully articulated.

Just as one's sex, gender, race and so on, can interlock to create a unique experience of social *disadvantage* – for example, as in the case of cis-hetero-misogynistic abuse, mentioned above – so too can group membership interlock to create a unique experience of social *advantage*.[56] That means, in actual times and places that are structured by oppressive social dynamics, there will be a specific collective of subjects who are centred at the intersection of *all* socially privileged groups. This group, Gelber's approach implies, *cannot* experience hate speech at all in the circumscribed context, no matter what is said to or about them. This is a consequence of the approach being *functional* rather than *linguistic* or *expressive*.[57] Should that maximally socially privileged group be targeted with discriminatory speech they may very well be insulted or offended, but this speech does not and *cannot* oppress them. Just who is so advantaged and who is so disadvantaged is an empirical question, and changes from context to context. In the Australian context (and the Anglosphere more generally), it will come as no shock to see that this maximally socially privileged group is white, cisgender, heterosexual, able-bodied, middle- to upper-class, sufficiently educated, Christian-secular, English-speaking, adult (but not elderly) men. Unless it can be demonstrated that discriminating speech acts are occurring in a milieu among other group-directed forms of subordinating discrimination, we cannot class this *group* as harmed by *hate speech*.[58] The concept and term 'hate speech' are circumscribed by a specific normative aim: identifying and objecting to expressions that result from and contribute to a group's oppression.

Now, to the benefits of Gelber's systemic discrimination approach. First, this definition 'does not rely on the presence or detection of an emotion of "hate" in the speaker' for some expression to count as 'hate speech'.[59] A speaker who simply reiterates unquestioned norms, habits and symbols that figure a stigmatised group subordinate is thus *hate speaking*, even when their speech act is not consciously motivated by malice or an aim to harm in the speaker. Second, this approach 'does not rely on the use of vituperative speech, epithets or profanities to define hate speech'.[60] This, Gelber believes, is important because oppressive speech is sometimes sneaky and hard to spot.[61] There are many faces of oppression, after all. Third, this approach is context sensitive. It recognises 'that not all group identities suffer from systemic discrimination'.[62] This, Gelber thinks, is where we should draw the line between discriminatory speech which is legally regulable and that which is not. Hence, its benefit is in its clarifying and circumscribing the concept.[63] Fourth, this approach 'render[s] visible power imbalances that are too often invisible in debates about free speech. It illuminates, rather than disregards, the deeper structural inequalities that produce and maintain' the lived experiences of diverse groups of people.[64] Finally, though she does not elaborate upon the claim, Gelber believes that this way of approaching 'hate speech' is suggestive of different legislative strategies we may employ to block, dissolve or otherwise punish the oppressive act of the speaker. She writes:

> While there is no room to develop this point further here, it is important to note that in recognizing how it is that hate speech harms, this framework makes it possible to imagine institutionally supported, discourse-based responses to hate speech that could empower and give voice to those who would otherwise be marginalized by hate speech.[65]

In other words, while this speech *does* warrant a government policy response, Gelber is 'not presenting an argument here as to the form that policy response can or should take', except to say that we need not limit our imagination to hate speech bans.[66] The right response to 'hate speech' (meaning, the most pragmatic response in light of our aim: creating a just society) might come in the form of counterspeech (more on which in chapter 5).

NARROWING THE CONCEPTION FURTHER

I find Gelber's approach to determining what constitutes 'hate speech' to be very compelling. Understood in this functional way, 'hate speech' could become one of the most important normative categories in anti-oppression politics today. Insofar as our societies are still stratified by hierarchies of oppression and privilege, and insofar as subordinating comments with coherences of breadth, depth and kind are still occurring, the need for a concept that names up these acts is pressing, for we cannot fight what we cannot identify as specially problematic.[67] Indeed, the very point of such a concept is not only to put a name to a shared experience, it is to be able to *communicate* that these acts are part of the system of oppression in which certain groups are stratified. Its purpose is simultaneously epistemic, affective, moral, and political. 'Hate speech' enables the marginalised to say: this is a specific, systemic action committed against us, it is wrong, it is harmful, perpetrators should be ashamed and it needs to stop. And to do this is, in itself, to 'fight to gain equal access to the power . . . to construct knowledge, social meaning, ideology, and definitions of who "we" are'[68] – in short, it is to fight to become an equal participant in the shaping of the dominant social imaginary within which one dwells and which so negatively affects one's life.[69]

With that said, I still think 'hate speech' needs to be further refined. While all oppressive speech is, of course, unjust, I believe we should narrow 'hate speech' to those speech acts that oppress through the face of violence. This does not mean that they cannot *also* oppress through other faces of oppression simultaneously. It is just to specify that its being an act of systemic violence is a necessary condition of a speech act's being 'hate speech'. But why make the concept narrower in this way? To answer this question, let us compare some actual instances of oppressive speech from my data set (more of which in the next chapter).

---

grow up little miss. (Man)	*Women MP's hey, can't live with 'em, can't shoot 'em. (Man)*
They all talk about gender inequalities. Where exactly is this inequality? We have laws against it already. (Man)	*Feminist scum. (Man)*
Sadly the MeToo movement has abandoned victims and become a weapon to be abused. (Man)	*You're obviously too ugly that guys don't make unwanted sexual advances against you. (Man)*

I believe that each of these comments oppresses women. If this is correct, Gelber's systemic discrimination approach would classify each as instances of 'hate speech'. I do not think we should accept this conclusion.

In the left-hand column, the first comment is directly condescending, and this condescension has more gravity insofar as it is preceded by a history of my milieu treating women as essentially infantile as compared to Men. The second expresses a political statement: women claim to be unequal but there are laws banning this, therefore the women's equality movement is disingenuous. Hence, the commentator denies the facticity of women's experiences of oppression. It circumscribes what will count as evidence against one's reality. It is thus culturally imperialistic. The third expresses an opinion. This opinion contributes to the oppression of women insofar as it perpetuates the myth that women lie about sexual assault. Like the second commentator, this man denies the facticity of women's experiences of oppression and so is culturally imperialistic. But while the comments on the right express very similar meanings to those on the left, there is something distinctive about their formation. The comments on the right, I posit, all oppress through the face of violence. This is not to say that they necessarily intimate violence against women (though two of them do); rather, what is distinctive about these comments is that they are *abusive*, and 'abusive comments are not intended to facilitate or begin a dialogue with the victim, but rather represent attempts to shut down and restrict female speech or movement through public spaces'.[70] At least in the case of the comments on the left, it is possible to provide counter-evidence for the claim that women are already equal, or the claim that women tend to lie about the occurrence of sexual assault and harassment. We can even complain about condescension, which is a rude way to treat *anyone*, not just women. The same is not possible with violent speech.

This expressive violence is a group violence and '*a social practice*. It is a social given that everyone knows happens and will happen again'.[71] It 'is a mechanism of power and oppression, intended to reaffirm the precarious hierarchies that characterize a given social order. It attempts to re-create simultaneously the threatened (real or imagined) hegemony of the perpetrator's group and the "appropriate" subordinate identity of the victim's group'.[72] Having made this clear, I also find here an opportunity to reconsider what the 'hate' in 'hate speech' is referring to. I want to suggest that we consider 'hate' as a referent to *the affective tenor of the environment for the target in the face of such expressions*. As Sarah Sorial says, 'speech can be harmful . . . by helping to constitute a degrading, hostile, or demeaning environment, which prevents persons from acting in the ways they otherwise could have'.[73] The affect that comes to permeate the environment – hostility – is carried in the images of Woman that are repeatedly reiterated in public, social spaces. Here, the impressions are that Woman is *abject* (disgusting, filthy, ugly) and that Woman is incompetent (tacitly, compared to the exemplar Man). This also helps to clarify the harm that women (and other groups marked with a tracker stigma) experience, for note McGowan's recent observation that a hostile environment 'does the very same thing that other acts of gender discrimination do: it systematically and unfairly harms and it does so on the basis of membership in a legally protected class'.[74] What's more, the environment (that is, *any* social space) is always already potentially hostile. It is so because violence 'is always at the horizon of social imagination'.[75]

Note that violence is especially egregious because it traps a group within, or coerces a group back into, their subordinate place. To help convey this harm, I turn to Vittorio Bufacchi and Jools Gilson's claim that violence is not only an act done by an agent, it is an experience of the agent so acted upon – and 'experience is characterised by a temporal indeterminacy . . . with much broader and unclear boundaries'.[76] That is to say, the after effects of violence keep going; 'the experience of violence lingers on beyond the act'.[77] To convey this aspect of violence's nature they turn to a metaphor: 'after the act of throwing a stone in the water comes to an end, the ripples on the water carry on'.[78] Branching off this point, since we are always born into social worlds with their own contextual histories, being a member of an oppressed group often involves immersion into a world where the ripples of violence are still felt from attacks on one's group throughout history. Each individual instance has the 'cumulative and reinforcing effect of countless similar messages' conveyed in a society where women's subjugation is ubiquitous.[79] These aren't ripples that women are born into, these are waves.

A second reason we should make this distinction is as follows. My experience of manually collecting instances of misogynistic and sexist comments in online discourses about gender in/equality today has led me to the conclusion that such misogyny and sexism is often disguised in ostensibly *egalitarian* speech acts. This is consistent with the way Claire Chambers describes contemporary patriarchy (as discussed in chapter 2): 'in Western liberal orthodoxy patriarchy rarely presents women as *inferior*; instead it presents women as *differently-choosing*'.[80] This means that actual evidence of inequality between men and women can be dismissed, as we see for instance in this comment: 'If it's [a seat in Parliament] not earned then *this* [quotas for women] is not the solution. Where is the proof that people are being overlooked because of gender? Just because the numbers aren't even? That's not proof' (Man). So, while I (and other feminists) can *read through* this comment and recognise the extent to which it is informed by patriarchal ideology, it will be very difficult to demonstrate this to persons who are affectively invested in this very specific ethico-political image of equality.

Now, those with an interest in gender justice (like me) want not only to *identify* instances of, but also to *put an end to* the social practice of harming women with words, including those instances when what is said does not appear to be woman-hostile. The question is whether calling ostensibly egalitarian speech acts that sneakily oppress stigmatised groups 'hate speech' will help to stop those very same speech acts. I don't think that it will, and this is due to widespread affective investment in the very image of equality with which patriarchy shields itself. I can already anticipate the response of outrage: '"Men and women are equal'; 'Jobs should be earned on merit' are now 'hate speech' in this new age of political correctness gone mad!" It may be factually incorrect that men and women are equal, and it may also be true that a standard of merit can coexist with a quota system, but no one is going to buy that statements such as these are really tantamount to hate speaking. *I* don't even buy it. I think that the concept of 'hate speech' is most useful if its use is confined to utterances that fall into a very specific normative category: systemically violent speech; speech which is *explicitly* inegalitarian and abusive. I also think *punitive* responses are the appropriate responses to hate speech, but it is hard to imagine support for a system where a user could be banned from a platform (for example) for repeatedly insisting that men and women are equal in the Anglosphere today.

In fairness to Gelber, I must reiterate that she does not argue we should necessarily penalise speakers whose utterances fall under *her* scope of 'hate speech'. In her own words (above): this framework makes it possible to imagine institutionally supported, discourse-based responses to hate speech. And I agree with her. I think counter-imaginal, discursive strategies for addressing oppressive acts of expression is necessary for the wider project of gender justice. But I also think some speech acts warrant penalties (of various sorts). And I think that making a finer-grained distinction between oppressive speech that warrants penalty (what I seek to call 'hate speech') and other oppressive speech acts (simply, 'oppressive speech'), will better serve that goal. With that said, all that remains to be discussed in this chapter is whether hate speech *online* presents us with any distinctive challenges that must be taken into consideration when developing countermeasures.

IS ONLINE HATE SPEECH DISTINCTIVE?

In closing, I want to raise for consideration the question of whether online hate speech is importantly different to offline hate speech. According to Alexander Brown, scholars tend to emphasise three features of digital hate: speaker anonymity, ease of access to technology and platforms, and the potentially vast audience size. Brown adds the feature of instantaneousness for consideration.[81] I will have more to say about digital anonymity in chapter 6, but for now let us simply note that the speaker's identity is not necessarily known or knowable when hate speech occurs offline. As Brown says, 'If person A walks up to person B on the street and calls them a "Fucking x", where x is a hate slur, and if A and B are strangers . . . then A is probably anonymous to B . . . and may have little means of finding out who A is'.[82] It is also not clear that hate speech is more impactful when it is anonymous. Anonymity is not a unique problem of cyberspace, then.

On the *reach* of online versus offline hatred, Frederick Schauer notes that something's appearance 'on a website, as opposed to in a book, a magazine, or even on television, increases exponentially the number of likely recipients of the information, and increases as well the duration of the information's availability'.[83] That is to say, the size of the audience that bears witness to online hate speech can be much more vast than its offline counterpart. Schauer is not alone in his concerns.[84] However, Brown thinks we should not overblow concerns about reach. While campaigns of online hatred have gone viral (think Gamergate[85]), and 'although virtually anyone can gain access to the Internet, it is not the case that virtually anyone can attract a mass audience of followers, likes and clicks'.[86] But focusing on any individual speaker's personal reach is inattentive to the reach of hate speech conveyed by multiple users in a single space over a steady period of time. In the course of six months, in monitoring one legacy news outlet's Facebook page, I collected 2,881 instances of hate speech against women. During this time, there was only *one day* when no misogyny or sexism was expressed. Given this, and once one considers how many online social spaces there are, whether or not individual users are capturing a wide audience is pretty much irrelevant. It may be the case that an individual can fire off a Tweet and only a handful of people see it, but that does not take away from nor undermine the impact of the steady onslaught of abuse by multiple users in multiple online social spaces over time. When you look at online social spaces from the target group's perspective, hate speech is always potentially coming in the next refresh of one's feed. That is why I describe online environments as *always already hostile* to women. Women know they are going to encounter gendered hate speech online. What they don't know is whether they will be personally targeted by it.

There is also a sense in which digital technologies mediating online communication make it 'easier' to engage publicly in hate speech. For one thing, 'the Internet is relatively cheap and easy to use'.[87] Of course, there is a real monetary cost for specific items (a modem, a smart phone, etc.) and for Internet access (cheaper plans may come with lesser data or worse service), and access to these is not equitable. However, access to certain platforms, be they social media, blogs, news websites and so on, are often free. Facebook, for example, generates its revenue from advertising, not directly from its users.[88] These Internet mediums also make a difference in another way: it is much simpler to post a public Facebook comment than it is to get a letter to the editor published in a newspaper.[89] This is because they often are not moderated before they go live, but also because there is no spatial cap on content. An editor will only publish so many letters; a comments section can go on and on by the thousands until people lose interest, the issue falls out of the news cycle, or until some sort of moderator or administrator shuts commenting off. This leads us to Brown's final feature, instantaneousness. On this point, I quote Brown at length:

> The Internet provides people with almost instantaneous publishing. On the Internet, the time delay between having a thought or feeling and expressing it to a particular individual who is located a long distance away, or to a group of likeminded people or to a mass audience can be a matter of seconds . . . My hypothesis, then, is that, as compared to offline modes of communication, the Internet encourages forms of hate speech that are *spontaneous* in the sense of being instant responses, gut reactions, unconsidered judgments, off-the-cuff remarks, unfiltered commentary, and first thoughts. Among the common types of online hate speech that may be spontaneous in this sense are uses of abusive or cruel insults or demeaning language or threatening words directed at or against a person or group of persons identified by their race, ethnicity, nationality, religion, sexual orientation, disability, gender identity, or other protected characteristics.[90]

He importantly clarifies, 'my hypothesis is not that online hate speech is always spontaneous and offline hate speech, including face-to-face hate speech, is never spontaneous. Rather, my hypothesis is that, as compared to offline modes of communication, the Internet encourages forms of hate speech that are spontaneous in virtue of the combination of qualities that online communication possesses'.[91]

I do not share the intuition that online communication encourages *more* spontaneous speech than offline communication. But I do think focusing on the often-spontaneous character of hate speech (wherever it occurs) is very revealing in another way. If Brown is right and the images of women circulated in hate speech are often 'off the cuff' comments – that is, if the reason there is so much woman-hostile speech online is attributable to the fact that the medium allows us to *react* and move on, without a second thought as to what we are really saying, whether we should say it, and what harm it might do – then we must seriously consider the possibility that *we* (the terrestrial creatures into whose lives Internet technologies have been integrated) *are habituated to misogyny*. For though it sounds paradoxical, spontaneity actually requires habit.

A NOTE ON SPONTANEITY AND HABIT

In positing that we are habituated to misogyny – its images and acts – I am closely following Ngo's take on habituation and habit. She says of subtle racist habits: 'The flinches, the tensing, the moving away, the calling toward, the panic – these are examples of habits insofar as they represent a kind of response that is *unthinking and nearby*; they are responses that reside within the body schema, such that they become called upon *readily and effortlessly* in navigating encounters with the racialized "other"'.[92] Like these racist gestures, I believe women-denigrating expressions are, in fact, part of a culturally shared arsenal that can be called forth and projected outward in an instant, readily and effortlessly – that is, spontaneously. Members of this milieu share access to and effortlessly make use of the same 'grab bag' of demeaning figurations of Women. The 'grab bag' has been established through a series of repetitions, the effects of which are cumulative rather than singular, reinforcing rather than isolating, and, with time, certain images of Women have become systemically embedded in the dominant Western social imaginary.[93] To be even more specific, I think that hate speech against women is spontaneous in that it is *a habituated mode of corrective* deemed appropriate in light of a disruption to the patriarchal status quo. That is, I contend that hate speech is just one mode of backlash to those who challenge the world-organising narratives and norms of patriarchy, which, as we have seen in chapter 2, remains a core component of the dominant Western social imaginary.

Habituation, so understood, also clearly aligns with a social imaginaries take on the phenomenon of hate speech and so is particularly helpful for bringing to the fore the need to challenge normative (i.e. habituated) images and practices in the fight for social justice. For these habits are shared; these 'habits are acquired and operative in a collective . . . environment'.[94] Tacit 'knowing how to act' (norms) and 'knowing what acts mean' (impressions, narratives) are socially learned from our environment; they are themselves formed of habituation. And these norms, impressions and narratives – these ways of seeing and inhabiting the world – become so engrained that they turn into a kind of 'second nature' about which hardly anyone thinks twice. But what we take for granted – what we so rarely consciously think about – still shapes how we behave (and, again, remember that speaking is *conduct*), giving meaning and purpose to the actions we undertake. What is taken for granted also generates *expectations* of particular others' behaviour, with strong affective investments in particular normative ways of life and allegiance to particular social narratives of who we are, what we do, what we value, what we are like and so forth. When these expectations are not met – for example, when a woman is stepping beyond her station per the contemporary ideology of patriarchy – one should expect backlash. For, as Moira Gatens reminds us, 'norms bite deeply into the identity of the individual and her/his place and status within the community'.[95] Hence I agree with Emma Jane's conviction that online expression is a good 'litmus test' for certain demographics' subliminal self-understandings and world-orientation.[96]

However, I will just point out a worrisome presupposition that may be hiding behind this observation that hate speech is often spontaneous, off the cuff: that if people only took more time to think before they speak, then there wouldn't be anywhere near as much hate speech to deal with.[97] It is true that not everyone who hate speaks against women takes themselves to believe that Women are, in their essence, naturally subordinate to Men. With that said, the 'stop and think' strategy implied by the above presupposition isn't necessarily going to help. The reason for this is precisely that the influence of imaginaries is so insidious we often fail to spot it in ourselves and in others even when we are trying to be more cognisant of our sedimented predispositions. So, we have some more work to do to counteract the presence of implicit biases and oppressive habits.

A final point. The description of misogyny as 'habit' does not in any way suggest that commentators cannot or must not be held responsible for their acts of gender oppression. I agree with Young, who says 'a conception of justice that starts from the concept of oppression must break with such a limitation of moral and political judgement to discursively conscious intended action'.[98] The threshold for acts deserving of punitive and/or reparative responses must change. As Ngo notes, there is a sense in which these habits are actively held. She writes, 'in geological sedimentation, the depositing of materials is passive insofar as surfaces do not solicit them – *but they do receive them. This entails a measure of material and compositional compatibility* such that the new material does not simply "run off" the existing surface'.[99] In other words, 'habits are *held*, not merely acquired', and they are held in a continuous and ongoing way.[100] Like Ngo, I want to emphasise explicitly that habituation to patriarchy and all that this entails – this holding of the body as always ready to (re-)act in misogynistic ways to status quo challenges and the threat of meaning vertigo[101] – is not simply a passive mode of existence. Such acts always involve *agency*, even though 'habit occupies the hazy space between conscious and non-conscious being', sitting 'in the grey region of acquired orientation'.[102] So, subjects are responsible for their actions, even when those actions are not in any way deliberate. Indeed, to quote Young once more: 'If social philosophy assumes that intended and deliberate action is the primary focus of moral judgement, it risks ignoring or even excusing some of the most important sources of oppression. Only moral judgement that extends to habitual interaction, bodily reactions, unthinking speech, feelings, and symbolic associations can capture much about oppression'.[103] Hence, we need not require that commentators are *deliberately* hate speaking to support the conclusion that hate speech needs to stop and that we are justified in pursuit of this aim, even by punitive measures.

ENCOUNTERING HATE SPEECH ONLINE

While there may not be anything fundamentally different between virtual and terrestrial hate speech in terms of the harms it generates, it certainly has the scope to harm vast amounts of people and to further sediment patriarchy as an overarching influencer in the dominant Western social imaginary today. In the next chapter, I evidence this claim by analysing instances of hate speech against women online. But, to anticipate what will come in chapter 6, I want to explicitly note one approach we can and should adopt in light of the widespread social practice that is hate speaking. We should ask *what are our dominant images of cyberspace*, and *do our images of cyberspace obscure our route to gender justice*? By attempting to address these questions head-on, we may generate some of the epistemic and affective frictions we need to imagine new ways of living in this world we share.

NOTES

1. Marilyn Frye, *The Politics of Reality: Essays in Feminist Theory* (Freedom: The Crossing Press, 1983), 2.
2. Alexander Brown, 'What is Hate Speech? Part 1: The Myth of Hate', *Law and Philosophy* 35 (2017): 419. In addition, when one looks to hate speech

scholarship in particular, one finds an absence of analyses centring gender, particularly in the literature produced by philosophers. However, exceptions include: Lauren Ashwell, 'Gendered Slurs', *Social Theory and Practice* 42 (2016): 228–239; Quill Kukla, 'Slurs, Interpellation, and Ideology', *The Southern Journal of Philosophy* 56 (2018): 7–32; Mary Kate McGowan, 'Oppressive Speech', *Australasian Journal of Philosophy*, 87 (2009): 389–407. Philosophers have also discussed pornography as hate speech. See, e.g.: Rae Langton, *Sexual Solipsism: Philosophical Essays on Pornography and Objectification* (Oxford: Oxford University Press, 2009).

Outside philosophy, feminist scholars have done some work on the issue of gendered hate speech. For instance, see: Tanya D'Souza, Laura Griffin, Nicole Shackleton, and Danielle Walt, 'Harming Women with Words: The Failure of Australian Law to Prohibit Gendered Hate Speech', *UNSW Law Journal* 41 (2018): 939–976; Donna Lillian, 'A Thorn by Any Other Name: Sexist Discourse as Hate Speech', *Discourse and Society* 18 (2007): 719–740; Anjalee de Silva, 'Addressing the Vilification of Women: A Functional Theory of Harm and Implications for Law', *Melbourne University Law Review*, 43 (2020): 1–46; Sarah Sobieraj, 'Bitch, Slut, Skank, Cunt: Patterned Resistance to Women's Visibility in Digital Publics', *Information, Communication and Society* 21 (2018): 1700–1714; Kylie Weston-Scheuber, 'Gender and the Prohibition of Hate Speech', *QUT Law and Justice Journal*, 12 (2012): 132–150.

Generally, though, research on hate speech against women online tends to get swept up amongst broader discussions of online misogyny. See, for example: Danielle Keats Citron, *Hate Crimes in Cyberspace* (Cambridge: Harvard University Press, 2014); Emma Jane, 'Gendered Cyberhate as Workplace Harassment and Economic Vandalism', *Feminist Media Studies* 18 (2018): 575–591. Emma Jane, *Misogyny Online: A Short (and Brutish) History* (Los Angeles: Sage Swifts, 2017); Karla Mantilla, *Gendertrolling: How Misogyny Went Viral* (Santa Barbara: Praeger, 2015); Jessica Megarry, 'Online Incivility or Sexual Harassment? Conceptualising Women's Experiences in the Digital Age', *Women's Studies International Forum* 47 (2014): 46–55; Martha Nussbaum, 'Objectification and Internet Misogyny', in *The Offensive Internet*, ed. Saul Levmore and Martha Nussbaum (Cambridge: Harvard University Press, 2010), 68–87; Anastasia Powell and Nicola Henry, *Sexual Violence in a Digital Age* (London: Palgrave Macmillan, 2017).

3. For instance, Frederik Stjernfelt and Anne Mette Lauritzen write: 'It is an all-purpose category with no clear limits, so it can be stretched to accuse points of view that are simply not liked'. See: Frederik Stjernfelt and Anne Mette Lauritzen, *Your Post Has Been Removed: Tech Giants and Freedom of Speech* (Cham: Springer Open, 2020), 153.

4. Ishani Maitra and Mary Kate McGowan, 'Introduction and Overview', in *Speech and Harm: Controversies Over Free Speech*, ed. Ishani Maitra and Mary Kate McGowan (Oxford: Oxford University Press, 2012), 1–23.

5. de Silva, 'Vilification of Women', 6n18.

6. Katharine Gelber, 'Differentiating Hate Speech: A Systemic Discrimination Approach', *Critical review of International Social and Political Philosophy* (2019): 1–22. https://doi.org/10.1080/13698230.2019.1576006. Gelber also argues that hate speech can *cause* harm to its targets and has undertaken empirical research proving

this is the case. See: Katharine Gelber and Luke McNamara, 'Anti-vilification Laws and Public Racism in Australia: Mapping the Gaps Between the Harms Occasioned and the Remedies Provided', *UNSW Law Journal* 39 (2016): 488–511.

7. Frye, *Politics of Reality*, 2.

8. Gelber, 'Differentiating Hate Speech', 15, my emphasis.

9. Note, also, Kukla's observation on a key difference between insults (as is "ostrich") and slurs (examples of which were discussed in Chapter 2). They write: 'I can insult someone *as an equal* ("Wow, you're being an asshole!") but I can't slur someone as an equal; the use of the slurring name not only reflects but constitutes a kind of subordinating speech, which positions the one slurred in a less empowered position than the one using the slur'. See: Kukla, 'Slurs', 20–21.

10. Gelber, 'Differentiating Hate Speech', 11.

11. Miranda Fricker, *Epistemic Injustice: Power and the Ethics of Knowing* (Oxford: Oxford University Press, 2007), 4.

12. Fricker, *Epistemic Injustice*, 4.

13. Gelber, 'Differentiating Hate Speech', 10.

14. Fricker, *Epistemic Injustice*, 27.

15. Fricker, *Epistemic Injustice*, 29.

16. Fricker, *Epistemic Injustice*, 27.

17. I take the term systematic to be processual, a repeated performance of the same act. Over time this comes to constitute a system, and what is systemic – spread throughout and engrained in the system – is hard to eradicate precisely because it is built into that system as a whole.

18. Gelber, 'Differentiating Hate Speech', 18n13.

19. Helen Ngo points out that 'there are specific epistemological conditions under which some things' – say, these patterns of treatment – 'can be perceived'. This is because 'one's experiences, framework, and embodied concerns play an active role in shaping one's perceptions'. See: Helen Ngo, *The Habits of Racism: A Phenomenology of Racism and Racialized Embodiment* (Lanham: Lexington Books, 2017), 19. This is due to the *situatedness* of the collective which experiences the treatment. Following Gaile Pohlhaus Jr., I maintain that knowledge developed from the margins can be shared by those in the centre; however, this does not mean those in the centre are able to access that knowledge in the same way. See: Gaile Pohlhaus Jr, 'Relational Knowing and Epistemic Injustice: Toward a Theory of *Willful Hermeneutical Ignorance*', *Hypatia* 27 (2012): 715–735.

20. Ngo, *Habits of Racism*, 19.

21. Ngo, *Habits of Racism*, 20.

22. Sara Ahmed, *The Cultural Politics of Emotion*, 2nd ed. (Edinburgh: Edinburgh University Press, 2014), 47.

23. Gelber, 'Differentiating Hate Speech', 15, my emphasis.

24. Gelber, 'Differentiating Hate Speech', 9; Ishani Maitra, 'Subordinating Speech', *Speech and Harm: Controversies Over Free Speech*, ed. Ishani Maitra and Mary Kate McGowan (Oxford: Oxford University Press, 2012), 94–120.

25. Gelber, 'Differentiating Hate Speech', 9; Maitra, 'Subordinating Speech', 94–120.

26. Michelle Zimbalist Rosaldo, 'Women, Culture, and Society: A Theoretical Overview', in *Woman, Culture, and Society*, ed. Michelle Zimbalist Rosaldo and Louise Lamphere (Stanford: Stanford University Press, 1974), 21n2.

27. McGowan, 'Oppressive Speech', 391, 402.

28. Fricker, *Epistemic Injustice*, 13, original emphasis.

29. Fricker, *Epistemic Injustice*, 11–12.

30. For example, Stjernfelt and Lauritzen write; '"hate speech" is not only a vague, politicized and subjective category. It is also full of double standards, because it does not equally protect all groups defined by race, gender, religion and so on' (Stjernfelt and Lauritzen, *Your Post*, 153).

31. Millicent Churcher and Moira Gatens, 'Reframing Honour in Heterosexual Imaginaries', *Angelaki* 24 (2019): 154.

32. As Amy Allen points out, 'Women's use of power is not necessarily benevolent; we are not unwilling or unable to use our power to hurt others simply because we are women'. See: Amy Allen, 'Rethinking Power', *Hypatia* 13 (1998): 31.

33. Amy Allen, 'Rethinking Power', 31.

34. Gelber, 'Differentiating Hate Speech', 10.

35. Gelber, 'Differentiating Hate Speech', 11, my emphasis.

36. McGowan, 'Oppressive Speech', 395.

37. McGowan, 'Oppressive Speech', 395.

38. Gelber, 'Differentiating Hate Speech', 15.

39. Gelber, 'Differentiating Hate Speech', 12.

40. Iris Marion Young, *Justice and the Politics of Difference* (Princeton: Princeton University Press, 1990), 42, my emphasis.

41. Young, *Justice*, 41.

42. Young, *Justice*, 41, my emphasis.

43. Frye, *Politics of Reality*, 10–11, original emphasis.

44. Young, *Justice*, 53.

45. Young, *Justice*, 53.

46. Young, *Justice*, 56.

47. Young, *Justice*, 59.

48. Young, *Justice*, 61.

49. Powell and Henry, *Sexual Violence*, 65. I also take it to be instructive that the pioneers of the "hate speech" concept frequently alluded to physical violence in articulating its impact on the target. (Susan Brison, 'Speech, Harm, and the Mind-Body Problem in First Amendment Jurisprudence', *Legal Theory* 4 (1998): 40) "Hate speech" has been described as 'assaultive speech', 'words that wound', speech that 'ambushes' and 'terrorizes', which constitutes an 'attack', a 'blow', a 'slap in the face' and so forth. See: Charles R. Lawrence III, Mari Matsuda, Richard Delgado and Kimberlè Williams Crenshaw, 'Introduction', in *Words that Wound: Critical Race Theory, Assaultive Speech, and the First Amendment*, ed. Mari Matsuda, Charles R. Lawrence III, Richard Delgado, and Kimberlè Crenshaw (Boulder: Westview Press, 1993), 1–16.

50. Young, *Justice*, 61, my emphasis.

51. Young, *Justice*, 62, original emphasis.

52. Note, also, that fear of violent reprisal is a further mechanism which 'functions to keep oppressed groups subordinate'. See: Young, *Justice*, 62.

53. Lawrence et al., 'Introduction', 1–7.

54. Lawrence et al., 'Introduction', 6, my emphasis.

55. Like Gelber, 'Differentiating Hate Speech', 18n13, I am 'aware of, but unconvinced by, arguments that groups such as men or white people do face systemic discrimination', for 'the case has not been made out with strong evidence and sound methods'.

56. Allen, 'Rethinking Power', 29–30.

57. de Silva, 'Vilification of Women', 6n18.

58. Note, however, what this definition does *not* imply. It does not imply this intersectionally privileged group is the only group that can *commit* acts of hate speech. Indeed, the fact that one can be a victim of 'hate speech' does not mean that one is unable to victimise others. Inter-group oppression and intra-group oppression are possible too. Moreover, this approach does not preclude the possibility of the presently intersectionally most privileged group from coming to be marked by tracker stigmas in the future. Finally, nothing about this conception suggests that the intersectionally privileged group can have their speech automatically silenced.

59. Gelber, 'Differentiating Hate Speech', 16.

60. Gelber, 'Differentiating Hate Speech', 16.

61. McGowan, 'Oppressive Speech', 394.

62. Gelber, 'Differentiating Hate Speech', 16.

63. Note, though, that Gelber's view of what legal regulation could look like is open ended. She is not only (or necessarily) advocating for legislative hate speech bans.

64. Gelber, 'Differentiating Hate Speech', 16.

65. Gelber, 'Differentiating Hate Speech', 16–17.

66. Gelber, 'Differentiating Hate Speech', 17.

67. An inability to articulate a widely shared experience is called a 'hermeneutical gap'. See Fricker, *Epistemic Injustice*, chap. 7.

68. Lawrence et al., 'Introduction', 14.

69. It is to compel moments of epistemic friction within and across central and marginal social imaginaries, creating opportunities for critical reflection, and to enable the imag(in)ing and production of a better future. See: José Medina, *The Epistemology of Resistance: Gender and Racial Oppression, Epistemic Injustice, and Resistant Imaginations* (Oxford: Oxford University Press, 2013), chap. 6.

70. Megarry, 'Online Incivility', 52.

71. Young, *Justice*, 62, my emphasis.

72. D'Souza et al., 'Harming Women', 967.

73. Sarah Sorial, *Sedition and the Advocacy of Violence: Free Speech and Counter-Terrorism* (London: Routledge, 2013), 103.

74. Mary Kate McGowan, *Just Words: On Speech and Hidden Harm* (Oxford: Oxford University Press, 2019), 174–183.

75. Young, *Justice*, 62.

76. Vittorio Bufacchi and Jools Gilson, 'The Ripples of Violence', *Feminist Review* 112 (2016): 32.

77. Bufacchi and Gilson, 'Ripples of Violence', 35.

78. Bufacchi and Gilson, 'Ripples of Violence', 35.

79. de Silva, 'Vilification of Women', 27.

80. Claire Chambers, 'Feminism', in *The Oxford Handbook of Political Ideologies*, ed. Michael Freeden, Lyman Tower Sargent and Marc Stears (Oxford: Oxford University Press, 2013), 578.

81. Alexander Brown, 'What Is So Special About Online (As Compared to Offline) Hate Speech'? *Ethnicities* 18 (2017): 297.

82. Brown, 'What Is So Special', 300.

83. Frederick Schauer, 'Recipes, Plans, Instructions, and the Free Speech Implications of Words That Are Tools', in *Free Speech in the Digital Age*, ed. Susan Brison and Katharine Gelber (Oxford: Oxford University Press, 2019), 80.

84. Susan J. Brison and Katharine Gelber, 'Introduction', in *Free Speech In The Digital Age* (New York: Oxford University Press, 2019), 5; James Weinstein, 'Cyber Harassment and Free Speech: Drawing the Line Online', in *Free Speech in the Digital Age*, ed. Susan Brison and Katharine Gelber (Oxford: Oxford University Press, 2019), 52.

85. Soraya Chemaly, 'Demographics, Design, and Free Speech: How Demographics Have Produced Social Media Optimized for Abuse and The Silencing of Marginalized Voices', in *Free Speech in the Digital Age*, ed. Susan Brison and Katharine Gelber (Oxford: Oxford University Press, 2019), 159.

86. Brown, 'What Is So Special', 303.

87. Brown, 'What Is So Special', 302; James Curran, 'The Internet of Dreams: Reinterpreting the Internet', in *Misunderstanding the Internet*, ed. James Curran, Natalie Fenton, and Des Freedman, 2nd ed. (London Routledge, 2016), 25.

88. Ben Gilbert, 'How Facebook Makes Money From Your Data, in Mark Zuckerberg's Words', *Business Insider Australia*, April 12, 2018, accessed June 4, 2020, https://www.businessinsider.com.au/how-facebook-makes-money-according-to-mark-zuckerberg-2018-4?r=US&IR=T.

89. Mary Anne Franks, '"Not Where Bodies Live": The Abstraction of Internet Expression', in *Free Speech in the Digital Age*, ed. Susan Brison and Katharine Gelber (Oxford: Oxford University Press, 2019), 141.

90. Brown, 'What Is So Special', 304, my emphasis.

91. Brown, 'What Is So Special', 306.

92. Ngo, *Habits of Racism*, 23, my emphasis.

93. de Silva 'Vilification of Women', 17.

94. Ngo, *Habits of Racism*, 10.

95. Moira Gatens, 'Can Human Rights Accommodate Women's Rights? Towards an Embodied Account of Social Norms, Social Meaning, and Cultural Change', *Contemporary Political Theory* 3 (2004): 285.

96. Jane, *Misogyny Online*, 34.

97. Katharine Gelber and Susan Brison, 'Digital Dualism and the "Speech as Thought" Paradox', in *Free Speech In The Digital Age* (New York: Oxford University Press, 2019), 19.

98. Young, *Justice*, 150.

99. Ngo, *Habits of Racism*, 38, my emphasis.

100. Ngo, *Habits of Racism*, x, 40.

101. Ngo, *Habits of Racism*, 5; Filipa Melo Lopes, 'Perpetuating the Patriarchy: Misogyny and (Post-)Feminist Backlash', *Philosophical Studies* 176 (2019): 2531.

102. Ngo, *Habits of Racism*, 3, 25.

103. Young, *Justice*, 150.

Chapter 4

Analysing Hate Speech against Women Online

Social inequality is substantially created and enforced – that is, done – through words and images. Social hierarchy cannot and does not exist without being embodied in meanings and expressed in communications.

—Catharine MacKinnon[1]

There is a growing body of feminist scholarship pertaining to various kinds of online misogyny;[2] however, *hate speech* against women online has been little studied.[3] Hate speech, I argued in chapter 3, is a material practice sustained by social imaginaries, which targets specific identity-based group traits, occurs systematically (i.e. it is done by many and done repetitively – it has coherences of breadth and depth) and occurs among a constellation of other acts (e.g. physical violence, exclusion, undue control, grooming, etc. – that is, coherences of kind), which perpetuate the subordination of an identity-based group. This chapter discusses the ways women are figured in acts of hate speech in news comments sections on social media. These are particularly important sites because on 'matters of legitimate public concern', which legacy media are supposed to report, 'we wish to promote an ongoing public dialogue that involves a common search for meaning in light of shared facts'.[4] Comments sections are key sites where this dialogue plays out today. Thus, I have chosen to collect data from one platform (Facebook), and specifically from one legacy newspaper's page (*The Australian*), for while legacy media have 'colonised the news segment of cyberspace',[5] they have done so only insofar as social media platforms have facilitated the hosting of its content, being designed in such a way as to enable user discussion and interaction. Social media sites are now widely recognised as key sites of news consumption, providing both the fuel and a platform for public dialogue.[6] While no reader will be surprised to find out that these spaces frequently ended up devolving into ad hominem attacks and other forms of online incivility, this chapter will demonstrate that these spaces are not just unpleasant or offensive to women with delicate sensibilities, but that they are sites where social identity power dynamics are embodied, enacted and enforced.

First, I detail my research questions and method of data collection. Second, I deliver a qualitative analysis of the images of woman projected in the instances of hate speech I discovered. It is worthwhile reiterating that we can understand imaginaries (like the central sexual imaginary – including the power structures that inhere in the relationality between the imagined subjects therein) by analysing the images they use.[7] By analysing these images – whether they are aimed at individual women, Bad Women or Women as such – and by paying attention to their circulation, we may reveal why women are endlessly subjects of hostility. Third, I discuss the impact of this imaginal repetition for women as a group. To that end, I employ the concept of bodywork and the analogy of the videogame to refigure the group harm of hate speech.

METHOD AND RESEARCH QUESTIONS

As mentioned already, my data are publicly available Facebook users' comments responding to posts made by *The Australian* on their Facebook page. Facebook was chosen as the site of collection because it is the largest social networking platform with 2.41 billion monthly users worldwide[8] and 11 million Australian daily users, 9 million of which access Facebook on their mobile device.[9] I chose to collect comments responding to posts by *The Australian* because Australia is the Anglospheric region with which I am most intimately familiar, and this is Australia's only daily *national* broadsheet. *The Australian*'s Facebook page had over 845,000 Likes as of December 2019.

Before progressing further, two important issues must be commented on. First, *The Australian* represents a conservative worldview (but generally presents this as 'the mainstream norm, rather than right-wing'[10]). Since *The Australian* is a conservative publication, it is possible that it elicits more hate speech commentary (or other types of online incivility) than more liberal news pages.[11] With that said, I make no assumptions about the political leanings of the commentators themselves, for misogyny can be found right across the political spectrum.[12] I also make no claim that these comments are representative of Australians' *general* attitudes towards women. (A great many of the commentators may not even be Australian.) My interpretation and discussion of the data proceed from undertaking a political aesthetics approach;[13]

asking what message or impression would women reasonably derive about their place and worth *as women* in their milieu given the look, sound and feel of this space? Is this space explicitly woman-hostile? Second, it must be noted that articles published by *The Australian* are behind a paywall. At the time of writing, Facebook users could view one article per day for free before being prompted to subscribe to the newspaper. However, those unwilling or unable to pay for a subscription to *The Australian* can still glean information from (and thus make assumptions about) current affairs from the headline, the post (a brief snippet of text summarising the focus of the article), and accompanying thumbnail image. To be clear, I do not assume that all commentators have read the articles on which they are commenting. I am taking their responses to the post as they appear on Facebook, not *The Australian*'s own platform.

My data ranges from September 2018 to February 2019. Starting September 2, 2018, I proceeded to read and manually document in an excel spreadsheet the sexist and misogynistic comments that had been left in response to articles shared by *The Australian* in the previous 24 hours.[14] I sought to collect this data manually for two reasons. First, humans are endlessly creative in the ways they communicate; they can outsmart automated detection software – for example, humans have been known to use 'deliberate misdirection, such as inserted punctu@tion and furking misspellings'.[15] Manual collection, therefore, offered the strongest possibility of a robust data set, especially one which captured instances of hate speech that were not obviously vituperative.[16] Second, I wanted to inhabit this nook of cyberspace, to conduct a political aesthetic analysis of these linked comments sections – that is, to ask what it is like, as a woman, to inhabit a space that looks, sounds and feels the way it does, not only in terms of what commentators posted, but in terms of the affective 'mood' (or 'tone') generated by the choice of thumbnail, headline and post itself.[17]

The downside of manual data collection is that one person can only gather so much material. Thus, I applied screening criteria to the articles posted by *The Australian*, collecting comments only from those which were either (A) written by or about a woman; (B) featured an image of a woman in the accompanying thumbnail or (C) whose content centred on gendered issues (e.g. the gender pay gap; sexual assault; gender quotas; 'toxic' masculinity; 'having it all'; etc.). Once the six-month collection period was over at the end of February 2019, I set the data aside. I began drafting the early, theoretical chapters of this book, revisiting the data in 2020, where I refined my data set by testing each comment against the standard for 'hate speech' developed in chapter 3. At that point, I sought to determine how much hate speech against women amassed over a six-month period (RQ1), what the seeming gender division was among the hate speakers (RQ2)[18] and what figurings of women consistently emerged in the data set – that is, how women were imaged

(RQ3).[19] Now, onto the results. Note that each indented comment is made by a unique user.

HATE SPEECH AGAINST WOMEN ON
THE AUSTRALIAN'S FACEBOOK PAGE

After eliminating all comments which did not meet the benchmark for my proposed systemic violence approach to hate speech, I was left with 2,881 comments posted over 181 days by 1,342 seemingly distinct Facebook users. This is an average of almost sixteen instances of hate speech against women per day (15.92 comments). In fact, while undertaking data collection, there was only one day – October 28, 2018 – where no sexist or misogynistic comments appeared at all. After narrowing the data set, I determined the number of comments posted by users with masculine usernames, feminine usernames and ambiguous or non-specific usernames (e.g. a page name, gender-neutral name or a shared profile). While usernames in no way guarantee the gender of the user, it appears as though 71.09 per cent of comments were made by men, 20.41 per cent by women and 8.50 per cent by ambiguous and non-specific users (see figure 4.1). Previous research has found that men are about twice as likely as women to produce online hate, but this includes other types of hate beyond online misogyny.[20] My research finds that for every one hate speech comment left by a woman user, over three (3.48) hate speech comments were made by men. Men users also outnumber women users by almost 3 to 1 (2.89–1). In short, there appear to be 891 men users responsible for 2,048 instances of hate speech against women online (71.09%), an average

Total Comments: 2,881

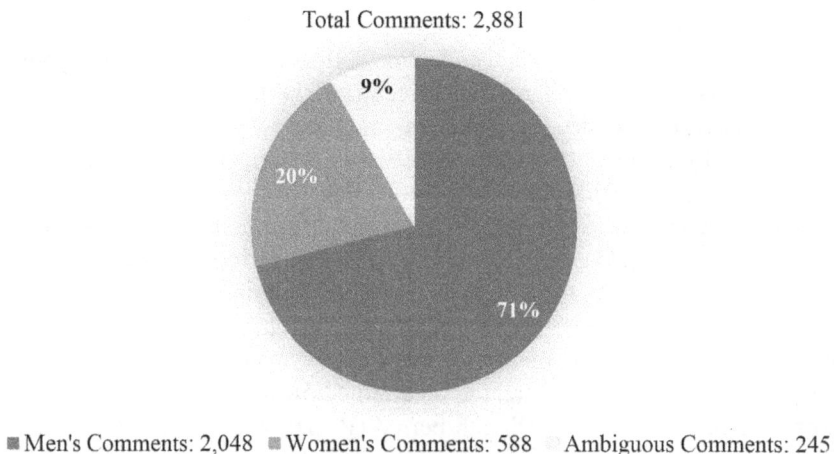

■ Men's Comments: 2,048 ■ Women's Comments: 588 Ambiguous Comments: 245

Figure 4.1   Total Hate Speech Comments Broken Down by Gender.

of 2.29 comments each; 310 women users appear to be responsible for 588 instances of hate speech against women online (20.41%), an average of 1.90 comments each; finally, 137 ambiguous users appear to be responsible for 245 instances of hate speech against women online (08.50%), an average of 1.79 comments each. These results are summarised in table 4.1, answering RQ1 and RQ2. The recurring figurations of Woman in these acts of online gendered hate speech are treated thematically in the remainder of section 2, wherein I provide exemplary quotes for qualitative analysis. Discussion of these provides an answer to RQ3.

Woman as Sex Object

As argued in chapter 2, the imagined subjects of the patriarchal sexual imaginary of the Anglosphere are cisgender, heterosexual Men and Women. These subjects' relation to each other is structured by a hierarchy of sexual social identity power: Men (are supposed to) desire Women, and Women (are supposed to) desire being desired by Men. Thus, it was no surprise to find instances of sexual objectification in my data set. At times, such speech would appear 'complimentary' rather than violent. For instance, take the following comment, responding to a thumbnail image of public figure Peta Credlin:

• 'She's very tidy. Reckon she'd taste like seedless Victorian watermelon' (Man).

Or consider this comment, said of Randi Zuckerberg, Facebook founder Mark Zuckerberg's sister, who appeared in a thumbnail image accompanying an article focusing on lack of diversity at the company:

• 'Geez . . . I'd pork her' (Man).

That these men deem Credlin and Zuckerberg fuckable – which accords them a certain social value (namely, they succeeded in being 'hot' in the eyes of

Table 4.1   Hate Speech Discovered in *The Australian's* Facebook Comments Sections

Gender	Users	Comments	Average	% Comments
Men	895	2,048	2.29 comments	71.09
Women	310	588	1.90 comments	20.41
Ambiguous	137	245	1.79 comments	08.50
Total	1,342	2,881	2.15 comments	100.00

men) – could be interpreted as a 'compliment'. But the fact is that comments such as these function by 'reminding her and those around her of what she *is* and what she is *for*'.[21] Of course, the 'she' in question is neither Credlin nor Zuckerberg as specific individuals. One should recognise that Credlin and Zuckerberg are merely representative targets 'standing in imaginatively for a large swathe of others'.[22] Any woman may be treated this way precisely because she is a Woman; this is not reserved for celebrities, public figures or the especially attractive (whatever that may mean). Furthermore, comments like this fix Woman in her specific hierarchical relation to Man: the *object* of a *subject's* desire. So, what is being provided here is not just a specific image of Woman but also a tacit yet specific image of Man, too. The men commenting are sexual agents, and they exhibit their agency *through* their objectification of women.[23] To say 'I would fuck this woman' is to say 'I am a Man'.[24] It doesn't matter all that much who the specific women are.

Then there are expressions of *antagonistic* (as opposed to complimentary) sexual objectification. Here, 'sexuality becomes a vehicle for expressing both power and anger toward women'.[25] The aim is not for a man to display or imply his virile masculinity (and in so doing subjugate women as objects of desire); it is instead, variously, (A) to tell a woman how *unfuckable* – read: worthless *because* undesired by Men – she is; (B) to discursively create a scene of, or to advocate for forced sexual activity wherein a woman is figuratively rendered powerless (tacitly, *to a man*) or (C) to figure a woman as engaging (or having previously engaged) in a certain sex act, thus diverting attention away from any other important activity she has undertaken. Women's unfuckability (A) is evidenced in exchanges like the following:

- 'Why are those lesbian vegans cranky, I couldn't be stuffed reading' (Man 1).
  r. 'I don't think they are lesbian' (Woman).
  r. *'Of course they are. I mean take a look at them, do you really think males would be interested in that lot?' (Man 2).*

The comments were left in response to a post stating that The Greens, a political party, 'are confronting crises in two states, with members leaving over comments against women and allegations of violence'. The accompanying thumbnail image shows four young white women, three with short hair and all with neutral facial expressions conveying discontent for such misogynistic acts and this culture. While the first man's comment engages in lesbian-baiting (more on which in 'Failed Women', below), the second man's comment perfectly exemplifies 'unfuckable objectification'. The tone of this comment suggests it is perfectly obvious that these women are sexually undesirable to *all* men, the implication of which is that these women have no value whatsoever. They have failed in one of their most fundamental service work roles: being attractive for Men; thus, they are not wanted by Men. Once more, Men are figured as the only real (sexual) agents, since all Men *can*, but never *would* choose to fuck that 'lot' of (Bad) Women. These types of speech acts undercut unfuckable women's autonomy generally but note the additional impact such speech can have in light of its context. These women are not objecting to just anything. They are attempting to exercise agency in the face of persistent sexual harassment and a culture of entrenched misogyny in contemporary Australian politics,[26] and their actions are met with speech acts that say this 'lot' of women aren't worth shit anyway because no one wants to fuck them. The subtext is, of course, that any woman who dares to look or act like them – you know, 'the type' – will be similarly denigrated. But it also says to women *we don't care about the sexual violence you face*, a violence that is itself a manifestation of patriarchy.

Unfuckable objectification can also be put to other uses. Some commentators use women's perceived sexual desirability to evaluate the likelihood that women's allegations of sexual assault are plausible. Women who are deemed too undesirable are thought not just unfuckable, but 'unrapable' or 'unassaultable'. For example, in response to the Australian Broadcasting Corporation's (ABC) former managing director Michelle Guthrie's allegation that former ABC chairman Justin Milne inappropriately touched her back, one commentator said:

- He couldn't get that drunk to want her. (Man)

In this his view, Guthrie's appearance universally ensures she cannot be sexually assaulted. This comment not only denigrates her on the basis of her appearance, but it does additional damage insofar as it perpetuates rape culture. It does this by creating the false impression that women's looks trigger sexual assaults and that, vice versa, Men only assault Women to whom they are sexually attracted. This misrepresents rape as being borne of sexual desire and obscures that rape is an exercise of power through sex. These myths can undermine the credibility of complainants who make public their experiences of sexual assault.

Next, consider an example of discursively created forced sexual activity wherein woman is rendered powerless (B):

- hello snowflake would u like 2 suck my C[ock] u need something 2 shut u up leftard. (Man)

This comment is an instance of an 'ad hoc encounter'.[27] This 'offer' – a veiled threat, an intimation of physical sexual violence – was a reply to a woman commentator, who complained 'Can always rely on *The Australian* to draw out stupid and ignorant comments' on a post pertaining to the UK prime ministership. Taken in its entirety, the comment intends three things (in the phenomenological sense). (1) To take a political stance (to dismiss 'the Left,' which is importantly associated with progressive social movements like feminism). (2) To demean; this is achieved through the use of insults ('snowflake', 'leftard') and through the proposition of a sex act which involves a Man's sexual pleasure and a Woman's sexual service (hence, submission). (3) To silence; his cock is not just an instrument of (sexual identity) power, it is a figurative a gag. She is told to suck his cock *because she needs to shut up*, and this is how he will enforce silence upon her.

Now, this is an instance of hate speech where the subject and target are one and the same. But there are instances of this type of objectification of women when the subjects of the speech act are highly unlikely to ever witness them. For instance, one man commented:

• Pauline needs to be raped and murdered! (Man)

This was in response to the post '[Federal Senator] Pauline Hanson tells us what she thinks about a schoolgirl's refusal to stand for the national anthem'. That's a pretty low threshold for this allegedly deserved punishment. But, then again, advocacy of violence against women with 'unlikeable' opinions is hardly new. 'Rapeglish', as Emma Jane calls it, was being used by men on the internet well before we all jumped aboard social media platforms.[28] Like the aforementioned ad hoc comment, the message is that Hanson, or rather, *women like Hanson* (again, Bad Women), need to be silenced – that's the murder part. The rape is simply sexualised punishment imaginally meted out to remind her of her powerlessness and vulnerability at the hands of Men.

The third form of antagonistic sexual objectification (c) can be seen in the following comment.

• She went to China to suck Chinese little red knobs because that's all she can do. This ranga [red-head] is completely out of her depth and totally unqualified for the role. (Man)

This comment was made of Australian federal minister of foreign affairs Marise Payne in response to the post: 'Marise Payne will meet China's foreign minister today in a meeting which could help "mend broken fences" with the country'. It too figures a woman as engaging (consensually, but nonetheless degradingly) in a sex act, but this is an indirect assertion, not an offer nor dictate. Still, we once again see the use of fellatio to symbolise Woman's submission to Man. In this case, the men in question are also targets of derision, emasculated on the basis of a racial stereotype (that Asian men have small penises),[29] which is somehow even more disparaging to Payne – she's not just sucking *any* dicks, she's sucking little (read: inferior) Chinese dicks. What does that imply of her? While this comment clearly refers to the (in)capacity of Payne to succeed in her political role, it spreads this message by trading on the loose association Woman – sex – Bad. Payne is figured as not only about to engage in a subordinating sex act, but as *good for nothing other* than performing that sex act. And though its target is a specific woman, this is a gendered attack, deliverable only because she is a woman. Any other woman (who takes up that role in the future) could be figured just the same because sucking dicks is what sexual subordinates do – and women users reading the comments understand this.[30]

Promiscuous Women

The border between licit and illicit sexual conduct for Women is heavily policed in online hate speech, maintaining the well-worn whore/virgin dichotomy.[31] As we saw in chapter 2, Women's role in sex is primarily imaged through a commodity-exchange model. The Good Woman will 'give it up' for a Man in exchange for marriage, financial security, children (licit sex). Although, to be fair, some resent women for even this usually licit form of exchange. Witness:

• It was never realistic to expect women to fully engage in the entirety of the job market. They have no motivation to do so. *They know the pussy pass will grant them an easy life sponging off a man.* Men know they have to earn a good living to attract a decent woman that doesn't look like a womanatee. So they've take any risky job they can because they're forced to.

    (Man, responding to the post: 'Men still pick "blue" jobs and women "pink" jobs. Does it matter that the labour market is so sex-segregated'?)

The usual imagined 'transaction' between Men and Women is, to this commentator, something that privileges Women; Men suffer comparatively (because it is hard to find a sexy woman – that is, a woman that does not look like a manatee – to settle down with, and even harder to find a woman who refrains from playing her 'pussy pass' at every opportunity, hence Men's willingness to work more dangerous and high-paying jobs).

More straightforward transactions (e.g. sex for direct financial gain, or 'giving it up for free', that is, for pleasure's own sake) are, of course, the domain of the Bad Woman. These Women have illicit sex; they are 'sluts', 'slags', 'tarts', 'whores', 'slappers', 'smutty'. For instance, consider comments made of Stormy Daniels, a pornographic film actress (who famously had sex with former U.S. president Donald Trump in 2006):

- The woman sounds like a gumboot full of water when she walks. (Man)
- #SLAG. (Man)
- $20 is $20. (Man)

Feminist writer Clementine Ford explains, what people mean when they intimate a woman is readily promiscuous 'is that she deserves to be fucked as if
she's nothing. She deserves to be degraded, violated, and humiliated, because
she's worth nothing'.[32] In this central patriarchal imaginary, if a woman
engages in sex for money – or even for pleasure – she has been used, and so
she becomes worth less (worthless). Above, we see a tacit logic something
roughly like this: Daniels is a sex-worker; sex work is degrading (because
women who give it up for free or a fee are *morally* worthless); therefore,
Daniels has little-to-no worth and is thus not owed respectful treatment.

This attitude that women sometimes 'deserve' sexual degradation is conveyed in the following comment intimating promiscuity, which is also a
contribution to a victim-blaming rape culture. Witness:

- That dress really shows what sort of respect she is looking for 🙂. (Woman)

This was said in response to a thumbnail image of Australian Federal Senator
Sarah Hanson-Young (mouth agape, finger pointed and cleavage showing),
accompanying the headline 'Show the Women Some Respect'. The same
rationale is also used to cast doubt on women's accusations of sexual assault,
too. Consider this comment:

- [Christine Blasey-]Ford's nickname at school was bike rack. (Man;
  responding to the headline 'Why feminists fear Brett Kavanaugh')

The unstated punchline to this 'joke' is that 'everyone has had a ride'. In other
words, the commentator is saying that Blasey-Ford had sex with basically
everyone in her schooling years, when her assault by Kavanaugh was alleged
to have happened. But, because Blasey-Ford was such a slut, we have little
reason to believe her encounter with Kavanaugh was not consensual, like all
the imagined others. Again, this is a contribution to rape culture.

What is particularly interesting about accusations of promiscuity, though,
is that these are levelled at women in all sorts of settings, including when
there can be no perception of a woman's moral character or her sexual history.[33] Examples abound:

- 'NO THANKS. WE DON'T WANT THAT SLAG HERE. CHUCK HER
  IN THE OCEAN FOR THE SHARKS'. (Man, said of New Zealand Prime
  Minister Jacinda Ardern)

- 'dozzie old tart'. (Man, said of Anna Wintour)
- 'Slapper'. (Man, said of former Federal MP Julie Bishop)
- 'im not sure if i should call you a Carnt [cunt] or a Dirty Hor [whore]'. (Man, ad hoc comment to a woman)
- 'Cripes, what a bunch of slappers'. (Woman, ad hoc comment in response to a thumbnail image showing seemingly drunk young women at a horse racing event)

Because Woman's imagined primary relations to Man are sexual and service based, and since Man is imagined the superordinate gender, it is not surprising that impugning women on the basis of their *sexual* and *sexed* worth is such a common, stable, ready-to-hand act. But a woman's actual sexual conduct is not predictive in whether she will be denigrated in this way. Hence, we should not read such comments as *mere* moral disapproval of taboo sexuality, but 'a recognition of, and response to, vulnerability generated in an unequal society'[34] – specifically, vulnerability to subjugation by the forces of Men's social identity power (embodied and institutionalised in the Anglosphere) where 'sex' (both body and act) is core to the centrally shared identity-based image of what and who a Woman can be: Good, or Bad.[35] Women who read or hear such messages 'understand that they could be the "next victim"' because all women know, at least tacitly, that one could be construed (rightly or wrongly) as a Bad Woman.[36]

Woman as Body

Though 'a woman's worth lies in her sexual appeal to men', her derogation, ironically, is often tied to her 'sex saturated female anatomy'.[37] We saw above the way images and imputations of *sex acts* are used to derogate women. Here, we see a different type of *sexed objectification*.[38] This is conveyed in hate speech comments in several ways. This includes (A) allusions to female primary and secondary reproductive organs (e.g. 'pussy', 'twat' and of course, 'cunt'); (B) the reduction of women to or inordinate focus on mere body parts (vaginas, breasts, wombs, etc.) and (C) their reduction to bodily capacities (e.g. breastfeeding, gestation). The effect of each is to emphasise the inescapably corporeal existence of womanhood. Her person is always brought back to her female sex (for, remember, patriarchy's image of gender is biologically essentialist).

For example, (A) to news of former Australian Federal MP Julie Bishop's retirement from parliament, one commentator wrote

- See you next Tuesday. (Man; read: '*C U Next Tuesday*', that is, he called her a cunt)

Elsewhere, when it was rumoured that actress Angelina Jolie could sidestep into politics, one person said:

• She is a UN Globalist cun*. (Man)

Then there were comments reducing women to their body parts (B). For instance, consider:

• Bwaaaahaaaa Half Term Tony's mistress *looks like she has a couple of beaver tails hidden in a dress.* OMG!! you go for the slu*y look. Talk about TARTS. Old horse head has it in spades. (Man)

This commentator is using the same tactic of antagonistic sexual objectification described above, and is also moralising about former Prime Minister Tony Abbott's former Chief of Staff Peta Credlin's (alleged) promiscuity, but he is doing so by homing in on one of Credlin's secondary sex characteristics – her breasts – asserting that they are an 'undesirable' shape. Breasts are 'supposed' to be rounded and supple, not long and deflated.[39] Hence, not only is she reduced to her body, her body is rendered undesirable. Then there's this. In response to an article's thumbnail image featuring a t-shirt that reads 'there are only 2 genders', one commentator riffed:

• There
are only
2 holes©. (Man)

Note: '2 hole' is a relatively new slang term for 'Woman', but it follows the same old pattern of metonymy where genitals are the attribute that represents the entire group.[40]

Finally, (C) sometimes commentators would denigrate women's reproductive capacities. Not infrequently, terms such as 'breeder', 'spawn', and 'mate', would appear, bestialising women via their fecundity (more on which below), but also implying that the capacity to reproduce is dangerous. One says of 'lefty women'

• Don't let them breed. (Man)

In addition, such comments were also on occasion instances of racialised misogyny, betraying a lasting allegiance to the idea of white racial superiority. For example, consider these comments, responding to the post: 'Pregnant British ISIS bride Shamima Begum, 19, has already lost two children to illness and malnutrition under the caliphate but is pleading to keep her third if allowed to return to the UK':

- Should be compulsory tubes tied so it can't breed. (Man)
- Sterilize her and drown the mutt she gives birth to. (Man)

Notice the way Begum is dehumanised by being denied the feminine pronoun, instead being described as an 'it', the term used for objects. She is viewed as a mere reproductive vessel, yet she is also an imminent danger to the world we know and love; hence, violence against her would be justified.

Woman as Beast

As Jacqueline Broad reminds us, we share in a longstanding 'idea that human beings and animals occupy different levels of grades of being'.[41] From this, we can understand why bestialising people is *generally* offensive, for it impugns subjects are subhuman. However, given the history of Women's subjugated status, bestialising women does more than merely offend. As we saw in chapter 2, in the patriarchal sexual imaginary Man is thought to have 'greater moral and intellectual competence compared to women' and a 'rational soul'.[42] Thus, Woman has oft been figured as *more* animal, closer to nature and thoroughly immanent as compared to Man, who is instead a civilised subject that can transcend his (few) bodily limitations. That is, Woman is 'ranked just slightly above the beasts and slightly below men in the created order'.[43] So, in other words, while Man is fully human, Woman – insofar as she is naturally more bestial – is subhuman. Early calls to recognise women's dignity were thus, unsurprisingly, predicated on the claim that, just like Man, Woman has 'the high ontological status of a human being, rather than say a brute animal (or a plant or rock)' – indeed, the claim was that Woman is '*just as far* above the beasts' as Man.[44] This was not just an intellectual but a visceral plea, for there is honour attached to the image of the noble civic subject (the Individual).[45]

Given this, it was unsurprising to find frequent repetitions of women being cast as beasts in my dataset, in particular beasts with a sedimented history of application such that the terms now can be considered gendered slurs. Here are just a few examples, the first of which is 'cow'.

- Thank god this cow has gone . . . she is a disgrace. (Man, speaking of Julie Bishop)
- Tell the stupid cow to 'get stuffed'. (Man, responding to the post: 'Jacinda Ardern has lashed out over deportations of New Zealanders while standing with Scott Morrison, after a "frank" exchange')

- P[i]ss off savva Bitter old cow. (Woman, directed to local journalist Niki Savva)
- Silly old cow get back in your paddock and eat grass. (Man, directed at Greens senator Rachel Siewert)

It is clear from their tone that each of these comments intends to insult. Since she is a cow, she need not be recognised as having, nor to be treated with the dignity afforded to human persons.

Like 'cow', another more emphatic term that was used to express disdain for a woman (or for women more generally) was 'bitch'. Such instances include:

- 'I'd back both of these bitchs over a fu#king cliff!' (Man, referring to Federal Deputy Opposition Leader Tanya Plibersek and former president of the Australian Human Rights Commission Gillian Triggs)
- 'Sucked in you stupid big mouth biatch.' (Man, responding to the post: 'She was wooed from Fox News by NBC in a blaze of publicity. Two years later Megyn Kelly's star power has burnt out after comments this week about blackface')
- 'No one would believe this lying bitch😡'[46] (Woman, said of Christine Blasey-Ford's allegations of sexual assault against U.S. Supreme Court Justice Brett Kavanaugh)
- 'Whinging lefturded biatch.' (Woman, said of former Federal MP Julia Banks' exit from the Liberal Party and her comments about the 2018 Liberal Party leadership spill).

What draws the ire of commentators varies from case to case, but here, as with 'cow', note the way in which bestialising takes place alongside displays of contempt for these women's platforms and what they have to say. This – describing Women as cows and bitches – is a way of silencing through degradation. Such abuse creates a hostile environment, even potentially a chilling effect for women users who might otherwise dare to act like or show support for these women.[47] After all, bitches and cows are not worthy of respect, so no one needs to listen to what they have to say, nor respect the issues they take a public stance on.[48]

Then there is the gendered image 'mole'. While less common than 'bitch' and 'cow', its appearance was not infrequent. Witness:

- 'Let's hope she is voted out in the next election. Far left mole.' (Man, speaking of former Federal MP Kerryn Phelps)
- 'Whatever mole.' (Man, regarding Serena William's defence that she was not cheating during the 2018 U.S. Open women's final match)

- 'Shut it you dumb little mole.' (Man, responding to the post: 'To political leaders at the UN climate meeting, teenager Greta Thunberg issues a warning from the front line of forces pulling children from school around the world'.)

Again, note how these gendered insults are accompanied by the message that Women (and girls) should be quiet, are liars, and are undeserving of positions of power. It is also worth noting that 'mole' (the animal) and 'moll' (a gendered slur indicating a promiscuous woman) are homophones, and while 'moll' did sometimes appear, for example:

- 'Molls'. (Woman; responding to the post: 'Exclusive Sydney girls school Kambala has apologised "unreservedly" to its former principal, Debra Kelliher, and settled a defamation case she brought against it after two teachers sent several emails to staff attacking personal integrity'.)

I think it plausible to suggest that casting a woman as a 'mole' not only diminishes her human standing (her dignity) by making her subhuman, it also conveys a negative normative judgement that impugns a woman's (sexual) character.

Woman as Monster/ous

Women were imaged as monsters or monstrous persistently in the data; they were called 'witch', 'hag', 'banshee', 'harpy', 'succubus' and simply 'creature', among others. We might, following Barbara Creed, term this the 'monstrous-feminine'.[49] To illustrate, one commentator responds to an article about former UK Prime Minister Theresa May with the violent instruction

- 'Burn the witch'. (Man)

The exact same instruction was given by another man, targeting Queensland Premier Annastacia Palaszczuk.

Another example. In response to the headline: 'Uproar as Gay School Vote Delayed', featuring a thumbnail image of Australian Federal Senator Penny Wong with mouth agape and pointing a finger, one commentator wrote:

- 'She's a vile Harpie [*sic*]'. (Man)

A harpy is a mythical creature with a female body and a bird's wings, but it is also a short-hand term for a mean, foul-tempered woman. (Not only this, but the adjective 'vile' works to *abjectify* Wong too, figuring her as disgusting and to be avoided, more on which below.)

In the same vein, women were likened to evil or villainous characters. For instance, Julie Bishop is referred to by three men as the 'Wicked Witch of the West', as is Nancy Pelosi by one woman. Anna Wintour was called 'Cruella', the infamous villain of *101 Dalmatians*, by one woman and 'Cousin It' by a man. This comparison of Women to mythical, monstrous and evil figures, I contend, must also be read as expressive denigration since women are, again, denied the full status of human persons. In this regard, such insults are quite like bestial insults.

Woman as Abject: Ugly, Diseased, Decrepit

Commentators (and sometimes headlines and posts) draw upon abjectionable substances in describing women, which strongly conveys aversive affects.[50] Most famously elaborated by Julia Kristeva, abjection entails revulsion from the unclean/impure, disgust at the possibility of contamination, and the retaliatory impulse towards purification, which is coextensive with the social and symbolic order of the time (i.e. dominant and central imaginaries).[51] In Iris Marion Young's words, 'abjection is the feeling of loathing and disgust the subject has in encountering certain matter',[52] in this case, the 'matter' is *Women* both cis- and transgender, heterosexual and queer. Put slightly differently by Sarah Ahmed, 'abjection names that feeling of sickness caused by the proximity of an object that is already designated as disgusting, a sickness that may involve gagging or pulling away'.[53] Hence, by 'abjectify', I mean that commentators render Women grotesque, decaying, and 'Other' (i.e. not-me, not-us).[54] More specifically, commentators use their words to both *reflect* and to *trigger* that nausea, disgust, horror, towards women *qua Women*.

The affect of disgust is most evident in the use of 'nausea' and 'vomit' emoji: 🤢 🤮. Comments containing these were posted by men and women in response to articles on – and with thumbnail images of – high-profile women such as: Lady Gaga, Jada Pinkett Smith, Alicia Keys, Michelle Obama and Jennifer Lopez; Kerryn Phelps, Julia Banks and Rebekha Sharkie; Tanya Plibersek and Gillian Triggs; Jacinda Ardern; Julie Bishop; Ita Buttrose; Hillary Clinton; Amal Clooney; Angelina Jolie; Cate McGregor; Angela Merkel; Gina Rinehart; Amanda Stoker; Serena Williams . . . the list goes on. The scope of meaning conveyed by these emoji is not fully fixed, but used in this way they twine Women to the guttural gag of revulsion. So, it is reasonable to infer commentators intend (but may not deliberately mean) to express such notions as 'I don't like this', 'This woman is nauseating', 'This woman makes me sick', 'This woman is disgusting', and even 'Get it (her) away from me/us'!

Some commentators combined both emoji and text, making the intended meaning of the expression clearer. For example, one wrote:

- I wish there was a vomit 🤮 reaction for this washed up hag! (Man)

This comment, responding to the post 'Stormy Daniels' lurid details of her liaisons with Donald Trump will put you off mushrooms. We've read her memoir so you don't have to', abjectifies Daniels via the reference to vomit, her sullied body ('washed up'), and use of the nauseated emoji. This comment *also* makes out Daniels as monstrous ('hag'), and, in light of Daniels' work in pornography, the comment must be read as drawing a clear connection between sex work, contempt, and the affect of disgust. In another example, one commentator targets Cate McGregor, former senior Australian Defence Force officer and an openly trans woman, who had appeared on the Australian TV show *Q+A* as a guest alongside notorious Jordan Peterson,[55] writing:

- 'Hey Cate. You need yours ADAMS APPLE SHAVED 🤮'. (Woman)

Here, the commentator is using the vomit emoji and capitalisation, describing a masculine bodily feature to convey a trans-misogynistic message: that trans women's bodies are both flawed and sickening.

It was not only trans women's bodies that were cast as sickening in various ways. To abjectify women, commentators would also make comments about cisgender women's aged appearance, their body shape (being both 'too fat' and 'too thin'), and other accusations of gross ugliness or decay. For example, witness the following:

- 'Looks like a corpse!' (Woman, responding to a thumbnail image of Federal Greens Senator Rachel Siewert)
- 'If I had a FACE like that I would NEVER LEAVE THE HOUSE. Ugly ugly fat, frumpy moll.' (Ambiguous, responding to the Post: '[Former Federal MP] Kelly O'Dwyer says the Liberal Party is widely regarded as "homophobic, anti-women and climate-change deniers"').
- 'Horrible dress and how skinny can she get.' (Man, responding to a thumbnail of former Miss Universe Jennifer Hawkins)
- 'fukn idiot then. Go shave ya armpits sewer rat.' (Man, ad hoc comment in reply to a woman's sarcastic comment '#metoo' – he clearly missed the tone and mistook the commentator for a feminist).

These comments work to denigrate and subjugate because the central sexual imaginary conveys the impression that 'women need to be young, thin, pretty, and heterosexual to be desirable', and excludes 'those female bodies that are deemed too big, too old or simply too different'.[56] It also excludes bodies that are 'spent'. For instance, take this comment:

- 'that's why you don't be a stepdad to some *roasties* spawn'. (Man, responding to another man's comment claiming the social role of fatherhood is
  more important than biological fatherhood)

Apparently, cis women's labia become so enlarged and discoloured with every
new sexual partner that they end up coming to resemble 'roast beef'.[57] Hence,
spent women are not only morally worthless, their sex is literally *grotesque.*

It is not at all surprising to find abjectification a ready weapon with which
to attack women. The reason one aims to render a woman abject is that, 'in
a paradigm where women are consistently valued by their attractiveness to
men, unattractiveness is thought to be the highest form of insult'.[58] To be
ugly, old, diseased, infirm, decaying or otherwise disgusting is not (just)
a personal failure – *it is failure as a Woman.*[59] And since this is a context
where 'women are taught to consider their bodies as always somehow inadequate, always imperfect, and in constant need of work, products, treatments,
rehabilitation, and surgery',[60] and one where men (come to) feel that (at least
some) women owe them a desirable body, women are particularly vulnerable
to this type of attack. Since to be deemed 'beautiful' (i.e. desirable, alluring)
as a Woman is to be affectively regarded as both desired and worth something
in the patriarchal sexual imaginary, we must read this casting of women as
variously abject as devaluing women via the implication that desirability of
such women is absent and/or could never be present. Hence, its intention is to
produce aversion to (specific) women *affectively*, not only to say something
denigrating about (specific) women.

Failed Women

Women are imaged as 'failed women' through cis-hetero- and trans-misogynistic comments, too. In previous research, I defined cis-hetero-misogyny
as follows:

> Cis-hetero-misogyny is primarily a property of social systems or environments
> as a whole, in which sex-, gender-, and orientation-diverse persons, as well as
> some cis-het women, will tend to face hostility of various kinds because they
> are sex-, gender-, and orientation-diverse persons in an androcentric, sexually
> dimorphic, cisgenderist, heterosexist world (i.e. a cis-hetero-patriarchy), who
> are held to be failing to live up to cis-hetero-patriarchal standards, or because
> they actively challenge these standards in some way, including by being visu-
> ally Other.[61]

Forms of cis-hetero-misogynistic expression include lesbian-baiting (accusing
a presumed cis-het woman of being a lesbian, or drawing attention to a cis

woman's being a lesbian), assertions of gender non-conformity (accusing a presumed cis woman of being 'too masculine'), misgendering women (accusing presumed cis women of being men, rather than being *like* men), missexing women (accusing presumed cis women of being male), and androgynising (feigning uncertainty about a cis woman's gender identity). Identity denial (refusing to acknowledge and accept trans women as women) is a form of trans-misogyny. All of the comments in table 4.2 are 'used as a means to police gendered performance and behaviour', to show other users what a Failed (i.e. Bad) Woman looks like.[62] Though there is of course nothing wrong with being queer (or with being accused of being queer), nonetheless such *figurings* of women as queer should be recognised as acts of hate speech because the meaning they communicate in a cis-hetero-patriarchal context is disparaging; they work to discredit and demean women in the context of our central sexual imaginary. Though it is achieved through different figurations, every tactic images Women as somehow *lacking* in the domain of sexual orientation, gender status and gender expression, and therefore Failed, Bad. Either women have not, in fact, lived up to the social image of Womanness (especially regarding their bodily build, styling and sexual activities) and this is used as an opportunity to deride them, or else women are *accused* of such 'failings', usually in an effort to undermine women in their other pursuits or to express general animus for them. In other words, cis-hetero-misogynistic hostilities are often employed to *visibly* non-normative women, since sex-, gender-, and orientation-diverse women present an imaginal challenge to patriarchy's ideology and so too its dynamics of social identity power. Normative-looking cis-het women, by contrast, face such hostilities selectively, depending on whether they are perceived as Good Women or Bad Women.

Cultural Stereotypes of Woman

Commentators aren't always aggressive in their takedowns of women. Not only does 'humour' play a role, the commentators also 'seem to be having *fun*' punching down against women.[63] One common method of punching down is calling up longstanding stereotypes to exclude, denigrate or impugn a woman. Unsurprisingly, the image of Woman as 'homemaker' was deployed by commentators with frequency to figure women as belonging in the private, and therefore not in the public, sphere. This was achieved in comments such as:

- 'Will someone please think of the sandwiches 🍞.' (Man, responding to coverage of the 2019 Sydney Global Women march)
- 'Hmmm . . . better sandwiches?' (Man, responding to the headline: 'What difference do women make?' and a thumbnail image of three Australian women politicians)

Table 4.2   Cis-Hetero-Misogyny in *The Australian's* Facebook Comments Sections

Type	*Example of Cis-hetero-misogyny*
Lesbian-baiting	'Phelps is a carpet munching muesli eating sandal wearing leftist shitcunt'. (Man, referring to former Federal MP Kerryn Phelps)
	'Not sure what a lesbian gender activist has in common with coal miners and construction workers . . . perhaps the union movement is out of touch'?(Man, referring to Sally McManus' role as Secretary of the Australian Council of Trade Unions)
Gender non-conformity	'Obama looks like a man'. (Woman, commenting on Michelle Obama's appearance at the 2019 Grammy Awards)
	'No problem with more women in parliament, what we do not need is more women who look like men, dress like men and think like men'. (Man, said of Kerryn Phelps' immanent election to the House of Representatives in 2018)
Misgendering	'What's this blokes problem'. Man, responding to the headline: 'Misogyny Speech was Overdue: Julia Gillard')
	'Anna Wintour? Never heard of him'. Man, in response to Wintour's suggestion that Margaret Court Stadium be renamed due to Court's hostile views of the queer community)
Missexing	'Im sure this beast stands to piss'. (Man, directed at Annastacia Palaszczuk, in relation to news of the Brisbane Tattersall's Club allowing women to join in 2018)
	'I see someone say that is a female. No way, that is an ugly bloke'. (Man, responding to a thumbnail image of Sally McManus)
Androgynising	'Well ze's got the high Neanderthal forehead so I guess the non binary cis gender is perfect for the token appointment lolololololol'. (Man, responding to news that Prime Minister Scott Morrison recommended the appointment of Dr Kirstin Ferguson as the deputy ABC chair)
	'she should go straight to Tasmania where she can work out her gender'. (Man, on the release of Bali Nine heroin smuggler Renae Lawrence from jail in Indonesia, in light of changes to the process of recording gender on birth certificates in that state)
Identity Denial	'Can you please stop calling this man a woman. He's not a woman, he just dresses like a woman and puts on make -up. His 'Adam's apple' is very obvious'! (Woman, responding to Cate McGregor's scheduled appearance with Jordan Peterson on the ABC's Q+A)
	'Looks like an ugly man pretending to be a woman'. (Woman, responding to a thumbnail image of Tasmanian queer rights activist and openly trans woman Martine Delaney)

- 'If you can't stand the heat! Get out of the kitchen. In this case get back in the kitchen!' (Woman, responding to the Post: 'Julia Banks joins a growing list of women in Canberra who whine about sexism when things don't go their way')

As can be seen here, the delivery of such comments could be described as 'light-hearted', but they still figure Women as obliged to conduct the duties of service work. Such jokes should be read as sexist-cum-misogynistic. That is to say, these stereotypical ideas of femininity are 'consistently used in a derogatory manner'.[64] While their 'logic' (the presumptions assumed but not stated which make the joke both comprehensible to others and 'funny' to some) is sexist, their expression creates a hostile environment for women entering comments sections because women immediately know how they can be treated – namely, as the sorts of people from whom personal service work can be rightfully demanded.[65]

There were other familiar tropes that appeared across these comments sections, some of which impugn the motives of Women as Men's partners, others which assert, for instance, an inevitably lonely life. For example, consider these comments about Meghan Markle and Prince Harry:

- 'Odd couple. She'll dump him as soon as the gold is secured. #GoldDigger'. (Man)
- 'Meanwhile she is sharpening her shovel ready to dig gold 😆'. (Man)
- 'He married a Gold Digger 😂'. (Man)

Not only do these comments call into question Markle's motives for marriage, the use of these laughter emoji suggests that Markle's gold digging motive is obvious and Harry is an idiot for failing to see this. Similar comments were made about other women, such as Melania Trump:

- Melania [Trump] . . . well done. A true lady. (Woman)
  r. Don't you mean a moron, nude model, gold digger . . . since when does this equate to a lady . . . hahahaha what a dropkick you must be. (Man)
- She's a classy lady . . . Good on her. (Woman)
  r. She's a gold digging tramp with all the class of a nightclub toilet floor. (Man)

Note how both commentators also degrade Melania Trump on the familiar ground of alleged sexual promiscuity, with the latter comment abjectifying her too. Still others accused Christine Blasey-Ford of lying about her alleged sexual assault by Kavanaugh, and the reason some posited for her supposed 'lie' was that:

- she loves money 💲 like all women. (Man)

This comment, in particular, implies that *any* Woman could be a gold digger. Hence, every Woman is a potential threat to Man who must be approached with extreme caution, lest she rob him of his due.

Besides being 'gold diggers', Women were repeatedly figured as lonely through the repetition of the stereotype of the '(crazy) cat lady'. A 'cat lady' is a single, older woman who keeps the company of cats because she cannot land a partner and does not have any children (or even any friends). Consider the following examples:

- 'The poor cats all left at home while their owners march'. (Man, responding to the headline: 'Marchers demand women's equality')
- 'What a laughing stock of freaks and lonely cat ladies'. (Man, responding to the headline: 'Marchers demand women's equality')
- 'go back to your cats love . . . you're embarrassing yourself with your utter ignorance 🐱 🐱 🐱 .' (Woman, in ad hoc encounter regarding Blasey-Ford's sexual assault allegations of Kavanaugh)
- 'From Cat Suit to Cat Lady'. (Man, on Serena Williams' loss at the 2018 U.S. Open)

To call a woman a 'cat lady' is to either denigrate her by casting her as 'unwanted' (i.e. she never managed to achieve her ultimate purpose, which is to get married and have babies), or to dismiss her as 'crazy' (or, more precisely, irrational or stupid). Note how the first comment has a punitive intonation. It says, for the gains of the feminist movement (which have empowered women throughout the Anglosphere) you must now suffer loneliness and a life without meaning. The second comment works by aligning the 'cat lady' with the 'freak' – an obviously denigrated identity not too far removed from the abject. The third comment, on the other hand, intends to call into question a woman's credibility. The subtext is that this woman keeps the company of cats because she is too ignorant to be able to maintain human company. Finally, the last comment shows how becoming a cat lady is a fall from grace; it entails a loss of respect, a lessening of status.

The final stereotype I will discuss here – though there were other (less frequently occurring) stereotypes too: that Women are terrible drivers, that Women get 'baby brain', and so on – is the stereotype that Women are incapable leaders. This figuration most commonly arose in the context of political leadership, but it also emerged in the context of CEO and Board positions. Here are a few typical examples:

- 'So wait, I'm confused. Does the UN get a daycare centre now or what? This is why world leaders should be men . . . 😵 🐧.' (Man; responding to the headline: 'Jacinda Ardern's baby gets front row seat at UN')

Here, the commentator directs hostility (eyeroll emoji) towards Jacinda Ardern for caring for her newborn child at work. The implication is that it is not possible to successfully mother and do one's job simultaneously (hence the need for a day care centre at the UN, during the general assembly). Since

Women are, and always will be mothers, women should leave governance to Men. Or consider this comment:

• 'One must ask why it is only women [in Australian politics] who are complaining of being 'bullied'? Maybe they just do not have the calibre of fortitude necessary to be productive MPs?' (Man, responding to the post 'The Liberal Party does now have a women's problem: a group of disgruntled women MPs intent on whipping up a crisis at any cost, writes Janet Albrechtsen')

Similar to the quote above, this man questions women's capacity to succeed in politics – Women are too delicate for the work, unlike thick-skinned Men who know how to handle a little criticism. The comment implies that men politicians cop as much internal and external criticism as women, only they let these remarks slide off them like water off a duck's back and get on with their work. In other words, Women really are too emotional, too soft, for politics.

These comments undoubtedly sit at the limits of the category 'hate speech'. I contend that they function to abuse women because they are hostile, degrading *stereotypes*, and that they are so *even when someone holds them as genuine political beliefs*. Their being stereotypes (stigmatised images), expressed in a context where women have been historically excluded from and remain underrepresented in powerful leadership roles, functions to reaffirm the impression that *Men are superordinate to Women*, and thus that women should either stop complaining or (ideally) get back to the other social roles they are actually suited for.

Cancerous Feminazis

Finally, I would be remiss not to discuss the pervasive antifeminism displayed by many hate speakers. As Andrea Dworkin explains, 'Antifeminism is a direct expression of misogyny; it is the political defense of woman hating. This is because feminism is the liberation movement of women'; adding further: 'Woman hating is the passion; antifeminism its ideological defense'.[66] However, as discussed in chapter 2, patriarchy in the Anglosphere today is well hidden beneath the veneer of ostensibly neutral images with (alleged) equal applicability to all sorts of agents. Dworkin herself recognised as much in the 1970s, writing:

Antifeminism can accommodate reform: a recognition that some forms of discrimination against women are unfair to women or that some kinds of injustice to women are not warranted (or entirely warranted) by the nature of women.

But underneath the apparent civility, there are facile arrogant assumptions: that remedies are easy, the problems are frivolous; that the harm done to women is not substantial nor is it significant in any real way; and that the subordination of women to men is not in and of itself an egregious wrong.[67]

And the facile, arrogant assumptions that Dworkin speaks of are still alive and well today, particularly in the impression that Western (i.e. *white*) Women have already fought for *and have obtained* social equality with men, except, of course, when they *choose* to be unequal. Lucy Nicholas and Christine Agius put it plainly: 'the assumption that to be feminist is to discriminate against men, or privilege women, rests on an implicit premise that there is already equality, and feminism aims for something more'.[68] Hence feminists – women who simply will not shut up about *alleged* gender injustice – are the natural target for hostilities in service of maintaining the patriarchal – but ostensibly egalitarian – status quo.

A toxic blight on a precariously egalitarian society, spread through gender studies degrees and various other propaganda, feminism (and its agents, Feminists) are coming for men. They have an agenda. Feminists want a world where men are downtrodden, where they have no rights, no freedoms. For Feminists, it has never been about 'equality' – it has always been about domination. Some feminists may claim this isn't true, but their actions and arguments show that they are hypocrites. This view is evident in statements like these:

- 'They don't want to be treated the same. Feminism exists to ensure they're never treated the same – always better. That's the whole point.' (Man, replying to another man's comment: 'Women are men's equal. How about we treat them that way. Women aren't special delicate creatures that require special treatments and dispensations. They are normal human beings, how about we act like it'.)
- 'it's a bit hypocritical that all the gender neutral politics go out the window when the feminazis want only women in politics'. (Woman, responding to the headline 'A man may take [former MP Kelly] O'Dwyer's seat')
- 'I am thankful I have daughters that know Feminism is Cancer.' (Man, responding to the post 'Donald Trump says Brett Kavanaugh's story could happen to any man')

Interestingly, some people are less rigid with their hostilities towards feminism. They make a distinction between the feminism(s) of the past, where Women's struggles were fair and indeed necessary, and the feminism of today, which aims to privilege Women and destroy society as we know it. In doing this, commentators display 'a resistance to the idea that individuals are shaped by anything bigger than themselves, that neutrality may not be neutral, and that harmful sexist outcomes do not require consciously misogynistic intention'.[69] This is the accommodation Dworkin was talking about. Witness:

- 'Feminism. It's all based on third wave feminist theories. Second wave feminism was a good movement, a well needed movement. Feminism was hijacked by the hysterical, the bigoted, biased and the sexist. It's now just poison. However if you see what 3rd wave feminism's final goal is it is no surprise they want to discredit our society.' (Man, responding to the head-line: 'Rabbit hole of identity politics')
- 'Fourth wave feminism is a cancer in the West.' (Woman, responding to the headline 'Women, like men, lie on occasion')
- Gender equality in the workplace is unethical. I'd be pretty embarrassed to get a job based on what's between my legs instead of my ability. In fact it goes against the feminism earlier generations fought for. Every time I hear the words 'gender equality' I hear women screaming for special treat-ment. (Woman, replying to the post 'Victorian Premier Daniel Andrews has unveiled his new 50 per cent female cabinet, dumping Philip Dalidakis to make way for more women')

At least today, feminism is variously something to be afraid of, something to detest, something that is fundamentally opposed to *our* social values (i.e. equality, autonomy and freedom), and something that (misleadingly) makes Women believe they are 'better' than Men. Hence, any attempt by women to improve their lot can be misinterpreted (sometimes wilfully) as an instance of 'special treatment', or of 'double standards', as evidence that Women are, in fact, the privileged group in this milieu.[70]

In this context, I would go so far as to say that merely *accusing* a woman of being a feminist functions like some of the above-mentioned slurs (like 'dyke' or 'bitch' or 'slut'). Because of the imaginative associations between the fig-uring of The Feminist and the figurings of Bad Women, sometimes calling a woman a Feminist functions as an act of linguistic violence tending to systemic discrimination. This is certainly so with the affect-laden portmanteau 'feminazi' (seen eighty-one times in the data), a term that also alludes to feminists 'real' moral character: pure evil.[71] By aligning the feminist movement with Nazism, feminists are presented as evil dictators dedicated to the elimination and sup-pression of those who do not conform to or agree with their vision for a new world order. They are taking 'man-hating' to a whole new level, apparently.

Note further the way in which the Feminist Woman is imaged. She is ugly, has a non-normative and/or 'unfeminine' appearance (e.g. hairy), she's fat, she can't get a Man and she's always shrieking about something (tacitly: something overblown, something melodramatic).[72] She is the paradigm opposite of the Good Woman. Or so the widespread cultural stereotype goes. Witness:

- 'Why am I not surprised you have blue hair and probably hate all men.' (Ambiguous, ad hoc response to a woman's comment 'Thank God there's this man to explain to me how women operate. Now I know')
- 'Femininity has been replaced by feminism. Both are completely at odds with each other.' (Man, responding to the headline 'Greens in crisis on women and violence')
- 'Unhappy overweight feminists making there [*sic*] mark on the world by destroying Western society in the name of there [*sic*] Equality Cult.' (Man, responding to the headline: 'Gender game rotten to the core')

Here, the Feminist Woman does not only represent the ultimate Bad Woman in her continued attempts to disrupt the status quo; she is also thoroughly abject. The aim of this image is to reorient women away from feminism and towards the Good Woman pedestal through aversion, disgust, and even fear and anger. This comes as no surprise. As Kate Manne points out, the natural targets of misogyny are feminists, because it is they who push back hardest against patriarchal norms.[73] And even though one may object that antifeminist speech does not necessarily equate to anti-woman speech (because one maintains a modicum of respect for the Good Woman), I am with Dworkin: 'It is *right* to see woman hating, sex hatred, passionate contempt, in every effort to subvert or stop an improvement in the status of women on any front, whether radical or reform', and that is what these comments do.[74]

As a final point, it must be emphasised that the specific content of hate speech acts targeting women 'are situational: chosen and applied not to show what she is in her essential self but to intimidate her in a particular situation'.[75] While these above-discussed images of Woman may at times seem disparate and disconnected, they all convey the same message: '"This is a Woman". "You are a Woman". "She is a Woman"'.[76] The terminology may evolve (e.g. 'roastie' or '2 hole'), or commentators may choose less crude words (e.g. 'cow' instead of 'bitch'), but the imaginal root of this denigration remains unchanged. And the function of these violent speech acts against women is meant to be a corrective, to force Women back in their place, subjugated to Man.[77]

DISCUSSION: HARM, BODYWORK
AND THE VIDEOGAME

It is hard to find words to describe what it is like to inhabit space that feels (because it looks) generally hostile. The difficulty in describing the harm of hate speech is partly because, in our central ethico-political imaginary, harm is generally understood to be – or is *seen as* – 'direct and measurable, and what causes it is relatively straightforward: A hits B, and B hurts'.[78] Such a narrow figuration makes it difficult to comprehend, let alone bear witness to, indirect, diffuse and especially group, harms. But such environments put one 'on guard', waiting for the next act of hate speech (or patriarchy-enforcing speech more generally) that one knows will eventually come, if not now, then soon.[79] 'The fear or reality of such abuse is an ever present subtext of women's private and public lives', and this includes their digital lives.[80] Indeed, encountering hate speech against women online is a daily reality even in a forum (namely, a newspaper's comments section) that is supposed to be – but is not in practice – structured by a liberal ethic of equality, civility and non-discrimination. This *should be* surprising to women, but it is not 'because it happens frequently and lies as a constant possibility at the horizon of social imagination'.[81] This results in what can be described as an 'existential stress', recognition of oneself as 'seen-*as* a series of pre-scripted or pre-determined possibilities'.[82]

The status-based group harm I claimed hate speech engenders – *reinforcing and perpetuating hierarchies of identity-based oppression via systematically violent expression constituting a hostile environment* – does not neatly fit the above-described 'simplistic, cause/effect, unidirectional and individualistic understanding of harm'.[83] Some of us can recognise the harm of hate speech clear as day, but we struggle trying to articulate and convey exactly what it is that these spontaneous and sometimes flippant remarks do. Perhaps this explains why several hate speech scholars have gravitated to a particular metaphorical articulation of the harms of hate speech: hate speech as toxic environmental pollutant. For instance, Jeremy Waldron describes a well-ordered society as one wherein each citizen has a taken-for-granted assurance 'that there will be no need to face hostility, violence, discrimination, or exclusion by others', and that when this is so, the assurance 'is something on which everyone can rely, like the cleanness of the air they breathe or the quality of the water they drink from a fountain'.[84] He goes on to say that hate speech 'creates something like an environmental threat to social peace, a sort of slow-acting poison, accumulating here and there, word by word'.[85] Just like environmental pollution, we know that the tiny impacts of 'insignificant' actions can accumulate into a 'toxic effect'.[86]

Admittedly, there are some advantages to such a figuration of 'hate speech'. It mitigates the need to draw a direct causal line of harm from one utterance to one group (or, even better, to one member of that one group), and instead forces us to look at 'the big picture', the impact on the social environment as a whole. It also helps to convey why we should *care* about each and every instance of hate speech, even when some may try to dismiss them as jokes, or claim that the speech isn't harmful if its targets take no personal offence – either way, these are still a contribution to an environment that is becoming more and more toxic, less and less inhabitable.[87] Finally, there is a strong chance that this image will resonate with persons who are rarely (or never) the targets of hate speech, the intersectionally privileged actors who may otherwise be inclined to dismiss the speech acts as random and isolated, lending support to the corollary view that, because they are isolated, these incidents are inconsequential.[88] If you can 'get' how pollution works and why it is necessary to curb it, you can 'get' how hate speech works and why we need to eliminate the practice.

But there is also a problem with the image. It conveys the idea that we begin with a pristine environment that our speech is subsequently degrading. And this is far from reality.[89] *The groups who are the victims of hate speech, who are marked by identity-tracking stigmas, have never been accorded the status of equal moral worth in Western liberal democracies.* This matters. We are born and raised in an environment that is *already* degraded – already structured by hierarchies of power and oppression – and we are fighting to achieve a specific goal: dismantling those hierarchies and establishing equality among identity-based groups. Still, one may object, is it not true that our environment could become much more degraded than it is presently? Does this not make the metaphor a good one? Without doubt this is true, but it is not the point. The point is that justice, in the form of equality, is, and has only ever been, an aspirational ideal. *We need to make it a reality.* A new image and a new narrative can help us do that by accurately conveying the struggles of the oppressed.

An image that gets at hate speech being just one, among many, ever-present threats to one's living a secure life *as* a woman, or *as* a queer person, or *as* a person of colour and so on, is videogaming.[90] Videogames usually have an aim, a quest to achieve or a task for the agent to fulfil, and advancing beyond a certain number of challenges (e.g. levels of the game, or quests) will get the agent there. Here, the quest is a *just* society – no mean feat. This is the hostile environment within which every 'player' starts. But, crucially, recognise how videogames can often be played with differing degrees of difficulty. The greater the difficulty of the game, the harder it is to achieve the aim. Some agents, due to luck of birth and circumstance, get to play this game on Easy (less hostile). Others have to play it on Hard (more hostile). Not only this, avatars often come either with limited lives, or just one life with diminishing health. I put it to the reader to imagine acts of hate speech as blows that diminish the agents' 'health'. They are not the only kind of blows that players can receive – they exist in a web of other hostilities which the agent must keep at bay – but nonetheless they are something one must always be on guard for. The agent must always be *ready* to dodge the threat or put up defences to avoid that threat in the first place ('Don't read the comments'!).

I find a lot of resonance between this metaphor and Helen Ngo's discussion of the *bodywork* oppressed groups go through on a day-to-day basis just to get by and take care of themselves in what is, essentially, an *always-possibly* hostile environment.[91] In other words, she considers the phenomenological impact of living under the *threat* of attack (specifically, for racialised groups), which in itself deprives the subject both freedom and dignity.[92] Because hate speech (and other oppressive acts with coherences of breadth, depth and kind) is 'a social given that everyone knows happens and will happen again',[93] it ever-remains on the horizon of social imagination. Members of oppressed groups know they must employ certain strategies to mitigate their risk of becoming the target, a type of work that is undertaken (sometimes subtly and sometimes overtly) with the body. This includes playing up to or against the social expectations attached to your group: trying to look feminine or attractive by the standards of the male gaze as a cis-het woman ('playing up to'), or proving that one is (unexpectedly) exceptional at mathematics and hard sciences even though one is a woman ('playing against'), are examples. This bodywork is laborious. Because the risk is everywhere, bodywork is a constant necessity. And while we all do bodywork sometimes ('we all might comport ourselves differently for a job or bank interview – in other words, for *events* or *occasions*',[94] says Ngo), for members of oppressed groups 'this kind of work is operative even during the non-events of strolling through a park, walking the streets, or doing the weekly shopping'.[95] It is also operative in the non-events of reading the comments on the news, among other digital activities. In a social context stratified by hierarchies of privilege and oppression, this labour is unending. For some, it is not even limited to the public sphere, but follows them into their homes, manifesting in every area of life. And the point is, it is hard to persist, let alone flourish, in consistently hostile social spaces where there is a decent chance one might become the target, or at least the subject, of attack. Because of one's group memberships, this bodywork is always necessary (indeed, often it is the only line of defence one has against being targeted for who one is). Always on alert. Always ready for the next incoming attack. Just like the agent of the videogame.

(RE-)IMAGINING HER PLACE

Catharine MacKinnon argues that 'social inequality is substantially created and enforced – that is, done – through words and images'.[96] As this chapter has demonstrated, certain images of Woman, *images which are not new and did not originate with the internet*, are reproduced in hate speech against women online. These expressions do not just constitute an affective environment, they function to police women who (appear to) step beyond their station. In this respect, women do not have equal (or equivalent) access to online social spaces as compared to men, *ceteris paribus*. Hate speech puts Woman in her place through linguistic violence and sets her up for constant bodywork to pre-emptively fend off possible attacks. We must now ask, how can hate speaking against women online be reduced or eliminated (the narrow question), and how can we 'shift deeply ingrained habits of perception and feeling to ensure social reforms are rendered stable and enduring'[97] (the broad question). Chapters 5 and 6 aim to address these questions, in turn.

NOTES

1. Catharine MacKinnon, *Only Words* (Cambridge: Harvard University Press, 1993), 13, original emphasis.

2. See, for example: Kim Barker and Olga Jurasz, *Online Misogyny as a Hate Crime: A Challenge for Legal Regulation?* (London: Routledge, 2019); Bianca Fileborn and Rachel Loney-Howes, eds., *#MeToo and the Politics of Social Change* (Cham: Palgrave Macmillan, 2019); Debbie Ging and Eugenia Siapera, eds., *Gender Hate Online: Understanding the New Anti-Feminism* (Cham: Palgrave Macmillan, 2019); Emma Jane, *Misogyny Online: A Short and Brutish History* (London: Sage Swifts, 2017); Karla Mantilla, *Gender Trolling: How Misogyny Went Viral* (Santa Barbara: Praeger, 2015); Anastasia Powell and Nicola Henry, *Sexual Violence in a Digital Age* (London: Palgrave Macmillan, 2017); Jacqueline Ryan Vickery and Tracy Everbach, eds., *Mediating Misogyny: Gender, Technology, and Harassment* (Cham: Palgrave Macmillan, 2018) – this is not to mention the numerous journal articles currently being published on this very same subject.

3. Jane (*Misogyny Online*) and Powell and Henry (*Sexual Violence*) both discuss hate speech, but minimally, treating it as a form of harassment.

4. Robert Post, 'Privacy, Speech, and the Digital Imagination', in *Free Speech In The Digital Age*, ed. Susan Brison and Katharine Gelber (Oxford: Oxford University Press, 2019), 108.

5. James Curran, 'The Internet of Dreams: Reinterpreting the Internet', *Misunderstanding the Internet*, 2nd ed., eds. James Curran, Natalie Fenton, and Des Freedman (London Routledge, 2016), 23.

6. Emily Harmer and Sarah Lewis, 'Disbelief and Counter-Voices: A Thematic Analysis of Online Reader Comments About Sexual Harassment and Sexual Violence Against Women', *Information, Communication and Society* (2020) https://doi.org/10.1080/1369118X.2020.1770832.

7. Marguerite La Caze, *The Analytic Imaginary* (Ithaca: Cornell University Press, 2002), 19.

8. Facebook Newsroom, 'Stats', *Facebook Company Info*, accessed August 14, 2019, https://newsroom.fb.com/company-info/.

9. Facebook Business, 'Aussies on Facebook: Mobile is the First Screen and Video is Exploding', *Facebook News*, July 9, 2015, accessed August 25, 2020, https ://www.facebook.com/business/news/Key-Trends-Australians-on-Facebook.

10. John Sinclair, 'Political Economy and Discourse in Murdoch's Flagship Newspaper, *The Australian*', *The Political Economy of Communication* 4 (2016): 13.

11. One study found that on Facebook between 2015 and 2016, 'liberal news on the social network elicited the highest proportion of civil discourse. Among uncivil comments, those on liberal-news and national-news pages were less likely to be extremely uncivil than those on conservative-news and local-news ones'. Note, though, that this study focused on U.S. news outlets. See: Leona Yi-Fan Su, Michael A Xenos, Kathleen M Rose, Christopher Wirz, Dietram A Scheufele, and Dominique Brossard, 'Uncivil and Personal? Comparing Patterns of Incivility in Comments on the Facebook Pages of News Outlets', *New Media and Society* 20 (2018): 3692.

12. See Andrea Dworkin, *Right-Wing Women* (New York: Wideview/Perigree, 1978), 198.

13. Jeremy Waldron, *The Harm in Hate Speech* (Cambridge: Harvard University Press, 2012), chap. 4.

14. I collected comments which could be classified as sexist or misogynistic per the definitions developed in my 2018 article, Louise Richardson-Self, 'Woman-Hating: On Misogyny, Sexism, and Hate Speech', *Hypatia* 33 (2018): 256–272. Following Bianca Fileborn's method, two readings of the data were undertaken, during which I highlighted exemplary quotes and identified emergent themes. See: Bianca Fileborn, 'Justice 2.0: Street Harassment Victims' Use of Social Media and Online Activism as Sites of Informal Justice', *British Journal of Criminology* 57 (2017): 1490.

15. Tarleton Gillespie, *Custodians of the Internet: Platforms, Content Moderation, and the Hidden Decisions that Shape Social Media* (New Haven: Yale University Press, 2018), 99.

16. I acknowledge that this method is far from perfect, though. Users *do* report offensive material, and it *does* (sometimes) get removed. Facebook also has tools that help page operators moderate what visitors can post, as well as providing the power to delete or hide content and ban users. It is entirely possible that more egregious content was reported and removed before I conducted my data collection each day, or never made it onto the post to begin with. See: Facebook Business, 'Admin's guide to moderating your Page', *Facebook*, 2020, accessed August 25, 2020, https://www.fac ebook.com/business/a/page-moderation-tips. In spite of these limitations, I still found many instances of hate speech.

17. I include headlines, posts, and descriptions of thumbnails as necessary to contex-tualise the comments herein. However, regrettably, there is not enough space to analyse how these headlines, posts, and thumbnails *themselves* contribute to the sustenance of the patriarchal sexual imaginary – this is an area where future analysis is needed.

18. While 'patriarchy has no gender', it is still interesting to note the extent to which men and women appear to be engaging in this violent conduct. See: Lucy Nicholas and Christine Agius, *The Persistence of Global Masculinism Discourse,*

Gender and Neo-Colonial Re-Articulations of Violence (Cham: Palgrave Macmillan, 2017), 37.

19. I find it noteworthy that I was left with a substantial remainder of speech acts which did not meet the stipulated threshold for 'hate speech', but which nonetheless proffered problematic, hostile figurations of women, bearing different faces of oppression (most notably, cultural imperialism). I am calling these surrounding comments the Dialogical Plexus of hate speech – an interconnection of related imag(in)ings regarding Women, Men, other genders, Rights, Fairness, Equality, Feminism, Oppression, to name only a few of the most prominent. As argued in chapter 3, I believe that the subtle differences in patriarchy-enforcing, and specifically woman-subjugating speech suggest different modes of redress depending on which face/s of oppression they bear. I think that 'hate speech', being violent, warrants a punitive response.

20. Matthew Costello and James Hawdon, 'Hate Speech in Online Spaces', in *The Palgrave Handbook of Cybercrime and Cyberdeviance*, ed. Thomas Holt and Adam Bossler (Cham: Springer Nature, 2020), 1409.

21. Dworkin, *Right-Wing Women*, 199, original emphasis.

22. Kate Manne, *Down Girl: The Logic of Misogyny* (Oxford: Oxford University Press, 2018), 58, my emphasis.

23. Martha Nussbaum, 'Objectification', *Philosophy and Public Affairs* 24 (1995): 275.

24. Men's homosocial bonding is, in part, 'predicated on women's sexualisation and subordination'. Here, 'through the sexual objectification of women, maleness is established as not only *different from* female but as *better than* female'. What's more, men need 'to demonstrate their sexual prowess and experience to do well in the masculine hierarchy'. See: Steven Roberts, Signe Ravn, Marcus Maloney, and Brittany Ralph, 'Navigating the Tensions of Normative Masculinity: Homosocial Dynamics in Australian Young Men's Discussions of Sexting Practices', *Cultural Sociology* 15 (2020): 3, 4, 16.

25. Jane Dolkart, 'Hostile Environment Harassment: Equality, Objectivity, and the Shaping of Legal Standards', *Emory Law Journal* 43 (1994): 181.

26. Sexual assault and harassment in Australian politics has come to the fore of public discourse in early 2021 (triggering massive protests around the nation in March) – indeed, there is even a Wikipedia entry compiling various accusations of misconduct. See: '2021 Australian Parliament House Sexual Misconduct Allegations', *Wikipedia: The Free Encyclopedia*, April 10, 2021, accessed 11 April 2021, https://en.wikipedia .org/wiki/2021_Australian_Parliament_House_sexual_misconduct_allegations.

27. Manne, *Down Girl*, xiv.

28. Jane cites her own email inbox to demonstrate to the reader what 'the rape-a-rific emails sent to a rowdy, sex-positive newspaper columnist in the late 1990s' looked like, noting that the 'e-bile algebra' proliferated well before the present era (Jane, *Misogyny Online*, 13, 35).

29. Alexander Lu and Y. Joel Wong, 'Stressful Experiences of Masculinity Among U.S.-Born and Immigrant Asian American Men', *Gender and Society* 27 (2013): 345–371.

30. Kylie Weston-Scheuber, 'Gender and the Prohibition of Hate Speech', *QUT Law and Justice Journal* 12 (2012): 142.

31. Caitlin Janzen, Susan Strega, Leslie Brown, Jeannie Morgan, and Jeannine Carrière, "'Nothing Short of a Horror Show": Triggering Abjection of Street Workers in Western Canadian Newspapers', *Hypatia* 28 (2013): 144; Millicent Churcher and Moira Gatens, 'Reframing Honour in Heterosexual Imaginaries', *Angelaki* 24 (2019): 157

32. Clementine Ford, *Fight Like A Girl* (Sydney: Allen & Unwin, 2016), 201.

33. Weston-Scheuber, 'Gender', 145.

34. Tanya D'Souza, Laura Griffin, Nicole Shackleton, and Danielle Walt, 'Harming Women with Words: The Failure of Australian Law to Prohibit Gendered Hate Speech', *UNSW Law Journal* 41 (2018): 943.

35. D'Souza et al., 'Harming Women', 971, remind us that 'vulnerability is also a state or circumstance that is constructed (socially, discursively and legally) and therefore changeable'.

36. Weston-Scheuber, 'Gender', 142.

37. Powell and Henry, *Sexual Violence*, 168.

38. Sarah Sobieraj, 'Bitch, Slut, Skank, Cunt: Patterned Resistance to Women's Visibility in Digital Publics', *Information, Communication and Society* 21 (2017): 1706.

39. Iris Marion Young, *Throwing Like A Girl and Other Essays in Feminist Philosophy and Social Theory* (Bloomington: Indiana University Press, 1990), 200–201.

40. See Urban Dictionary's Entry: https://www.urbandictionary.com/define.php ?term=2%20hole.

41. Jacqueline Broad, 'The Early Modern Period: Dignity and the Foundation of Women's Rights', in *The Wollstonecraftian Mind*, ed. Eileen Hunt Botting, Sandrine Bergès, and Alan Coffee (London: Routledge, 2019), 27.

42. Broad, 'Early Modern Period', 29.

43. Broad, 'Early Modern Period', 28.

44. Broad, 'Early Modern Period', 28, 30, my emphasis.

45. Janzen, et al., 'Triggering Abjection', 156.

46. This emoji is the 'Woman Gesturing Okay'.

47. Jane, *Misogyny Online*, 4.

48. There were many instances where women were described, for example, as 'bird', 'parasite', 'snake', 'pig' and 'rat'. I have not labelled these comments "hate speech" because these terms do not have gendered connotations. However, it may be plausible to argue that such bestialising nonetheless counts as 'hate speech' where it can be demonstrably shown that the woman is targeted *because* she is a woman.

49. Barbara Creed, *The Monstrous-Feminine: Film, Feminism, Psychoanalysis* (London: Routledge, 1993).

50. Janzen et al., 'Triggering Abjection', 143.

51. Julia Kristeva, *Powers of Horror: An Essay on Abjection* (New York: Columbia University Press, 1982). See also: Janzen et al., 'Triggering Abjection', 151.

52. Iris Marion Young, *Justice and the Politics of Difference* (Princeton: Princeton University Press, 1990), 143.

53. Sarah Ahmed, 'The Skin of the Community: Affect and Boundary Formation', in *Revolt, Affect, Collectivity: The Unstable Boundaries of Kristeva's Polis*, ed. Tina Chante and Ewa Ziarek (Albany: State University of New York Press, 2005), 102.

54. On the process of triggering, See Janzen et al., 'Triggering Abjection', 142–161.

55. *Q+A* is a weekly Australian talk show on ABC featuring a different panel of guest experts per episode.

56. Hannele Harjunen, *Neoliberal Bodies and the Gendered Fat Body* (London: Routledge, 2016), 92.

57. See Urban Dictionary's Entry: https://www.urbandictionary.com/define.php ?term=Roastie.

58. Jessica Megarry, 'Online Incivility or Sexual Harassment? Conceptualising Women's Experiences in the Digital Age', *Women's Studies International Forum* 47 (2014): 50.

59. Harjunen, *Neoliberal Bodies*, 9.

60. Harjunen, *Neoliberal Bodies*, 95.

61. Louise Richardson-Self, 'Cis-Hetero-Misogyny Online', *Ethical Theory and Moral Practice* 22 (2019): 574–575. Note that I do not discuss the phenomenon of identity denial as a form of trans-misogyny in this article, but I do point out that lack of alliance between cis and trans women only contributes to women's subjugation and so must be addressed.

62. D'Souza et al., 'Harming Women', 955.

63. Jane, *Misogyny Online*, 22.

64. Megarry, 'Online Incivility', 49.

65. Lynne Tirrell, 'Toxic Misogyny and the Limits of Counterspeech', *Fordham Law Review* 87 (2019): 2449; D'Souza et al. 'Harming Women', 955.

66. Dworkin, *Right-Wing Women*, 195, 201.

67. Dworkin, *Right-Wing Women*, 196.

68. Nicholas and Agius, *Global Masculinism*, 3.

69. Nicholas and Agius, *Global Masculinism*, 46.

70. On the problem with 'special rights', see: Louise Richardson-Self, *Justifying Same-Sex Marriage: A Philosophical Investigation* (London: Rowman and Littlefield International, 2015), chap. 3.

71. Sobieraj, 'Bitch', 1705.

72. See Christina Scharff, *Repudiating Feminism: Young Women in a Neoliberal World* (Surrey: Ashgate, 2012), chap. 4.

73. Manne, *Down Girl*, 51.

74. Dworkin, *Right Wing Women*, 197.

75. Dworkin, *Right Wing Women*, 198.

76. Sobieraj, 'Bitch', 1708.

77. D'Souza et al., 'Harming Women', 955; Manne, *Down Girl*, 69.

78. Bob Brecher, 'Andrea Dworkin's *Pornography: Men Possessing Women* – A Reassessment', in *Women and Violence: The Agency of Victims and Perpetrators*,

ed. Herjeet Marway and Heather Widdows (Basingstoke: Palgrave Macmillan, 2015), 151.

79. Helen Ngo, *The Habits of Racism: A Phenomenology of Racism and Racialized Embodiment* (Lanham: Lexington Books, 2017), 56–61.

80. Dolkart, 'Hostile Environment Harassment', 179.

81. Young, *Justice*, 62.

82. Ngo, *Habits of Racism*, 61, 64.

83. Brecher, 'Dworkin's *Pornography*', 157.

84. Waldron, *The Harm in Hate Speech*, 4.

85. Waldron, *The Harm in Hate Speech*, 4.

86. Waldron, *The Harm in Hate Speech*, 97; see also Tirrell, 'Toxic Misogyny', 2445.

87. E.g., Tirrell ('Toxic Misogyny', 2445) says 'A strong organism encountering a weak dose [of toxin] might not even notice it . . . harmful speech is taken without awareness of the cumulative effect of multiple doses'.

88. On this point, see Mari Matsuda, 'Public Response to Racist Speech: Considering the Victim's Story', in *Words that Wound: Critical Race Theory, Assaultive Speech, and the First Amendment*, ed. Mari Matsuda, Charles R. Lawrence III, Richard Delgado, and Kimberlè Williams Crenshaw (Boulder: Westview Press, 1993), 22.

89. Miranda Fricker reminds us: 'focus on justice . . . creates an impression that justice is the norm and injustice is the aberration'. See Miranda Fricker, *Epistemic Injustice: Power and the Ethics of Knowing* (Oxford: Oxford University Press, 2007), VII.

90. This is offered not as a form of comparison, but a way of 'seeing-as'. See Talia Morag, 'Comparison or Seeing-As? The Holocaust and Factory Farming', *Morality in a Realistic Spirit: Essays for Cora Diamond* (New York: Routledge, 2019): 194–214.

91. Ngo, *Habits of Racism*, 58.

92. Young *Justice*, 62.

93. Young, *Justice*, 62.

94. Ngo, *Habits of Racism*, 58.

95. Ngo, *Habits of Racism*, 58.

96. MacKinnon, *Only Words*, 13.

97. Millicent Churcher, *Reimagining Sympathy, Recognizing Difference: Insights from Adam Smith* (London: Rowman and Littlefield International: 2019), 5.

Chapter 5

Countermeasures against Online Hate Speech

The power of law should not be gainsaid, but to end misogyny and rein in the steady onslaught of misogynist discourse and images, we need so much more than what law can do.

—Lynne Tirrell[1]

The purpose of this chapter is to answer the narrow question: How might hate speaking against women online be reduced? Much ink has already been spilled on the question of whether speech can be legally regulated to prevent harm to others. Many believe that 'speech is to be granted special protection not accorded to other forms of conduct', namely, forms of conduct that bring about 'real harms – harms that, if brought by any other means, would be considered unjust and sanctionable', making its *justified* restriction very difficult.[2] However, as Katharine Gelber and Susan Brison point out, there is 'a deeper assumption underlying much political philosophy in this area. That is the assumption that speech deserves special protection because it is more like thought than like conduct'.[3] This is problematic because there is no plausible way to make a speech/conduct distinction: 'A thought or idea has no more life while unthought, or unread in a book, or unheard on a tape, than does an action such as a dance when unperformed'.[4] Gelber and Brison conclude, 'speech is a physical phenomenon, being instigated by agents, expressed by agents, and having physical effects on its listeners'.[5] Once the speech/conduct distinction falls down, we see there is no justified reason for protecting speech that harms agents in certain ways if we already prohibit other (physical) acts which harm likewise. What's more, the free speech principle 'is theoretically incorrect, because it rests on a paradox, in which speech is conceptualized as both harmless, because causally inert, *and* capable of causing harms and so

117

warranting protection not provided by a general harm-to-others principle'.[6] As we saw in chapter 4, hate speech – being a kind of oppressive speech – is harmful. Thus, on the basis of Gelber's and Brison's argument, I take restrictions on hate speech and the use of punitive measures to combat its presence online (and off) to be theoretically justified.

The most obvious punitive strategy to take is a legal approach. Anastasia Powell and Nicola Henry explain, 'Law is *a discourse of power* because of its claim to justice and truth, its construction of knowledge, and its shaping of social norms, beliefs and values'.[7] Indeed I agree that, in the dominant Western social imaginary, Law[8] is the most prominent image of a functioning, coercive, binding and supremely powerful tool that can orient (or, rather, enforce) individuals' and organisations' behaviour. Law exhibits powers over ordinary social agents, Law sets standards for permissible and impermissible conduct (i.e. norms) among a certain collective, and is even suggestive of shared *moral* rather than merely political standards ('our' values, that is, meaning-generating narratives) – standards which apply to all who are bound by its jurisdiction – to ensure a just society.[9] Thus, Law may seem a very appealing avenue through which to constrain user behaviour. But it is not our only avenue, and nor are we constrained to punitive responses (though they are warranted). This chapter looks at the pragmatics of possible user and platform-based approaches to dealing with the problem of hate speech against women online. None of them are a panacea. However, in concert, their (albeit imperfect) power cannot be gainsaid.

THE USER-TO-USER LEGAL APPROACH

Utilise Existing Law

In fighting hate speech, one may turn to applicable existing laws. In Australia, there is a federal telecommunications law – which is part of the *Criminal Code Act 1995* (Cth) – forbidding the use of a carriage service to menace, harass, or offend a person (s474.17). This law has been used successfully but sparingly to hold gender-based digital abuses to account. One such case involved the non-consensual live-recording of a sexual encounter, which came to be known as the Skype Scandal (2013). The jury ultimately found two men guilty of this offence, and both received good behaviour bonds as penalty (though it was possible for the judge to have sentenced the offenders with a maximum penalty of three years imprisonment).[10] A second case occurred in 2015. Facebook user Zane Alchin had made comments to two women (the original target and a friend who came to her defence) which consisted of statements such as: 'If you sucked my dick I'd slap your over the back of the head after it so you'd spit my cum out you ain't worthy of swallowing my jizz', and 'You know the best thing about a feminist [is] they don't get any action so when you rape them it feels 100 times tighter'.[11] Alchin entered a plea of guilty to this offence and was also sentenced to a good behaviour bond.[12] In Australia, at least, it seems as though women who are targeted with online abuses, including hate speech, *do* already have a legal solution at their disposal.

However, the legislation itself and the actions of police in pursuing such charges leave a lot to be desired. First, note that 'the rapidly changing nature of digital technologies, the difficulty of identifying perpetrators, [and] the cross-jurisdictional nature of the problem' means many women in like situations will be unable to rely on this law as a mechanism for redress.[13] In the case of Alchin, it was almost serendipitous that both perpetrator and victims resided within the same legal jurisdiction. Had Alchin made these comments while located in, say, Hawaii (as a U.S. citizen), charges could not have been brought against him. Second, this law is infrequently used. While reasons for its infrequent use sometimes come down to those aforementioned, unfortunately victims cannot yet rely on institutional actors (such as police) to actively support their rights. Indeed, as Emma Jane writes, 'The fact that police took action in response to a report of cyber VAWG [violence against women and girls] is extremely unusual'.[14] Much of the credit is owed to the women themselves who, alongside reporting to police, engaged in several acts of 'digilantism' – spreading proof of and criticising the oppressive nature of such acts publicly.[15] Third, as Millicent Churcher, following Adam Smith, explains:

> We, as sufferers, 'resent injuries not just to our possessions or bodies, but *also to our dignity as persons*'. According to Smith, the primary goal of our resentment [to the one who has harmed us] is not 'to make our enemy feel pain in his turn' but 'to make him sensible that the person whom he injured did not deserve to be treated in that manner'. In this context, punishment can step in to 'make the other "sensible" of our dignity, to feel respect for us'.[16]

However, the phrasing of this law implies that *misuse of the carriage service* is the wrong in question, rather than the *digital abuse of women*.[17] Thus, prosecution under this law is unlikely to restore dignity to women because it does not adequately recognise this *group* as being harmed. An adequate response must better approximate and address the recognitive issues these harmful acts perpetrate. Finally, it is unclear to what extent a claim could be brought protesting the examples of hate speech I analysed in chapter 4, many of which have subjects who are not direct targets. These statements are *about* women, but not necessarily directed *to* women. Pragmatically speaking, a law such as this may not be very useful in these cases. This returns us to the difficulty of making known the group harms of hate speech.

Ban Gendered Hate Speech

Proposing we use Law to explicitly ban online hate speech is an alternative that mirrors the approach many Western countries have taken to address offline hate speech.[18] But does banning offline hate speech work, and could it similarly work online? Currently, the evidence is inconclusive. As Maxime Lepoutre summarises:

> Hate speech is difficult to measure and often goes unreported; different countries and agencies may have different ways of defining and measuring hate speech; and even if we had data reliably comparing incidence of hate speech between countries that do and do not ban it, there are so many other cultural, social, and political differences between countries that it would remain extremely difficult to establish a causal connection between bans and reductions in hate speech.[19]

In short, we don't know how well or whether these bans work to discourage hate speech given threat of penalty.

Still, others argue, legal bans on hate speech matter because of their *expressive value*: because of what they say to the community about hate speech as a practice – namely, that it won't be tolerated, and, by implicature, it won't be tolerated because the practice is *wrong*, an *injustice*, *harmful*. For example, Anjalee de Silva argues that the introduction of laws prohibiting gendered hate speech 'may be seen to constitute a "counter-speech act" by the state that may mitigate the harms to women of sex-based vilification'.[20] In other words, the introduction of such a ban wouldn't just establish a new set of prohibited conduct, it would *also* express to all members of the community that the state not only strongly morally disapproves of violently misogynistic expressions, it disapproves of them so much that it will punish people who so hate speak. This will, importantly, 'dilute the authority of such [hate] speech' – its power to harm subjects – if the rules are broken.[21]

There is some intuitive plausibility to this argument when viewed from a specific contextual location, such as present-day Australia (which is de Silva's context, and my own), given a social imaginaries lens. This gets at Law's being a discourse of power, which is just to say that its contents have a role in shaping the imaginal outlook of a given collective. Since Australia already has civil and criminal bans on racist hate speech at federal and state levels, for instance, by parity of reasoning, gender-based hate speech should likewise be banned to that same extent.[22] After all, gender and race are both recognised under anti-discrimination laws.[23] So, were the government to introduce such a ban, that ban would certainly emit an express message to the community at large.[24] However, one problem with arguing for bans based on parity of reasoning is that this can cut both ways: as a community, we may feel the scope of existing hate speech bans is too broad, for example, because they inhibit free speech (for those invested in the aforementioned free speech principle). Thus, we would protest the introduction of any further restrictions and demand the repeal of others.[25] A second different reason people may be hostile to the introduction of legal bans on gendered hate speech regards efficacy. The Law might ostensibly express a particular message, but if, in practice, those laws are not applied or functional, the message will be too weak to have any real effect; thus, a different message is sent instead: this behaviour won't really be punished, it is not *that* serious.

A third problem with relying on bans to solve the problem of hate speech against women (online or off) is that laws get 'stymied by the principle of viewpoint neutrality'.[26] Recall my argument that Men's present social identity power over Women means that women *can* be the victims of hate speech *as Women*, but men *cannot* be victims *as Men*. Well, as Tanya D'Souza (and others) point out:

> If the broader socio-political context were one of matriarchy (where feminine traits were systematically ranked and valued as higher than masculine ones) then GHS [gendered hate speech] which is misandrist *could* exist in the same way that misogynist hate speech currently exists under patriarchy. But that is currently not the case in Australian society.[27]

For this very fact, it is necessary for laws (and policies) to be neutrally articulated. Should the context change, laws (and policies) still need to be fit for purpose under the new social condition. Just because women are *currently* oppressed in the Anglosphere does not mean we should legislate bans on (or otherwise prohibit) hate speech against *women*. Rather, if we should create such a ban at all, we should ban *gendered hate speech*. This is what the principle of viewpoint neutrality tells us, and pragmatically this makes sense.

But how does viewpoint neutrality then stymie women's efforts to eliminate gendered hate speech? Unfortunately, to enact such a 'neutral' ban is to open up the possibility of spurious claims of women engaging in misandrist hate speech against men *in the present*.[28] If a neutral law is established, it can be exploited to the ends of the socially powerful. What's more, some people may not even realise that such claims *are* spurious. They may believe that we are, in fact, living in an egalitarian, or even a matriarchal, rather than patriarchal society, which is to say that people are living under different *gestalts*. There is trouble further still if the ostensibly neutral law is *applied* (but not articulated) partially so that it recognises utterances denigrating women as 'hate speech' (e.g. 'Women are scum'), but identical utterances denigrating men ('Men are scum') are seen as 'permissible speech'. On the basis of our central impressions about equality and fairness, one can easily see a chain of reasoning which leads to the conclusion that men are the victims of double standards. This take misrepresents the social identity power structures of the milieu, but, given the shape of contemporary antifeminism, it is not uncommon to see tacit presumption of the impression that gender equality has already been achieved in Western liberal democracies.[29] The fact that this is false does not make it any less meaningful for those who think it true; for, from their imaginal orientation, this is *obviously* the way the world really is, and any evidence to the contrary can be explained away.

With all of that said, I do support introducing legal bans on certain speech acts (both online and off) for the imaginally revolutionary role Law may have in reorienting our social norms, institutions and material practices within Australia, and potentially within the broader Western milieu. I'll call bans that apply the principle of neutrality 'bans on vilifying speech' to distinguish them from the normative ethico-political category 'hate speech', which I have argued does its best normative work when conceptualised as partial.[30] Banning gendered vilification is a form of state intervention 'which can support women's agency, especially their discursive and political agency in public spaces'.[31] However, introducing it will also enable users to bring spurious claims. This is a consequence I am prepared to accept for the institutional support it can bring to women. Now, to bypass such claims, lawyers and the judiciary must be trained to discern *harm in context*.[32] Even with this caveat, however, we must acknowledge that there *will* be members of the general public who will interpret this as women's privilege, as evidence that men are the oppressed class today. This is a problem seeking an urgent solution, and it is a problem of *shared meaning*.

LEGAL STRATEGIES INVOLVING PLATFORMS

Ban Cyber-Abuse

Interestingly, the Australian Government has recently proposed to introduce a Bill for an Act relating to online safety for Australians. This includes the 'world-first cyber-abuse take down scheme for Australian Adults'.[33] The core expectation of the proposed *Basic Online Safety Expectations* framework is that the platform enables end-user safety by taking reasonable steps to minimise cyber-bullying, cyber-abuse and non-consensual sharing of intimate images, among other things.[34] Platforms must provide a reporting or complaints system for their content. Platforms should also report to the E-Safety commissioner on various issues.[35] Is it possible that *this* law would recognise and remedy the harms of hate speech against women online? What is encouraging about this approach is its jurisdictional reach: take-down notices and other penalties can be applied to international offending parties (whether they be users or the platforms themselves). Thus, it is an improvement on the carriage service law. However, there are issues with the Bill. Here, note the definition of 'cyber-abuse' in Section 7(1). Subsection (b) stipulates that something is cyber-abuse when 'an *ordinary reasonable person* would conclude that it is likely that the material was *intended* to have an effect of causing serious harm to a *particular* Australian adult' (my emphasis). There are three concerns.

First, is the standard of an 'ordinary reasonable person' the most appropriate standard for determining whether serious harm was (intended to be) occasioned? As has been persuasively argued by feminist legal theorists and critical race theorists, 'reasonableness has no specific content' but can only be given meaning in a specific context.[36] However, in Western contexts, 'the dominant neutral principles of law . . . [reflect] white, male, heterosexual, middle-class norms'.[37] Insofar as some people are targeted with cyber-abuse *because* they belong to an oppressed group (e.g. because they are women, or because they are people of colour – that is, because they are *not* members of the socially dominant group), the 'ordinary reasonable person' standard is at risk of failing to fully comprehend the severity of the harm that the abuse has caused. This is especially true for the evaluation of 'offensive' material. Scholars who advocate against hate speech bans (and who usually happen to be dominant group members) consistently misconstrue 'hate speech' as simply 'offensive speech', and this is not helped by state legislation using the term in its description of the objectionable conduct.[38] But what appears as mere offence to these dominant group members actually forms part of a connected web of harmful practices within which marginal groups find themselves stuck on a day-to-day basis. As Jeremy Waldron explains, the aim is not to legislate against 'aspects of feeling, including hurt, shock, and anger', rather the concern is with 'objective or social aspects of a person's standing in society' – that is, their group status as equals.[39] Thus, it would be better that subsection (b) be reworded as follows: 'an ordinary reasonable person *in the position of the target* would conclude', because the members of the target group know what it is like to live a life marked by a tracker stigma.

Second, I question the extent to which it is appropriate to include in subsection (b) the phrase 'the material was *intended* to have an effect'. Although I have consistently used the phenomenological interpretation of 'intentionality' to characterise hate speech in this book – which is simply to say that the speech is oriented towards an oppressed group – it is more likely that the term would here be interpreted as a *deliberate action*; that is, that *mens rea* was present. However, misogyny is generally habituated and institutionalised, such that the perpetrators of such abuse (if, indeed, a perpetrator can be identified) are often simply following social scripts. As Tirrell writes: 'Ubiquitous in patriarchal societies, misogyny is inherent in the structural norms that shape gender identities, relationships, economics, and politics – it is woven into the very fabric of society'.[40] That is, mens rea is often *not* involved in misogyny's function.[41] Yet, if it is possible to demonstrate that the material in question has in fact caused or constituted a substantial harm, why is this not sufficient for determining an instance of cyber-abuse? I am in agreement with Vittorio Bufacchi and Jools Gilson, who critique the taken-for-granted standard way of thinking about violence, figuring it as something 'perpetrator-centred, intentionality-centred [i.e., deliberate] and time-specific'.[42] I see no reason for *accidentally harmful material* to be classed outside the scope of cyber-abuse and thus for the user or service provider to be protected from a removal notice. So, I propose that subsection (b) be reworded as: 'the material *had an effect*'. This would be consonant with a victim-centred approach to understanding 'harm'.[43]

However, there is still further cause for concern. Hence, third, I note some limitations with the provision that the material has 'an effect of causing serious harm to a *particular* Australian adult'. The offending material must be menacing, harassing or offensive leading to serious harm, where 'serious harm' is understood, under Section 5, to be either physical harm or harm to a person's mental health, wherein that may be serious psychological harm or serious distress. While it is undoubtedly true that individuals who are cyber-abused can experience extraordinary distress, and that cyber-abuse can be used to target people indiscriminately (for any individual can suffer from abuse), it is also true that certain collectives – again, women, people of colour and others – face a heightened risk of encountering hostilities *about* their social group which are not aimed at them as direct targets in online spaces. This is due to the ongoing web of discriminatory practices and prejudicial attitudes this stigmatised group has endured in the past, and which continues to affect it in the present. Specifically, the problem with the phrasing of the subsection is that it is too individualistic to reckon with the ripples of violence emanating from hate speech against groups.

It is important to recognise that when harassing, menacing and offensive material takes groups as its subject, it is not necessarily the case that specific individuals are harmed in the ways specified in the exposure draft. Harm to groups is both a dignitarian harm, but also inheres in the maintenance of unjust social hierarchies in contexts of already-existing inequality. Hierarchies are maintained, in part, by the very creation and sustainment of hostile environments, so the maintenance (or constitution) of *a hostile environment ought itself to be seen as a form of unjust discrimination* and thus a harm. A hostile environment – and the lingering sense that one is at risk of attack – can stop people from participating in public debate, from visiting particular platforms, and even from having a 'public presence' online altogether. That leaves women with the 'choice' to leave (i.e. to miss out on the goods the internet has to offer), or to create a highly sanitised, private space for themselves to minimise their own risk of attack (i.e. to retain some of the internet's goods, but to have far less freedom than other users simply due to gender). So, while it is immensely encouraging to see that the Australian Government is taking proactive steps to ensure the online safety of its residents; it is important for legislative approaches not leave any members of our community more vulnerable than others. Yet, such vulnerability remains when group harms like hostile environment are not explicitly considered.

Treat Platforms akin to Publishers, Not Conduits.

There are other ways in which speech can be curtailed on social media platforms – platforms like Facebook. Facebook, at the end of the day, is a terrestrially located organisation, which means that terrestrial laws apply to it. One suggestion, then, is that section 230 of the *Communications Decency Act 1996* (the United States) be either repealed, modified or reinterpreted, forcing companies like Facebook to take a more proactive approach in ridding their site of hate speech. S230(c)(1) states that 'no provider or user of an interactive computer service shall be treated as the publisher or speaker of any information provided by another information content provider'. In other words, s230 'has been broadly interpreted as protecting interactive computer service providers from liability for the actions of their users'.[44] Thus, Frederik Stjernfelt and Anne Mette Lauritzen conclude, with the enactment of this law 'the principle that control implies liability was dissolved'.[45] But Mary Anne Franks disagrees. First, s230 does not apply to 'violations of federal criminal law, intellectual property law, or communications privacy law'.[46] Second, s230 does not apply to all online entities, only those which themselves create content. Now, it is obvious that 'when people use Facebook to post defamatory comments or harass other users, this is not the same as Mark Zuckerberg engaging in defamation or harassment', which is to say that Facebook is the conduit of harassment but not the origin of that harassment.[47] However, while 'Facebook may not be "speaking" through a user's posts . . . it is earning revenue from them', so, 'while it may be wrongheaded to treat Facebook or similar entities as speakers or publishers of third-party content, it seems equally wrong-headed to treat them as though they had no relationship at all to such content'.[48] Indeed, we must not forget that s230 predates Facebook and a host of other social media sites, and thus is not nuanced enough to suit the conditions of cyberspace in the present context.[49] If amendments to s230 – to treat social media platforms as more akin to publishers and less akin to conduits, or to create some new status in between – would help big tech companies take a more active approach to content moderation, of which they are already legally permitted to engage,[50] then surely this should be pursued, for internet users could more confidently 'rely on general site managers to serve as bulwarks against hate on their platforms'.[51]

Treat Certain Users as Publishers, Not Conduits.

A different approach, but one which is compatible with removing or refining s230, would be strengthening the duties Facebook page admins have insofar as they are disseminating their own original publications. This would mean news outlets (like *The Australian*) could become accountable for user-generated content (i.e. comments) responding to their posts on their own social media pages.[52] The onus of moderation would sit largely with admins, who already have the capacity to block words, use a profanity filter, restrict photo and video posts, hide posts, delete posts, ban users and remove users. If a page admin fails to maintain these standards, then Facebook can remove the page and/or ban the user, meanwhile it may be possible to hold admin's (or the organisations they represent) legally responsible for the presence of certain content. This approach was recently undertaken by Dylan Voller, a young Australian man, who has sued Fairfax News, Nationwide Media and Sky News on grounds of defamation. Voller's mistreatment while incarcerated at the Don Dale Youth Detention Centre made headlines in Australia during 2016–2017, but these publications were not defamatory; rather, the content of the replies by users on these outlets' Facebook pages was defamatory. In this case, New South Wales Supreme Court Justice Stephen Rothman 'ruled the media organisations could be considered publishers of the third-party comments and were therefore liable for them'.[53] He reasoned: 'Each defendant was not merely a conduit of the comment . . . [They] provided the forum for its publication and encouraged . . . the publication of comments'.[54] While some scholars do see 'hate speech' as a kind of group defamation,[55] if a nation has banned hate speech then those laws can be invoked as an alternative benchmark of accountability.

By ranking those who run certain pages as, effectively, publishers (whether they are pages for legacy news, politician's blogs, or special interest pages), admins may be pressured to more tightly police user comments with the methods described above, ensuring stronger compliance to avoid civil suits. Dealing with this pressure may simply mean hiring more content moderators for the page (at the expense of the publishing page) or otherwise recruiting volunteers.

Adopting and Enforcing Clear Community Standards

The next most obvious approach to solving the problem of hate speech against women online – one that would be mandated by Australia's proposed cyber-abuse laws – is for platforms to develop and enforce codes of conduct. This must be accompanied by user-ability to 'report' hate speech (and other materials) to the platform directly. The most popular social media platforms already have bans on 'hate speech', among other conduct, but they are not uniform.[56] Thus, I focus on Facebook, the largest social networking site and subject of my research. They provide the following rationale for their hate speech ban:

> We believe that people use their voice and connect more freely when they don't feel attacked on the basis of who they are. *That's why we don't allow hate speech on Facebook.* It creates an environment of intimidation and exclusion, and in some cases may promote offline violence.
>
> We define hate speech as a direct attack against people on the basis of what we call protected characteristics: race, ethnicity, national origin, disability, religious affiliation, caste, sexual orientation, sex, gender identity and serious disease. We define attacks as violent or dehumanising speech, harmful stereotypes, statements of inferiority, expressions of contempt, disgust or dismissal, cursing and calls for exclusion or segregation.[57]

This is similar to the definition of 'hate speech' argued for in this book except, first, that it treats dehumanising speech, harmful stereotypes, statements of inferiority, expressions of contempt, disgust or dismissal, cursing and calls for exclusion or segregation as *distinct* from violent expression, whereas I have argued that these can be *kinds* of violent expression, and second, that it applies a principle of neutrality though Facebook is not legally (or morally) bound to do so.[58] So theirs is really a ban on 'vilifying speech'.

Facebook's current approach to banning vilifying speech will bring with it the issue of spurious claims, as discussed above. Leaving this issue to the side and homing in on the specifics of Facebook's standards for classifying some content 'hate speech', one soon notices great opacity. Users do not necessarily have a clear understanding of what will be tolerated thanks to Facebook's 'tiered' level to policing hate speech. Tier 1 forbids dehumanising speech and generalisations; Tier 2 conduct involves cursing, expressions of contempt and generalisations of inferiority; Tier 3 involves calls for exclusion and slurs. The existence of tiers seems to suggest that Tier 1 acts (e.g. 'men are scum') are the most severe. But the presence of two other tiers makes one wonder, to what extent is each type of hostile speech tolerated? And (why) are Tier 1 acts so much more severe than those in Tiers 2 and 3? There is no clarity on why certain acts belong in each tier or how severe violations of various tiers are seen to be. A convincing rationale for the tiered approach needs to be provided, and the difference between consequences for contravening tiers must be clarified, or else the community standards must be reformed.

Even still, should a satisfactory normative distinction between the tiers be forthcoming, one may argue that tech giants like Facebook, which are arguably internet monopolies, should not have such a grand power over so many people (effectively, a capacity to determine who out of billions gets to speak and what they can say). Granted, Facebook *has* established a binding, independent oversight board to uphold or reverse Facebook's own content removal decisions.[59] But will this be adequate for policing mundane, everyday occurrences of hate speech? I think not. To that end, forcing Facebook to comply with local laws around the world seems a good way to keep that power in check. While some go so far as to say that Facebook's terms of service should be refined to approximate the U.S. standard of the First Amendment and legal interpretations thereof[60] – after all, Facebook is an American company – we needn't go that far. For one thing, there is good reason to believe that such standards do not adequately protect *everyone's* freedom of speech;[61] for another, Facebook has already shown that it can and will comply with some local laws. For instance, in 2018 a German law, the *Network Enforcement Act*, came into effect forcing social media networks (including Facebook) to regulate hate speech as defined under German law.[62] But I note again that Australia does not have a national law prohibiting hate speech on grounds of gender with which Facebook must comply. Perhaps having one would make a difference. Perhaps the deterrent effect would increase. But it still remains true that 'we cannot . . . rely on government-imposed regulation to solve *all* the problems of the internet'.[63]

Now, all of this must also be considered alongside the question of efficacy. Whether conforming to the laws of specific nations, or trying to police the site by its own standards, how successful is Facebook at removing online hate speech? Counterfactually, if Facebook's own ban on hate speech (which does include gender) was a successful deterrent to committing acts of hate speech, then I shouldn't have been able to enumerate such an extensive data set. It seems Facebook's ban on hate speech is clearly *not* a successful deterrent to woman-hating, then. So, is there any point to the ban? Maybe not. But perhaps this is an unfair conclusion. Perhaps the effect of Facebook's ban on hate speech can only be evaluated in the context of its overall numbers. In fourth quarter 2017 and first quarter 2018, removal of 'hate speech' (of all kinds) went up from 1.6 to 2.5 million cases over the course of the two quarters.[64] That is a substantial improvement. A slightly weaker conclusion one could draw, then, is that *if* bans are having some deterrent success, the success rate is not strong enough to prevent women users from frequently and repeatedly encountering misogynistic hate speech on this platform. So, what further improvements might we make?

EXTRA-LEGAL APPROACHES

More Moderators, Better Algorithms

Perhaps Facebook's (and other social media companies') ban on hate speech would be more effective if it hired more content moderators and/or had better algorithms capable of 'pre-censorship' (i.e. removing a post before it becomes visible to other users).[65] First to algorithms. This avenue presents several difficulties, including the fact that technologies are continuously evolving. This means there are evolving technology-enabled opportunities to mask online hate.[66] Note the further issue that 'algorithms are manmade and thus not necessarily fair, objective or neutral'.[67] Because of this, any algorithm fit for purpose is likely to capture some instances of harmful speech but not others.[68] Add to this the fact that hate speech does not necessarily include vituperative terms or slurs, making automated detection incredibly difficult. Add to this still further the fact that humans creatively adapt to obstacles like automated deletion and word filters with great ease.[69] While algorithms may assist in detecting and removing hate speech, it would be foolish to hang all our hopes on this method of eradicating misogyny from the internet; we 'can never eliminate the need for human oversight and adjudication'.[70] Thus, these types of algorithms seem unlikely to be a plausible lone-standing solution.

This leaves moderation. Data shows that Facebook largely becomes aware of hate speech on its platform thanks to its flagging system. In Facebook's 2017 Q4 and 2018 Q1, 'only 23.6% and 38% [of hate speech cases], respectively, were found by Facebook itself. The majority of these were identified by flagging users'.[71] This means that content moderators are doing the grunt work of reviewing and deciding on whether something breaches Facebook's community standards. But there are concerns with the efficacy of this approach too. As articulated by Stjernfelt and Lauritzen, 'We still do not know much, however, about the safety and security staff [at Facebook], at present counting some 30,000 people, and their training, qualifications and working conditions, or what equips them to perform this task so crucial for the public'.[72] That's a mere 30,000 people hired to moderate the content of a site that is used by over two billion people and is accessible 24/7, year-round. Add to this the time pressure associated with removing harmful content.[73] Add to this further still that 'many of the content moderation departments of the tech giants work mostly for a low pay (3–500 dollars a month) in third-world countries like the Philippines and under non-disclosure agreements'.[74] So, better training, care, and compensation is surely a must. While hiring more moderators is a necessity, one wonders whether there are (or could ever be) enough adequately trained people, who are familiar enough with the relevant context, who could be relied upon to accurately rid Facebook of such hate while also consistently avoiding wrongful removals.[75]

But the significant issue here is this: we know that *humans* are reporting most of the prohibited content Facebook removes, and that *more humans still* review said content to decide whether it stays or goes. But by the very fact that a human has usually reported the material (and where that material is indeed an instance of hate speech), *the harm has likely already occurred.*[76] The point I'm getting at is that you can't un-ring a bell. Once it is experienced (by users *and* by moderators), the damage is done. Removing, blocking or hiding hate speech *after* it has made it to Facebook (or to a moderator's screen) doesn't stop it from harming people. And through all of this we must remember that moderation takes a toll on people's well-being. Repetitive exposure to horrific material online, not just instances of hate speech, is emotionally taxing and can be deeply scarring.[77] And the best that flagging and removing 'hate speech' can do is dampen the chime of that bell, assuming the material hasn't already been copied elsewhere, screenshot, sent out via email, immortalised in a news article or so forth. The same goes for offline hate speech too, of course, but online misogyny is especially urgent because its reach is more expansive. So, this seems to turn us back to the proposed imperfect solution of algorithms. It may be the case that humans intending to hate speak will always find ways to get around the automated strategies platforms put in place to limit such behaviour, but surely every little bit these algorithms catch helps. Thus, even though these will never capture all instances of hate speech, and even though what constitutes hate speech changes from context to context and at different points in history, still we should continue to employ (and keep amending and updating) these automated detection algorithms.

We should also turn our attention towards different algorithms. Specifically, we should consider the phenomenon of 'personalisation'. In 2009, Google changed its algorithm from PageRank to personalized search for everyone. Formerly, when users would search for a key term, the most well-connected websites would show up for anyone conducting the search. This is no longer the case.[78] As Stjernfelt and Lauritzen point out, 'many people might still assume that when a word is googled the results will be objective and the same for everyone'[79] – in the case of Google, I, for one, certainly did. Those users are wrong. Now, it *may* be possible to argue that personalisation by Google is justified (or justifiable). But that is not so for social media companies. Facebook uses personalisation to help advertisers reach their target audience (i.e. users likely to purchase their products).[80] The problem is that when personalisation is used on a site like Facebook – a site we not-infrequently use to engage in political dialogue and to receive news – this 'restricts information and creates filter bubbles, confirmation bias and echo chambers'.[81] The problem is, 'the user is led to believe that the individual's bubble makes up the whole relevant world',[82] so they remain ignorant of others' perspectives, of certain information, and other material not already conforming to the user's preferences. Facebook is showing you what it thinks you will like (and what advertisers think you will buy); it isn't necessarily showing you what you need (or ought) to see, or the different perspectives particular content is seen from. I believe we should campaign to depersonalise social media – that is, *abandon* certain algorithms – so we might pop the filter bubbles, escape our echo chambers and ward off confirmation bias through confronting a diverse array of content not tailored to our preferences. We must pop these personalisation bubbles so we do not lose 'the beneficial habit of attempting to understand why others have the opinions they have and fall back on assuming that other viewpoints are simply crazy, stupid, pathological or evil'.[83]

Make Users Pay for Platform Access

The massive uptake of paid streaming services like Spotify and Netflix, not to mention other sites like OnlyFans and eHarmony, demonstrates that people are willing to pay for different kinds of internet services. If Facebook (and Twitter, and Instagram and Reddit, etc.) suddenly started charging users an account fee, would people follow the community standards more closely? While users can be banned from Facebook (and other similar social media), it is presently not challenging to create a new email address and set up a new profile (and that's if the site even requires you to have a linked email account).[84] If a suspension of one's profile came with the additional burden of financial loss, as well as the inconvenience of setting up a new paid account, this might act as more of a deterrent than bans under present conditions. Of course, this would be a risky move. Users could walk away from the platforms now intending to charge them and congregate somewhere else, though a possible deterrent to mass abandonment might be making the platform advertisement-free for paying users (as with Spotify Premium), and so encourage users to stay. It is certainly worthwhile investigating the extent to which people would be willing to pay for presently-free platform use, and under what conditions.

Counterspeech, or 'Speaking Back'

Some believe that the best way to mitigate the harm of hate speech is to 'speak back', and in so doing block or challenge (through disagreement) the assertions that are made about the oppressed collective by the hate speaker.[85] Speaking back does have an important role to play in the fight against oppressive speech acts like hate speech. This is because 'with every conversational move we make, hearers tend to *accommodate* the presuppositions and assertions of speakers'.[86] Thus, 'if we do not challenge false assertions, biased presuppositions, and . . . other biased speech, we let their license stand. Others can easily take them up and run with them'.[87] In other words, 'counterspeech is the primary way we stop bad inferences in their tracks'.[88] However, counterspeech – imagined as the *target* or *subject* 'speaking back' – is an imperfect solution, too. As Matthew Costello and James Hawdon explain, 'attempts to personally confront hateful actors can result in the proliferation of hate'.[89] This is partly because social identity power plays a role in whose speech (i.e. which *imagined subject's* speech) is recognised as 'credible' and worth listening and deferring to (i.e. showing epistemic humility towards) in the first place. Indeed, the identity-power structured dominant Western social imaginary shapes people's 'capacities for listening properly and for assigning adequate levels of credibility and authority',[90] and given that credibility-attribution never happens in a vacuum but in a society structured by a complex system of social relations and practices, as well as the fact that 'credibility' has a comparative and contrastive quality (i.e. if some people get more, then other people get less),[91] it seems highly unlikely that counterspeaking members of oppressed groups will be recognised as *authorities* on their own oppression.

These differentials in power dynamics are precisely why scholars have argued that we need hate speech bans – because the voices of the superordinate group are so much stronger, they overpower the voices of the subordinated group, effectively silencing them.[92] In Lynne Tirrell's words,

> Counterspeech has limited power and reach, and often the most vulnerable targets of nasty speech are not in a position to reply with 'more speech'. This raises the issue of which social positions are graced with the power of 'more speech' and which are denied such power; it also raises the question of how to change these imbalances.[93]

However, what has been little considered is what 'counterspeech' might be if we did not imagine it simply as the target (or subject) 'speaking back'. This is not to say that targets speaking back does not ever work; it is to say that its success is largely against the odds.[94] Thus, one must ask, what else might counterspeech be?

Institutional and Counterpublics' Counterspeech

Some scholars have begun to reimagine who should practise 'counterspeech' and what acts of counterspeech might look like. Beyond the image of the lone individual target speaking back to their aggressor, we might instead think about the power of *collective speaking up*; this is counterpublic counterspeech, collectively rebuking injustice *en masse*.[95] Alchin's targets and their supporters engaged in this as well as their engagement of law enforcement, through establishing 'an advocacy group called Sexual Violence Won't Be Silenced to combat online sexual harassment'.[96] Such speech may be powerful enough to reorient the way at least some members of the public think about a particular issue. The hashtag activism of #MeToo is exemplary of this collective speaking up, raising global awareness on the extent of sexual harassment and assault.[97] Likewise, the 2015 #EndAllViolenceAgainstWomen campaign, which involved the mass Tweeting of hundreds of screen captures of abhorrent misogyny, did much the same.[98] However, such 'digilantism' by counterpublics can inspire a doubling-down on the very practices and world-orientations these campaigns protest, so we must remember that the capacity to harm and be harmed is not eradicated by collective speaking up; the group's status in the community is not necessarily raised up to the level of dignified recognition and respect through these campaigns.

More formally, Katharine Gelber has proposed we think about counterspeech in terms of 'a [*state-*]*supported response* to contradict the message contained within hate speech and its effects, insofar as it includes silencing or marginalization or disempowerment'.[99] We have seen de Silva propose that hate speech bans could be understood as an act of counterspeech by the state. Lepoutre makes an effort to further reimagine the types of state acts that can be considered expressive. The state might 'implement federal holidays honoring civil rights leaders, erect monuments celebrating those leaders, or fund private groups devoted to supporting targets of hate speech'.[100] This could instigate both imaginal and institutional transformations and may offer the beginnings of broader answers as to how to deal with the problem of hate speech, that is, in suggesting '*what* should be done, and *who* should do it'.[101] On the question of who should be engaged in counterspeech, our options are not limited to the state. Gelber, for one, proposes states' expression here because '*fostering* full and open debate is a permissible role for the state',[102] but there is no reason to limit our imagining to this body advancing this sort of remedy. Any agent powerful enough to generate impactful counterspeech should be considered.

Peter Molnar picks up on this idea in suggesting *art* and *education* are the key avenues via which we can address and prevent the harms of hate speech.[103] He champions these 'because prohibitions cannot reach the roots of hatred or even its symptoms'.[104] His focus on entrenched stigma as the *root* of hate speech is consistent with the evaluation I have offered in this book.[105] I have argued that we – those in my milieu, the Anglosphere – are habituated to misogyny, and that habituated (and sometimes consciously endorsed) misogyny underscores hate speech against women online. This habituation is itself a consequence of living in and through an enduring patriarchal sexual imaginary that cleverly effaces its own existence within the larger narratives of the dominant Western social imaginary using the tools that our central liberal ethico-political imaginary provides. Like Molnar, I think we will not have enduring success – by which I mean eradication of the phenomenon – until we have dealt with the roots of the problem. But *the roots of the problem are imaginal*, so we need counter-imaginings that work in the service of gender justice to be sedimented in this milieu.[106] This requires *thick* critical engagements with multiple publics and institutions and with society at large – engagements that are not only cognitive and argumentative but also affective, imaginal and action-oriented.[107] Thus, the project involves much more than speaking – even when it is institutional actors or organisations doing the talking. The project of education, as one might describe it – for example, ensuring users are 'equipped with the critical and literacy skills necessary to rebuff the hateful messaging'[108] – is not meaningful (and cannot be successful) without an imaginal revolution that manages to capture *who* is a victim of injustice, the *nature* of that injustice, how *we* are connected to that injustice, and *why* we (ought to) want to disrupt or put an end to the social practices and norms that sustain that injustice. To that end, I encourage us to move beyond the image of 'speaking back' as a remedy to hate speech to ask what broader counter-imaginings might be needed for enduring social change that will see an end to the social practice of hate speech against women online? To upend and replace problematic and harmful images, we must first *make those images visible*, or visible in a *new way*, and we must also *offer alternative imag(in) ings* that undermine the prejudice and eradicate the stigma inhering in our presently central images, while simultaneously avoiding meaning vertigo.[109]

FACILITATING IMAGINAL TRANSFORMATIONS

So we arrive at the broad question: how can we 'shift deeply ingrained habits of perception and feeling to ensure social reforms are rendered stable and enduring'.[110] If my analysis in chapter 3 is correct – that we are habituated to misogynistic behaviours (which includes hate speaking), that we're born into and made out of misogyny, that patriarchy is our inheritance and, without intervention, will also be our legacy[111] – it is obvious that all of the measures suggested here are band-aid solutions to a much deeper problem. If it really is the case that misogyny is thoroughly woven into the norms and practices of society, including our digital social spaces, as I have argued, then so long as people remained habituated in this way, and so long as certain images in the dominant Western social imaginary remain central, the oppression of women will continue. In the final chapter, I explore how central images of cyberspace itself figure hate speech against women online as an intractable problem. I do so with the aim of generating some epistemic and affective friction, a spark for the imaginal revolution that we so desperately need.

NOTES

1. Lynne Tirrell, 'Toxic Misogyny and the Limits of Counterspeech', *Fordham Law Review* 87 (2019): 2433.

2. Katharine Gelber and Susan Brison, 'Digital Dualism and the "Speech as Thought" Paradox', in *Free Speech In The Digital Age*, ed. Susan Brison and Katharine Gelber (New York: Oxford University Press), 15, 16.

3. Gelber and Brison, 'Digital Dualism', 17.

4. Gelber and Brison, 'Digital Dualism', 19.

5. Gelber and Brison, 'Digital Dualism', 21.

6. Gelber and Brison, 'Digital Dualism', 27.

7. Anastasia Powell and Nicola Henry, *Sexual Violence In A Digital Age* (London: Palgrave Macmillan, 2017), 197, my emphasis.

8. I use the capitalisation to indicate a people's shared impression of state-wielded (or even international) power, not to refer to a specific jurisdiction's legislation.

9. For example, Lepoutre explains, 'Legal theorists often suggest that, at the very least, legally prohibiting and sanctioning conduct x . . . expresses strong moral disapproval toward x. This disapproval may be communicated to both the offender and the broader public'. See Maxime Lepoutre, 'Hate Speech Laws: Expressive Power Is Not The Answer', *Legal Theory* 25 (2020): 277.

10. Powell and Henry, *Sexual Violence*, 211.

11. Max Chalmers, '"Internet Troll" Zane Alchin Who Mocked Women Threatening Legal Action Enters Guilty Plea', *New Matilda*, 20 June 2016, accessed February 5, 2021, https://newmatilda.com/2016/06/20/internet-troll-zane-alchin -who-mocked-women-threatening-to-take-him-to-court-enters-guilty-plea/.

12. Emma Jane, 'Feminist Digilante Responses to a Slut-Shaming on Facebook', *Social Media and Society* 3 (2017): 1.

13. Powell and Henry, *Sexual Violence*, 172–173.

14. Jane, 'Feminist Digilante Responses', 8.

15. Jane, 'Feminist Digilante Responses', 1–10.

16. Millicent Churcher, *Reimagining Sympathy, Recognizing Difference: Insights from Adam Smith* (London: Rowman and Littlefield International, 2019), 56, original emphasis.

17. Powell and Henry make a similar point about indecency and obscenity laws. See: *Sexual Violence*, 213. Tirrell makes a similar point about incels and violence. See: Tirrell, 'Toxic Misogyny', 2439–2440.

18. By 'ban' I envision something like a clear statement of prohibited behaviour and a set of responses which may penalise the offender and/or aim to compensate those harmed. For a detailed discussion of such laws, see: Alexander Brown, *Hate Speech Law: A Philosophical Examination* (New York: Routledge, 2015), and

Natalie Alkiviadou, 'The Legal Regulation of Hate Speech: The International and European Frameworks', *Croatian Political Science Review* 55 (2018): 203–229.

19. Lepoutre, 'Expressive Power', 278.

20. Anjalee de Silva, 'Addressing the Vilification of Women: A Functional Theory of Harm and Implications for Law', *Melbourne University Law Review* 43 (2020): 7.

21. de Silva, 'Vilification of Women', 39.

22. Tanya D'Souza and others and de Silva both make this point, however D'souza et al. describe the phenomenon as 'gendered hate speech' (Tanya D'Souza, Laura Griffin, Nicole Shackleton, and Danielle Walt, 'Harming Women with Words: The Failure of Australian Law to Prohibit Gendered Hate Speech', *UNSW Law Journal* 41 (2018): 955), whereas de Silva ('Vilification of Women', 2n1) is interested in 'sex-based vilification' which, implicitly, extends only to cisgender women.

23. Hate speech against women is also not fully prohibited by state and territory anti-discrimination laws (D'Souza et al., 'Harming Women', 946). It could be argued that 'women' are a protected group on the basis of 'gender identity' in Tasmania's *Anti-Discrimination Act 1998* (Tas); however, the term 'gender identity' in Australian law usually refers to a person's gender *status* – namely, whether they are transgender – rather than one's identity as a woman or other subordinate gender (D'Souza et al., 'Harming Women', 950).

24. Lepoutre ('Hate Speech Laws', 276) argues that the counterspeech objection does not necessarily justify speech bans. I think bans are primarily justified on the immense power of Law as 'punisher' in the dominant Western social imaginary. However, he raises a good point, that other types of counterspeech beyond 'speaking back' are possible. I will return to the issue of counterspeech later on.

25. On debate over racial hate speech laws in Australia, see Luke McNamara, 'Explainer: What is Section 18C and Why Do Some Politicians Want It Changed?' *The Conversation*, 1 September 2016, accessed 6 April 2021, https://theconversation.com/explainer-what-is-section-18c-and-why-do-some-politicians-want-it-changed-64660.

26. Tirrell, 'Toxic Misogyny', 2435.

27. D'Souza et al., 'Harming Women', 956, my emphasis.

28. Elsewhere I have written about the phenomenon of white Australian men complaining of racial vilification under Australia's *Racial Discrimination Act 1975* (Cth). Fortunately, no such complaints have been successful yet, though they have made their way to court. See: Louise Richardson-Self, 'Offending White Men: Racial Vilification, Misrecognition, and Epistemic Injustice,' *Feminist Philosophy Quarterly* 4 (2018): 1–25.

29. As Jane Dolkart puts it, 'any kind of special treatment is a double-edged sword', hence, 'for all of its problems, the equal treatment approach remains preferable' for many. See: Jane Dolkart, 'Hostile Environment Harassment: Equality, Objectivity, and the Shaping of Legal Standards', *Emory Law Journal* 43 (1994): 170. For the record, I am not one of that many, though I agree that "special treatment" is a problematic image for women to be saddled with. See: Louise Richardson-Self,

Justifying Same-Sex Marriage: A Philosophical Investigation (London: Rowman and Littlefield International, 2015), chap. 3.

30. For another take on the benefits of having both an 'ordinary' conception of hate speech and a "legal" conception of hate speech (what I call here, 'hate speech' and 'vilification'), see Alexander Brown, 'What is Hate Speech? Part 1: The Myth of Hate', *Law and Philosophy* 35 (2017): 419–468, and 'What is Hate Speech? Part 2: Family Resemblances', *Law and Philosophy* 36 (2017): 561–613. Though I disagree with Brown's argument as to the content of these concepts, I agree that we need (at least) two to do the ethico-political (anti-oppression social justice) work we hope it can do.

31. D'Souza et al., 'Harming Women', 941.

32. Katharine Gelber thinks this can be achieved. Katharine Gelber, 'Differentiating Hate Speech: A Systemic Discrimination Approach', *Critical Review of International Social and Political Philosophy* (2019): 2. https://doi.org/10.1080/1 3698230.2019.1576006.

33. Australian Government, 'Fact Sheet – Online Safety Bill', *Consultation on a Bill for a New Online Safety Act*, 2020, accessed 4 February 2021, https://www.com munications.gov.au/have-your-say/consultation-bill-new-online-safety-act.

34. It also includes a 'blocking scheme' for material which is tantamount to, promotes, instructs, or incites abhorrent violent conduct. 'Abhorrent violent conduct' is specified in Subdivision H of Division 474 of the *Criminal Code Act 1995* (Cth); it includes terrorism, murder or attempted murder, torture, rape and kidnapping, making this a narrower conception of 'violence' than the one used throughout this book, hence hate speech against women online would not be captured under this label. See: Australian Government, 'Exposure Draft – Online Safety Bill 2020', *Consultation on a Bill for a New Online Safety Act* s95(1), 2020, accessed 20 February 2021, https:// www.communications.gov.au/have-your-say/consultation-bill-new-online-safety-act, and 'Online Safety Bill—Reading Guide', *Consultation on a Bill for a New Online Safety Act* 2020, accessed 4 February 2021, https://www.communications.gov.au/h ave-your-say/consultation-bill-new-online-safety-act.

35. Australian Government, 'Exposure Draft'.

36. Dolkart, 'Hostile Environment', 201.

37. Dolkart, 'Hostile Environment', 175.

38. See, e.g.: Miklos Haraszti, 'Foreword: Hate Speech and the Coming Death of the International Standard before It Was Born', in *The Context and Content of Hate Speech*, ed. Michael Herz and Peter Molnar (New York: Cambridge University Press, 2012), xv; Frederik Stjernfelt and Anne Mette Lauritzen, *Your Post Has Been Deleted: Tech Giants and Freedom of Speech* (Cham: Springer Open, 2020), 102, 124.

39. Jeremy Waldron, *The Harm in Hate Speech* (Cambridge: Harvard University Press), 106.

40. Tirrell, 'Toxic Misogyny', 2437.

41. Tirrell, 'Toxic Misogyny', 2441.

42. Vittorio Bufacchi and Jools Gilson, 'The Ripples of Violence', *Feminist Review* 112 (2016): 33.

43. Powell and Henry, *Sexual Violence*, 5; see also Bufacchi and Gilson, 'Ripples of Violence', 28–38.

44. Mary Anne Franks, '"Not Where Bodies Live": The Abstraction of Internet Expression', in *Free Speech In The Digital Age*, ed. Susan Brison and Katharine Gelber (New York: Oxford University Press, 2019), 138. See also Stjernfelt and Lauritzen, *Your Post*, 167.

45. Stjernfelt and Lauritzen, *Your Post*, 167.

46. Franks, 'Internet Expression', 141.

47. Franks, 'Internet Expression', 141.

48. Franks, 'Internet Expression', 142.

49. Stjernfelt and Lauritzen, *Your Post*, 169.

50. S230(c)(2)(a) of the *Communications Decency Act 1996 (USA)* states: 'No provider or user of an interactive computer service shall be held liable on account of any action voluntarily taken in good faith to restrict access to or availability of material that the provider or user considers to be obscene, lewd, lascivious, filthy, excessively violent, harassing, or otherwise objectionable, whether or not such material is constitutionally protected'.

51. Matthew Costello and James Hawdon, 'Hate Speech in Online Spaces', in *The Palgrave Handbook of Cybercrime and Cyberdeviance*, ed. Thomas Holt and Adam Bossler (Cham: Springer Nature, 2020), 1411.

52. Stjernfelt and Lauritzen (*Your Post*, 144) mention something similar with respect to the Danish Media Ethical Commission, though they are critical of it.

53. Jamie McKinnell, 'Former Detainee Dylan Voller Gets Court Win Against Media Giants Over Facebook Comments', *ABC News*, 24 June 2019, accessed February 10, 2021, https://www.abc.net.au/news/2019-06-24/court-finds-media-lia ble-for-facebook-comments-by-public/11240826.

54. Jamie McKinnell, 'Dylan Voller'. It is noteworthy that the High Court will hear an appeal on this decision, so it may be overturned. See: Michaela Whitbourn, 'High Court to Hear Appeal Over Controversial Facebook Defamation Ruling', *Sydney Morning Herald*, December 8, 2020, accessed February 9, 2021, https://ww w.smh.com.au/national/high-court-to-hear-appeal-over-controversial-facebook-defa mation-ruling-20201208-p56lnz.html.

55. Tirrell, 'Toxic Misogyny', 2439; Waldron, *Harm in Hate Speech*, 34–64. See also Powell and Henry, *Sexual Violence*, 221.

56. Stjernfelt and Lauritzen, *Your Post*, 90.

57. Facebook, 'Hate Speech', *Facebook Community Standards*, https://www .facebook.com/communitystandards/hate_speech, accessed 9 February 2021, my emphasis.

58. Simon van Zuylen-Wood, '"Men are Scum": Inside Facebook's War on Hate Speech', *Vanity Fair*, February 26, 2019, accessed February 16, 2021, https://www .vanityfair.com/news/2019/02/men-are-scum-inside-facebook-war-on-hate-speech.

59. Facebook, 'Oversight Board', *Facebook Community Standards*, no date, https ://www.facebook.com/communitystandards/oversight_board, accessed 9 February 2021. Note that this makes Facebook compliant with the Santa Clara Principles: 'Companies should publish the numbers of posts removed and accounts permanently

or temporarily suspended; Companies should provide notice to each user whose content is taken down or account is suspended about the reason; Companies should provide a meaningful opportunity for timely appeal'. See: Electronic Frontiers Foundation, *The Santa Clara Principles: On Transparency and Accountability in Content Moderation*, 2018, accessed February 18, 2021, https://santaclaraprinciples.org/.

60. Stjernfelt and Lauritzen, *Your Post*, 153, 264. They also write (*Your Post*, xiv): 'At present, only the United States and European Union possess sufficient political muscle to arm-wrestle the tech giants from a fundamentally democratic and freedom-oriented stance'. This is, perhaps, true.

61. Danielle Keats Citron, 'Restricting Speech to Protect It', in *Free Speech In The Digital Age*, ed. Susan Brison and Katharine Gelber (New York: Oxford University Press, 2019), 122–136.

62. Stjernfelt and Lauritzen, *Your Post*, xi; Sarah Roberts, *Behind The Screen: Content Moderation in the Shadows of Social Media* (New Haven: Yale University Press, 2019), 213.

63. Stjernfelt and Lauritzen, *Your Post*, 241.

64. Stjernfelt and Lauritzen, *Your Post*, 140.

65. Gina Masullo Chen, Ashley Muddiman, Tamar Wilner, Eli Pariser, and Natalie Jomini Stroud, 'We Should Note Get Rid Of Incivility Online', *Social Media and Society* 5 (2019): 2. For an argument against pre-censorship, see Stjernfelt and Lauritzen, *Your Post*, 163.

66. Costello and Hawdon, 'Hate Speech', 1411.

67. Stjernfelt and Lauritzen, *Your Post*, 32.

68. Tarleton Gillespie, *Custodians of the Internet: Platforms, Content Moderation, and the Hidden Decisions that Shape Social Media* (New Haven: Yale University Press, 2018), 99.

69. Gillespie, *Custodians*, 99.

70. Gillespie, *Custodians*, 107.

71. Stjernfelt and Lauritzen, *Your Post*, 140.

72. Stjernfelt and Lauritzen, *Your Post*, 133.

73. Stjernfelt and Lauritzen, *Your Post*, 134.

74. Stjernfelt and Lauritzen, *Your Post*, 133. See also: Roberts, *Behind The Screen*, 170–200.

75. Stjernfelt and Lauritzen, *Your Post*, 125. See also: Gillespie, *Custodians*, 111–140.

76. Gillespie, *Custodians*, 75. Feminists have pointed out, further, that Facebook's approach to reporting and removing content is 'essentially, built to accommodate harassment the way a young man is most likely to experience it: as a one-off episode of name-calling'. But that is not what women go through online, as my data set demonstrates. We are dealing with a bigger issue than singular harms occasioned to individual women. See Soraya Chemaly, 'Demographics, Design, and Free Speech: How Demographics Have Produced Social Media Optimized for Abuse and the Silencing of Marginalized Voices', in *Free Speech In The Digital Age*, ed. Susan Brison and Katharine Gelber (New York: Oxford University Press, 2019), 154.

77. See, for example, Roberts, *Behind the Screen*, chap. 2–5.

78. Stjernfelt and Lauritzen, *Your Post*, 32.

79. Stjernfelt and Lauritzen, *Your Post*, 33.

80. Stjernfelt and Lauritzen, *Your Post*, 33.

81. Stjernfelt and Lauritzen, *Your Post*, xiii.

82. Stjernfelt and Lauritzen, *Your Post*, 42. See also Costello and Hawdon, 'Hate Speech', 1404–1405.

83. Stjernfelt and Lauritzen, *Your Post*, 39.

84. I do not discuss the strategy of 'banning users' because hate speakers are just products of their environments. If the dominant social imaginary has institutionalised systemic oppression, then it is pointless 'purging a discrete number of individuals' from a platform, because the milieu will just keep producing more of them. See José Medina, 'Racial Violence, Emotional Friction, and Epistemic Activism', *Angelaki: Journal of the Theoretical Humanities* 24 (2019): 23.

85. Tirrell, 'Toxic Misogyny', 2443.

86. Tirrell, 'Toxic Misogyny', 2449.

87. Tirrell, 'Toxic Misogyny', 2450.

88. Tirrell, 'Toxic Misogyny', 2450.

89. Costello and Hawdon, 'Hate Speech', 1411.

90. José Medina, 'The Relevance of Credibility Excess in a Proportional View of Epistemic Injustice: Differential Epistemic Authority and the Social Imaginary', *Social Epistemology* 25 (2011): 27.

91. Medina, 'Credibility Excess', 18.

92. See, among others, Citron, 'Restricting Speech', 122–136; Katharine Gelber, 'Reconceptualizing Counterspeech in Hate Speech Policy (with a Focus on Australia)', in *The Context and Content of Hate Speech: Rethinking Regulation and Response*, ed. Michael Herz and Peter Molnar (New York: Cambridge University Press, 2012), 198–216; Catharine Mackinnon, *Only Words* (Cambridge: Harvard University Press, 1993).

93. Tirrell, 'Toxic Misogyny', 2435.

94. I know of only two cases where the target's speaking back has been successful in undoing the damage of online abuse. The first involved Reddit users mocking a Sikh woman, Balpreet Kaur, for her facial hair which she does not trim due to her faith. When Kaur replied to this abuse, explaining why she has facial hair and does not remove it, the original poster (OP) apologised for his actions and acknowledged that his comments were intolerant and ignorant. See: Karen Frost-Arnold, 'Social Media, Trust, and the Epistemology of Prejudice', *Social Epistemology* 30 (2016): 513–531. The second involved Reddit users mocking a woman, Carly Findlay, with two forms of Ichthyosis, giving the appearance of very red, shiny skin. Like Kaur, Findlay responded, explaining her condition. Again, the OP apologised (but backhandedly), and thousands of people up-voted Findlay's post (a sign of support for the content of the comment). See: Ginger Gorman, *Troll Hunting: Inside the World of Online Hate and Its Human Fallout* (Melbourne: Hardie Grant Books, 2019), 208–211. However, it is unclear to what extent this 'speaking back' has affected broader social identity power dynamics. Perhaps for a more widespread and long-lasting change some form

of 'counterspeech' that could be sustained by institutions, including the state, would be warranted.

95. A counterpublic 'stand[s] in conscientious opposition to a dominant ideology and strategically subvert[s] that ideology's construction in public discourse'. See Alex Fattal, 'Counterpublic', in *The International Encyclopedia of Anthropology*, ed. Hilary Callan (London: John Wiley & Sons, 2018), 1. Hence, some scholars describe feminists as counterpublic and note their presence in online spaces. See: Nancy Fraser, 'Rethinking the Public Sphere: A Contribution to the Critique of Actually Existing Democracy', in *Habermas and the Public Sphere*, ed. Craig Calhoun (Cambridge: MIT Press, 1992), 109–142. See also: Sarah Sobieraj, 'Bitch, Slut, Skank, Cunt: Patterned Resistance to Women's Visibility in Digital Publics', *Information, Communication and Society* 21 (2018): 1702; Sophie Sills, Chelsea Pickens, Karishma Beach, Lloyd Jones, Octavia Calder-Dawe, Paulette Benton-Greig, and Nicola Gavey, 'Rape Culture and Social Media: Young Critics and a Feminist Counterpublic', *Feminist Media Studies* 12 (2016): 1–17; Anastasia Powell, 'Seeking Rape Justice: Formal and Informal Responses to Sexual Violence Through Technosocial Counter-Publics', *Theoretical Criminology* 19 (2015): 571–88; Bianca Fileborn, 'Justice 2.0: Street Harassment Victims' Use of Social Media and Online Activism as Sites of Informal Justice', *British Journal of Criminology* 57 (2017): 1482–1501.

96. Jane, 'Feminist Digilante Responses', 2.

97. Bianca Fileborn and Rachel Loney-Howes, eds., *#MeToo and the Politics of Social Change* (Cham: Palgrave Macmillan, 2019). See also Powell and Henry, *Sexual Violence*, 281.

98. Verity Trott, 'Connected Feminists: Foregrounding the Interpersonal in Connective Action', *Australian Journal of Political Science* 53 (2018): 116–129.

99. Gelber, 'Reconceptualizing Counterspeech', 213–214, original emphasis. As examples of this, consider the Australian Government's campaign against violence and disrespect towards women: https://www.respect.gov.au/the-campaign/. Separate is the question of this campaign's efficacy.

100. Lepoutre, 'Hate Speech Laws', 281–282.

101. Tirrell, 'Toxic Misogyny', 2438, original emphasis.

102. Gelber, 'Reconceptualizing Counterspeech', 209.

103. Peter Molnar, 'Responding to "Hate Speech" with Art, Education, and the Imminent Danger Test', in *The Context and Content of Hate Speech: Rethinking Regulation and Response*, ed. Michael Herz and Peter Molnar (New York: Cambridge University Press, 2012), 183–197.

104. Molnar, 'Responding to "Hate Speech"', 184. Note, however, that 'theorists have highlighted the limitations of relying solely on cognitive remedies such as reasoned argumentation and explicit education to foster ethical concern for victims of marginalization and oppression' (Churcher, *Reimagining Sympathy*, xi). Thus, what we envision 'education' to entail must be free of this bias towards mere cognitive remedy.

105. Molnar, 'Responding to "Hate Speech"', 185.

106. Churcher, *Reimagining Sympathy*, 167.

107. Medina, 'Racial Violence', 23.

108. Costello and Hawdon, 'Hate Speech', 1411.

109. Filipa Melo Lopes, 'Perpetuating the Patriarchy: Misogyny and (Post-) Feminist Backlash', *Philosophical Studies* 176 (2019): 2531.

110. Churcher, *Reimagining Sympathy*, 5.

111. See Susan Brison, '"We Must Find Words or Burn": Speaking Out Against Disciplinary Silencing', *Feminist Philosophy Quarterly* 3 (2017): 9–10.

Chapter 6

Challenging Images of Cyberspace

The internet has the potential to assist the building of a more cohesive, understanding and fairer world. But the mainspring of change will come from society, not the smartphone.

—James Curran[1]

So far, this book has identified women as a group affected by tracker stigmas – that is, by prejudicial images. Feminists have long been in the business of challenging the images that constrain women's lives, both in terms of their capacity to pursue their individual aspirations, but also in their relational dynamics with various others. This work – of reimagining Woman, her relation to Man, children, public life, private life and so forth – is necessary and ongoing.[2] Images matter. Images can conceal problems, gaps, inconsistencies, contradictions and power dynamics within and between imaginaries, all while decreeing 'that's the way it is', thereby making possible alternative ways of seeing or conceptualising our world 'out of the question'.[3] They obscure because 'there is something about the use of images that invites or seduces the acceptance of the [agent]'.[4] However, images are not an enemy *per se*. Images can reveal our worlds to us in new ways, opening up greater possibilities for living for agents. Indeed, as Marguerite La Caze says, borrowed and new images 'can play a constructive role in developing new ideas', and new ideas lead to new ways of life and new systems of meaning.[5] New images (or borrowed, repurposed images) can be applied to specific imagined subjects, the hope of which is to develop new ideas about how we ought to live, who 'we' are, what we expect from one another, and so forth, and these changes can be empowering and liberatory. The journey towards justice may also elicit alternative imaginings when one runs up against problems, gaps,

143

inconsistencies, contradictions and power dynamics in the ordinary business of daily life. One such gap – at least, for members of oppressed groups – has been delivering an adequate impression of 'harm'. The classic liberal image of harm involving a deliberately acting agent directly affecting a specified target is simply unable to fully communicate the impact of hate speech on groups. It would be folly, however, *not* to explicitly consider our widely shared images of cyberspace, and, in particular, our impressions of social media platforms like Facebook (from where my dataset was drawn).

Today, we use the internet in myriad ways: instant messaging, emailing, video chatting, blogging, vlogging, streaming, banking, shopping, trading, conducting and disseminating research, and so much more. We have Alexa and Siri and Google Home; smart phones, smart watches, smart televisions. We're encouraged to mix new media with old: live-Tweeting reactions to pre-recorded and live television shows (#Survivor) or digitally subscribing to our preferred newspaper to receive email updates. There is a constant, ongoing interaction between our virtual (online) and terrestrial (offline) lives; more than this, they are *integrated*.[6] So, it makes sense to ask how the internet, its technologies and its platforms, have impacted the dominant Western social imaginary via changes to its constitutive central imaginaries. Some changes are immediately obvious. Consider the sexual imaginary. Apps like Tinder and Bumble have changed the ways we conceive of and practise dating. Smartphone technologies make sharing intimate content easy, but also open new avenues for sexual abuse and harassment (the unsolicited dick pic and sextortion come to mind).[7] The ubiquity of online pornography seems to have affected our self- and other-directed body image standards (e.g. genital size and appearance[8]) as well as what we imagine to be normal sexual activity (e.g. 'facials'[9]). The rise of Tube sites and pay-per-view sites like OnlyFans is changing the way we imagine sex work.[10] The list goes on. But the internet has done more than augment our existing central imaginaries. We have in fact constructed a new imaginary, a digital imaginary. Since we can begin to understand imaginaries by analysing the images they use,[11] my aim in this final chapter is to illuminate some of the most common impressions and to interrogate whether (and how) these images perpetuate the social practice of hate speaking against women.

CENTRAL IMAGES IN THE DIGITAL IMAGINARY

The images of cyberspace I analyse here are social media as the *new public sphere*; the internet as an *expansive zone for free speech*; cyberspace as the homeland of the *anonymous troll*; and, the internet as a space with *a dark side* – a chaotic, lawless land that impossible to regulate. It is immediately obvious that these images form two distinct pairs of dichotomous couplings that could be described as *idealist* (or utopian) and *realist* (or pessimistic):[12] Public Sphere *v.* Anonymous Trollscape; Free Speech Zone *v.* Lawless Land. I discuss each in turn.[13] In this discussion, keep in mind that images 'work to constrain debate and to exclude certain experiences and alternative views'.[14] This goes just as much for idealist, aspirational images, as for realist and even dystopian ones. The aim of interrogating images, then, is to uncover (or recover) what is rendered unimaginable in light of aiding the end of establishing cyberspaces as egalitarian.

The New Public Sphere

One dominant impression of the internet, and particularly social media spaces, is that it provides a new public sphere that 'can provide an equal and democratic social platform', since 'the internet is a politically neutral and inherently democratic space'.[15] The public sphere is imagined to be 'a space where citizens act out and critically debate the intricacies of political life through an open dialogue in which everyone is free to participate and raise their concerns'.[16] In it, we develop a 'public opinion' – a shared, public, critical stance – that is *reactive to* and *directed towards* governing bodies.[17] An interesting point to note, then, is that the public sphere itself is imagined to be 'essentially extrapolitical'.[18] The production of public opinion is deemed '*a debate outside of power*',[19] which is to say that the constituents of the public sphere's is 'a discourse of reason *on* and *to* power rather than *by* power'.[20] That is, within the public sphere, it is taken for granted that Individuals are not exercising power over one another: rational argument rather than coercive power is what steers public opinion. Traditionally, the preoccupation of the public sphere is the 'common good', that is, the interests we all supposedly share. Descriptions of the internet as the new public sphere are not hard to come by,[21] but what makes this image seem like such an organic fit? Media – and digital media especially – are what make it possible for us to *imagine ourselves as an interconnected public*, even though 'the conversation' can be asynchronous and nonlocal. Social media, in particular, are both a *conduit* for information transmission – that is, it is where we are provided with information relevant to our shared world in common – as well as a *medium* for public discussion and debate, through which we develop public opinion.[22] Sharing in this public debate is unifying – it creates an 'us'; a public.[23] It is easy to see why the image of the public sphere and its inhabitants – one which is central to our 'social self-understanding' in the Anglosphere[24] – has been readily applied to (aspects of) the internet. Technology like smart phones and infrastructure like underwater cables and cell towers keep us ever connected to friends, family, communities and the world, via social media platforms,[25] blogs, vlogs, email and so much more, and enable information transmission at a pace never before seen, compressing our experiences of both time and space.[26] Essentially, the internet provides us with a 'mega-marketplace of ideas', as well as space to share and debate our ideas, not just with the people that we know or the people in our city, but with other citizens of our state and of the world.[27]

That we – members of my milieu – imagine social media's place in our lives through the image of the public sphere is rendered evident by Facebook's recent actions in Australia. As I sit here finalising my manuscript, something extraordinary happens. On February 18, 2021, Australian Facebook users woke to find they were no longer able to post Australian news content to the platform and their past posts containing links to news content published in Australia had been deleted from their profile pages (though we could still post news that was not of Australian origin). Simultaneously, Australian news organisations (and others caught in the cross-fire) found that their pages had been wiped.[28] What once was there – including the data I had collected, which was still accessible through *The Australian* page's search function – was now gone. To be clear, Facebook didn't de-platform Australian news sites as a mechanism for eliminating 'harmful' content of any kind, whether contained in news articles themselves or to prevent certain user behaviour. It did so because, in addition to its cyber abuse laws, the Australian Government is also proposing a law that would require tech giants like Facebook and Google to pay news organisations to host their content. The Bill in question – the *Treasury Laws Amendment (News Media and Digital Platforms Mandatory Bargaining Code) Bill 2021* – has now passed in both houses of parliament.[29] However, before the Bill made it through the Senate, Facebook made good on its earlier issued threat to block us from sharing news.[30]

At the end of the day, Facebook is running its business exactly as one would expect a large privatised company to run under neoliberal capitalist logic. But the user experience of having Australian news content pulled from Facebook didn't *feel* like this. It felt like the public sphere had been broken, that this crucially important metatopical space had become fragmented, keeping us from important conversations, unenlightened and unawares. We had been disabled, stripped of certain powers of communication that we were used to exercising. This feeling was exemplified by a question posed on an episode of the ABC's television programme *Q+A* that same day by a member of the general public.[31] Critical of the government's proposed legislation, he said:

I think the government misunderstands what users go on to Facebook to do. They go there to get COVID public health updates, they go there for updates on bushfires, the list goes on. By introducing this code, and Facebook responding by stopping Australian news, *the government is doing the public a disservice by denying people access to news.* What can the government do to fix this problem? Because it's important the public gets access to news if they choose to get it on Facebook.

Note, here, how Facebook – conceptualised as a site of news consumption and thus central to the public sphere – is not figured as a corporation, a bearer of immense social power, even though it was they who chose to pull Australian news content from their platform. Instead, the commentator holds the Australian Government responsible for the injustice of fracturing our public sphere due to its overreach of power. The commentator says the government's legislation is illegitimate *because* it interferes in our public sphere; Facebook is simply the medium between two parties – state and public – in this figuration.[32] But this fracture in our public sphere was quick to heal. After an uncertain few days and some swift negotiations between Facebook and the Australian Government, Facebook has once more enabled users to post Australian news as a trade-off for certain amendments to the legislation, with the Bill passing the Senate on February 23, 2021. Everything is now back to normal.

A Free Speech Zone

Because of its reach, content and variety of platforms that enable user-generated content, the internet has also been 'posited as *a site of freedom*, a place where anyone and everyone could have their say'.[33] In other words, there is also a shared impression that the internet is fundamentally a free speech zone, and that online speech should not be inhibited by governments or any other powerful bodies, precisely so that the people can develop and then spread their collective opinions *to* governments or other powerful bodies. As members of the Anglosphere, 'we' believe that 'all persons [should] have access to places where they can speak and listen, and then, after reflection, speak and listen once more', and today those places are increasingly online.[34] As Danielle Keats Citron further explains, there is a shared but implicit impression here: 'the idea [is] that individuals who can freely speak and listen to others make more informed decisions about the kind of society they want to live in'.[35] But the centrality of this free speech image cannot be wholly explained by the prominence of the public sphere image.

The right to free speech, and investment in an 'independent free speech principle', has a long lineage.[36] And it is not just Western societies that see free speech as fundamentally important. Ashutosh Bhagwat reminds us that 'almost every written constitution in the world contains provisions guaranteeing freedom of speech . . . in nearly absolute terms', which leads him to assess that 'if there is *any* topic on which societies across the globe purport to agree, it seems it is the importance of providing strong protections for freedom of expression'.[37] As we saw in chapter 5, the independent free speech principle holds that 'there is a presumption against restricting speech, even if it causes harm that, if brought about by non-speech conduct, would justify restricting such conduct'.[38] Adherence to this principle is justified by the *value* of free speech, demonstrated by appeal to its role in a well-functioning democracy (as above), or else in truth-seeking and revelation, or else in fostering individual autonomy.[39] Importantly, it is now 'widely accepted' that internet platforms are a central conduit for free expression.[40] Given an already-shared investment in this free speech principle, it may well be fair to say that *this* image – the image of the internet as a (near-) absolute free speech zone – is the most prominent image within the central digital imaginary. Our shared, idealised image is of a 'free', boundless internet. The associated narrative is that it is appropriate and *right* to refrain from restricting digital expression, and that censorship is generally a very bad thing. Said differently, there is a presumption in favour of free expression unless a *very* strong case for censorship can be articulated. Hence, why debates on hate speech bans usually centre on whether this very strong case has been met.

But when it comes to the right to free speech, what freedom is being imagined by the Anglosphere's users? The contours of this image – the view of free speech that has come to prominence in the Anglosphere's central digital imaginary – stem from the United States' 'First Amendment exceptionalism'.[41] This is unsurprising, for 'much information technology originated in the United States and continues to be developed in Silicon Valley', so it is understandable that the internet, as we know it, bears the traces of an affective commitment to the 'tradition of First Amendment jurisprudence'.[42] The First Amendment has come to have a kind of 'mythic' status in the United States; it is treated as sacred, enveloped in emotion and any attempt to question it is held a desecration.[43] Notice, furthermore, how the U.S. imagining of the right to free speech is increasingly colouring the way Australian's imagine this right, even though we, unlike the U.S., have no constitutional protection for it (online or otherwise).[44] As Misha Ketchell points out, 'because we are so saturated in American culture, very few Australians realise that free speech in this country isn't really a thing'.[45] This demonstrates the power of one nation's particular interpretation of a core political value to contour the central digital imaginary, shaping relevantly similar others' (i.e. members of the Anglosphere's) experiences of the internet, and thus to shape the dominant shared Western social imaginary more broadly. (Indeed, this is why I speak of a dominant *Western* imaginary, rather than, say, a dominant *Australian* imaginary.)

Taken together, these two images, borrowed from liberal political imaginings, figure a utopian internet: an all-inclusive public sphere where we can speak our minds and participate in the shaping of our societies. How liberating this domain sounds! Yet, as Mary Anne Franks' notes: 'The internet's liberating potential was certainly real, but so was its oppressive potential'.[46] This has led to a different, *realist* impression that 'we cannot have both a safe internet and a free network'.[47] And certain users are more vulnerable in particular ways.

Anonymous Trolls

What gives us the impression that cyberspace is *unsafe* (tacitly: more so for certain sorts of people)? If you've ever been on the internet, you will have encountered more than pure rational discussion and debate. We know that human ignorance is a fact of life, that people display epistemic vices (like gullibility, closed-mindedness and superbia) in their online activities, and often aren't willing to engage in meaningful debate with people in social media spaces.[48] But worse than this is the fact that some people are willing, even eager, to behave immorally (and amorally) online.[49] As Franks notes, 'almost as soon as it became possible to use the internet to engage in mass communication, it was used to express decidedly anti-egalitarian sentiments'.[50] And, as we saw in chapter 4, not much has changed since then – at least, for women.[51]

Enter the offending agent: the Troll. The pre-internet troll of folklore has several figurations. In modern children's tales, trolls are monstrous creatures who live under bridges, harassing those who would cross and/or exacting a toll from them; in early Scandinavian folklore they were creatures of the night, living in castles and haunting the surrounding areas, being extremely hostile to humans.[52] A transposition is easy to make: under cover of darkness (anonymity) the Trolls haunt (harass, disrupt, antagonise, abuse) various digital subjects, and even exact tolls from them (e.g. engaging in 'sextortion'[53]) before leaving them alone. 'Trolling' also has piscatorial origins, being a method of fishing where a baited line is dragged through the water.[54] This offers an apt image for the internet's prankster-troll, the person who has 'gone fishing' for an incensed response by posting something outrageous, discriminating, offensive or disgusting, looking to bait (or 'trigger') as many people as possible.[55]

Nowadays, we tend to refer to mobs of people who engage in disruptive or antagonising online commentary, online aggression and even cyberbullying and harassment as Trolls – it's basically our 'all-encompassing term for being an ass on the internet'.[56] But, prior to this, the term 'troll' was taken on as a self-descriptor by the subcultural troll.[57] There *is* a difference between the subcultural troll – he (and it is almost always a 'he') who engages in 'highly stylized lulz-based trolling' – and 'other forms of antagonistic online behaviour', such as those described above, 'which may or may not also be *called* Trolling' by wider society.[58] Perhaps one reason for its spread and evolution is that 'the seemingly clear-cut distinction between those who Troll and those who do not' isn't so clear-cut after all.[59] I'm using the term Troll to describe someone whose 'being an ass' on the internet is not always, or necessarily just for the lulz, consonant with common usage. But trolling's subcultural origins are still relevant here, primarily because of the relationship between subcultural trolling and the view that attacks online are generally anonymous (or pseudonymous) and therefore largely unstoppable.

Anonymity is scary because, in theory, it is available to everyone and can be used by anyone to engage in aggressive, hostile, degrading and harassing online activities which may be genuinely harmful.[60] The possibility of anonymity on the internet is every person's own ring of Gyges, should they choose to use it.[61] Indeed, some say that the possibility of anonymity 'removes the social cost of making outrageous personal attacks, as well as shielding the attackers from legal liability'.[62] Others call anonymity a 'multiplier' for trolling behaviours.[63] And while anonymity can be used for good (think 'hacktivism'[64]), it seems equally true that online anonymity enables amorality and immorality, perhaps even emboldening Trolls or encouraging trolling behaviours, either due to the lack of accountability and punishment, or through desensitisation to the acts' harms via over-exposure to online incivility.[65] Clearly, the threat of anonymity (as well as pseudonymity) feeds the image of the internet as dangerous, as a place with a Dark Side, which I elaborate upon below.

The Dark Side of Cyberspace

By now everyone has heard of the 'dark web'.[66] But one need not sink to its depths to suddenly find oneself in the shadow lands. One may try, but 'techniques for avoiding online hate are not fool-proof, because online hate is commonly viewed inadvertently during the course of routine, mundane online activities'.[67] Perhaps this is why, at times, 'the internet is framed as a place that is inherently dangerous – like Mount Everest during a blizzard'.[68] This danger, the dark side of the internet, is no secret,[69] and the encroachment of this dark side has arguably been 'facilitated by the rise of social media platforms, which offer ordinary online user platforms to easily and efficiently broadcast information, including hate'.[70] Some people think that we have to tolerate what lurks in the shadows. Take, for instance, Stjernfelt and Lauritzen's endorsement of 'an old truth that "he who gives up his freedom for security is at risk of losing both"'.[71] But this image of the internet's having a dark side is not only conveyed through pleas to tolerate harmful online con-duct.[72] It is also present in defeatism about the possibility of regulating harm-ful conduct. Some believe that it is simply impossible to *adequately* regulate and, if necessary, penalise what happens online. If true (or, rather, *if taken to be true* – for a central image need not actually be true to nonetheless affect our engagements with the material world), one might expect to see persons take on their own risk management strategies at the individual level in terms of avoidance, especially via privacy settings and content filters.

There is good reason for users to be sceptical about the possibility of regulating and penalising harmful online conduct. After all, popular social media platforms have put in place sets of community guidelines with a range of ways for users to report or flag harmful content, and yet experience shows that this doesn't necessarily mean reported content will be taken down or a user banned. Worse, some content never gets reported and remains undetected (like the comments in my data set); it too is never removed from the site. What's more, platforms also offload their responsibility to ensure cybersafety for their users onto the users themselves. That is, individual risk management strategies are often built into the very structures of reporting systems on par-ticular sites. Consider Facebook: it currently presents users with the option to 'find support or report', but the only support offered if one does not wish to report the content is for users to 'Block' or 'Unfollow' the offending party. In the case of data like mine, it would mean snoozing the page or unliking it. A lack of reliable or practical avenues to respond to harmful or inappropriate conduct, or insufficient outcomes of reporting problematic content to the site, leaves us frustrated yet simultaneously resigned to our fate. The implication – the 'fact' that we must all accept – is that online hatred and obscenities are inevitable and are the price we (must) pay to secure the luxuries and goods the internet otherwise delivers.[73]

The view that platform based, or even legislative regulation is, at best, largely ineffective, and at worst, completely futile is both presupposed in, and also explains the development of well-known individual-oriented behavioural imperatives that are designed to pre-emptively protect us from harms, hurts and frustrations in digital spaces. Consider two: 'Don't feed the Trolls'! and 'Don't read the comments'! By saying that we should not 'feed' the Trolls – that is, engage with them – we are treating their activity as an inevitability. Trolls, unlike Average Internet Users (AIUs), are unreceptive to the voice of reason because they simply don't care to be receptive to the voice of reason. The only solution, then, is for 'us' (AIUs) to protect ourselves from 'them' by either refraining from engaging, relocating to another part of cyberspace, and/or making one's cyberspaces more secure – that is, *private* – if possible. Likewise, the imperative not to read comments also suggests that the voice of reason is unable to lessen intolerable or ignorant speech. There is no point in

trying to educate someone on the internet,[74] so we shouldn't go and get ourselves into a hot fuss by reading the daft things they say in the first place. This
is, essentially, an imperative *not* to join online conversations – the antithesis
of the imperative implicit in the image of the public sphere. What these examples actually demonstrate are individualised risk management tactics. Since
we can't count on laws and platforms to effectively regulate cyberspaces, we
need to come up with our own strategies of self-preservation. The AIU takes
on the onus of protecting themselves as much as they can – and if they don't
follow the rules about reading comments and feeding Trolls, well, they only
have themselves to blame for the aftereffects.

INTERROGATING THE IMAGES

The Realist Images of Cyberspace

In light of the above, it would be unsurprising to find the social practice of
hate speech against women online blamed on anonymous or pseudonymous
Trolls. The Troll stands in contrast to the tacitly assumed AIU who would
never even think to use internet mediums for the purposes of abuse. If we
could just rid the internet of these Trolls, one may reason, then maybe all
could experience equality online. Real name policies reveal this type of rationale. Witness Facebook, for example, which explains: 'When people stand
behind their opinions and actions with their authentic name and reputation,
our community is more accountable'.[75] The idea is that by requiring users
to be themselves on the internet, users will feel compelled to conduct themselves according to shared moral and civic standards for public debate. This
policy thus tacitly endorses and perpetuates the impression that anonymity
breeds trolling, as well as the inverse: identifiability breeds moral conduct.

Anonymity is a bit of a bogeyman, though. First of all, online sociability
comes with varying degrees of anonymity, and staying anonymous is easier
in some places and harder in others.[76] Second, our real selves are absolutely
everywhere online: in photo albums on Facebook, in Twitter feeds, on
Instagram, TikTok and YouTube, on Google Images, university websites,
Wikipedia. The list goes on and on.[77] Take note, for instance, of the way that
'many of the most popular platforms build gender relevance into their architecture, requiring users to identify by gender'.[78] (This is true of Facebook.)
Many, if not most of us, inhabit cyberspaces as our real selves – and not as
disembodied, impartial, unidentifiable, and/or dispassionate agents – and
engage with people who are not strangers to us, at least some of the time, in
part because we want to, in part because the structures of the platforms we
frequent encourage us to, and, in part reflexively, because we simply don't

think about it.[79] Third, and related to the second point, just because it is not immediately apparent who the person behind the screen is, that does not mean it is necessarily difficult (for law enforcement, or anyone else) to find out.[80] Finally, while acknowledging that people do not always follow real name policies (Facebook removes billions of fake accounts from its service annually[81]), it also turns out that the 'real names' policy isn't as discouraging as one might assume. Indeed, a great many people are willing to engage in trolling *even when they can be recognised as their real selves*.[82] Relatedly, *Trolls are not monsters*. They are ordinary members of one's social milieu, and they are habituated to certain forms of behaviour. These can include habituation to women's abuse in varying manifestations, including hate speech.

It is also untrue that the internet and its platforms are unregulatable. The acts of Trolls can be penalised, and platforms can be made responsible too. First, there are platform-level regulations (e.g. Community Guidelines and moderation practices), though, admittedly, these have been found lacking in the past. Beyond this, there is terrestrial law. As discussed in chapter 5, the Australian government has proposed to introduce a bill for an act relating to online safety for Australians which includes the 'world-first cyber-abuse take down scheme for Australian Adults'.[83] This recognises that it is possible to have harmful content removed from the internet, but it does take cooperation between governments, organisations, platforms, and providers, as well as a lot of manpower (the removal of child exploitation materials is an example that immediately comes to mind[84]). The aim here is just to illustrate that there is some falsity, and perhaps some disingenuousness behind the impression that the internet cannot be regulated, that Trolls cannot be pursued, and that the onus of protection from abuse necessarily falls on each individual user. Both free speech enthusiasts and defeatists alike know that it is possible and sometimes right to block, remove and trace digital content (again, as when child exploitation materials are removed). The image of the internet as unregulatable is both false and counterproductive.[85]

What is clear is that the popular image of the Troll (an anonymous and therefore unidentifiable, and therefore unpunishable user) accurately sheds light on aspects of some people's experiences of online abuse, but the image also obscures aspects of others' abuse. It is also clear that the persistence of the image of cyberspace as unregulatable only serves to sediment the view that that harmful online speech must be tolerated – not for any principled reason, but because effective regulation is seen as impossible. It also conveys, inaccurately, that abuse is inevitable and that the onus is on the individual to risk-manage their presence online. So, we can see how this 'realist' image of the internet comparatively serves the interests of men over women: if we imagine that abuse is the doing of Trolls, and if we acknowledge that 'the internet is a dangerous place for Women' because unregulatable, then actual women may feel that their only option is to try to live a life offline, or, more likely, to construct for herself highly securitised (i.e. *private*) cyberspaces. We need alternative images which better approximate what the experiences of encountering hate speech against women online are like for women. Much of this speech – as my dataset reveals – is not directed at specific women users (whom the Troll tacitly targets); (Bad) Women are primarily spoken *about*, and these evaluations of women are left free-floating on sites of public importance where other women (and men, and other genders) encounter them. The 'inevitability' of a harmful online environment also obscures from view the possibility of both punitive *and* non-punitive measures we can take which would make cyberspace less harmful.

The Idealist Images of Cyberspace

It is worth asking from where our shared images originate, since doing so can help open up space for the possibility of critical interrogation. Our prominent idealist images are new iterations of older liberal images, and it is worth pausing to reflect on them in greater detail. Assuming we already know what a utopian internet would look like – a metatopical space of free dialogue and debate – works, in my view, to exclude certain experiences or alternative visions of cyberspace. Recall that the public sphere is the imagined metatopical space where we can think and speak on matters of shared importance, coming eventually to form public opinion. However, one must reckon with the fact that public debate is often divisive, and many different values collide. Given this fact, why suppose it is possible for a set of Individuals to develop *a* public opinion online? One answer is developed with regard to the assumed traits of the public sphere's imagined subject. Its subject is a reasonable and reasoning agent, who will 'strive for a certain *impersonality*, a certain *impartiality*, an eschewing of party spirit' in their deliberations.[86] Indeed, 'impartial reason aims to adopt a point of view outside the concrete situations of action, a transcendental "view from nowhere" that carries the perspective, attributes, character, and interests of no particular subject or set of subjects'.[87] Note, then, that insofar as all are reasoning and reasonable agents, all are (taken to be) fundamentally alike. In the public sphere, any rational agent will 'strive to negate their own particularity and thus to rise above any private or partial view'.[88] Each will be rational, unbiased and open-minded. These agents aspire to impartiality, detachment and dispassionateness.[89] In this state, rational agents will discuss, debate and then settle on the most reasonable conclusion. They will be able to reach a conclusion because reasonable and reasoning minds think alike. So, essentially, Individuals are all interchangeable.

Here's the problem. Digital agents are not fundamentally alike nor interchangeable. The imagined subject of the central digital imaginary, the AIU, does not and *cannot* map onto all internet users. Thus, we must ask, who does our image of the AIU best approximate and thus privilege? Given that this image of cyberspace was pilfered from our central ethico-political imaginary, it should come as no shock that its original inhabitant – the Individual – is the tacit subject. When the inhabitants of cyberspaces (AIUs) are tacitly figured as *one sort of person* (Individuals), this obscures from view that there are *other subjects, other publics* who experience cyberspace in particular ways. Let us see how this is the case when it comes to freedom of speech. The idealised impression of the internet as a space for free and unfettered expression comparatively privileges men users over women users. One of the ways this is achieved is by making harmful online conduct look like the exception rather than the norm. To demonstrate, consider excerpts from John Perry Barlow's infamous *A Declaration of the Independence of Cyberspace*:

> Governments of the Industrial World . . . You claim there are problems among us that you need to solve. You use this claim as an excuse to invade our precincts. Many of these problems don't exist. Where there are real conflicts, where there are wrongs, we will identify them and address them by our means. We are forming our own Social Contract. . . . We are creating a world where anyone, anywhere may express his or her beliefs, no matter how singular, without fear of being coerced into silence or conformity.[90]

Here's how the trick is achieved. When Barlow references 'beliefs no matter how singular', he is producing an image of an 'us' and an 'other' by way of lateral association: *singular beliefs*, by definition, are not what 'we' (a plurality) believe. And since 'we' are in the business of building an egalitarian cyberspace (or so he says), *ipso facto* bigots are isolated individuals.[91] Through this lateral association, an impression is generated that online bigotry, obscenity, hostility, and so on are *isolated* – that is not patterned, pervasive or systematic – incidents.[92] But this certainly does not track reality for women users who are, as we saw in chapter 4, constantly made to witness how 'stereotypical ideas of femininity are consistently used in a derogatory manner'.[93] To promote the image of the public sphere as an ideal, without simultaneously questioning the ontological features of its subjects, ignores that 'embodied being and experience are always enmeshed in fields of meaning and power' – including social identity power – 'enabling and constraining the subject positions and opportunities of different bodies'.[94] While the public sphere is imagined to be essentially extrapolitical, where the speech exercised therein constitutes a debate outside of power, in fact, 'the public sphere is also a site where social meanings are generated, circulated, contested and reconstructed'.[95]

In sum, to idealise the public sphere 'as a free and open space for dialogue' by essentially interchangeable Individuals who can engage in even democratic playing fields simply does not 'account for the unique social situation of women in patriarchal societies'[96] – namely, that women *already* exist in a terrestrial world which subjugates them for their sex and gender, and that this is also true of their virtual world, *for these spaces are deeply integrated.* If the internet is meant to be an evolution of *the* public sphere, it is clear that women still do not have access to this sphere in the same way as men. As Sarah Sobieraj puts it, 'women's use of public space is shaped by the looming possibility of gender-based incidents that threaten to undermine their freedom, comfort and safety'.[97] It is worth noting that while forms of misogyny, including hate speech, do not necessarily drive women out of public cyberspaces, the environment's being poorly policed (whether by the platform itself, or by moderators) almost *requires* women to modify their cyberspaces so as to make it 'safer' for themselves to act. Sobieraj, on that note, articulates the choices women must always consider about their inhabitancy of cyberspace:

> What are the conditions under which it is safe(r) to share your ideas, opinions, preferences, expertise, and experiences online? What topics are likely to rile the trolls? How does the specter of digital misogyny hover over the keyboard? To what extent does the looming threat of digital misogyny serve as a cautionary tale, creating a chilling effect even for women who have not been on the receiving end of this kind of abuse.[98]

Here, 'the concept of vulnerability allows us to appreciate the ways in which women are impacted by such language, *even as they continue to act and to speak*'.[99] The fact is, 'online harassment', including hate speech, 'is remarkably heterosexist and geared toward reinforcement of rigid binary gender and sexuality norms', and this fact alone essentially ensures that 'the only group of people able to take *full* advantage of the internet's potential', including their enjoyment of the right to free speech, are those who embody the tacit traits of the Individual, who has now also come to stand in for the AIU.[100] I put it to the reader that the subject whose speech is freest is the subject who, thanks to the social identity power dynamics of the particular context, is the least likely to be abused on the basis of their identity. Indeed, that is what makes them so free to speak.[101]

However, this is not to say that we should throw the baby out with the bath water when it comes to the image of the public sphere, the value of free speech, and its application to the internet. But we shall only be able to maintain them as ideals if we can find a way to make them 'answer to a plurality of experiences and perspectives that cut across various lines of difference – for otherwise it will remain the case that only certain social groups, as well as certain members within those groups, will have the power to have *their* imaginings . . . act more forcefully' in the central digital imaginary.[102] I'm suggesting we start this investigation at the ontological level.

DIGITAL SUBJECTIVITY

Anya Daly argues that, when theorising about social justice, ontology must always be considered, because problematic ontologies can 'insinuate themselves into the workings and interpretations of [some] theoretical framework, inevitably having downstream consequences for practice and action', including those practices and actions to which we are habituated and which work to subliminally sustain systems of oppression.[103] Our ontological image of subjects in the dominant Western social imaginary is dualist.[104] Being is thought to involve both a mind and a body, and the self (*I* or *me*) is equivocated with the mind.[105] The dualism that has most deeply penetrated into our legal, ethico-political, medical and now digital spheres, though this runs counter to prominent views in contemporary philosophy of mind,[106] hails from Descartes and is captured by his well-known adage: I think, therefore I am.[107] Such ontological presumptions have consequences. For instance, if the body causes a harm that the mind (that *I*) did not deliberately inflict – say, in a passing comment I left on a newspaper's social media post – logic dictates that my blameworthiness is at least partly diminished. On this basis, responsibility for the consequences of one's actions applies most strongly to the deliberately acting subject, the agent who conducted themselves willingly and knowingly.

Indeed, as Moira Gatens says, 'it is not difficult to see the compatibility of Cartesian dualism with the legal notion of *mens rea*, along with exceptions to this rule. The soul (mind) that freely forms an intention to perform an evil act is deemed responsible for that act'.[108] We saw this very same logic applied in Subsection 7(1)(b) of the draft legislation prohibiting cyber-abuse of adults, for example (see chapter 5). But this ontology is not only to be found in long-standing legal notions like *mens rea* and in our moral practices of assigning blameworthiness and responsibility. It is more diffuse in Western culture. For instance, consider the well-worn genre of the body-swap: scenarios of a person's 'soul' or 'mind' entering another's body can be found in such diverse places as the Walt Disney films *Freaky Friday* (1972, 2003) and John Locke's *An Essay Concerning Human Understanding*.[109] Clearly, my consciousness is the real 'me'; my consciousness is who I *really* am.[110] The Body thus comes to be imagined, tacitly, as a mere receptacle or vehicle, a simple container of the self.[111]

Though allegedly inessential for identity, until the invention of the inter-net 'the self' seemed inescapably stuck with its body. Wherever 'the self' went, the body necessarily came, too. But now that we have the technol-ogy, it seems as though 'I' can finally *be* – that is, exist – in another realm, another world, one that is truly disembodied, a realm of minds alone. Indeed, in the words of Lucy Osler, 'if we wanted to craft a paradigm form of *dis-embodied* social interaction, online encounters seem a perfect example. Our online interactions, rather than taking place *in the flesh*, are mediated by our screens'.[112] Of course, it is true that the body remains necessary – for without it we could not perform the actions that allow us to inhabit cyberspace, like typing, or holding a smartphone, or sitting at a desk, or recording the verbali-sation of our thoughts – but the body does not occupy the same *space* as the self. While the Body is in terrestrial space, the Mind is in cyberspace: a com-ments section, a massive multiplayer online role-playing game, a news feed and so forth. So, we can see why Barlow pronounced in his manifesto that he 'come[s] from Cyberspace, the new home of Mind', and that cyberspace 'is a world that is both everywhere and nowhere, but it is not where bodies live'.[113] From its opening sentence, this 'revolutionary' declaration presents a clear dualist ontology.

This image, the notion that the internet *is not where bodies live*, may encourage us to invest in a view of cyberspace as the perfect medium for rational, impartial, public debate relating to the good of a people, which the images of the public sphere and the value of free speech facilitate and trade on. But this is problematic. Far from the new home of Mind, let us note that bodies are, in fact, everywhere on the internet. By way of proof, consider the never-ending amount of pornography. At 2011, it was estimated that porn comprised '12 percent of all Web sites and a quarter of all Web searches'.[114] Turning to PornHub – a Tube site where people can watch pornography online for free or a fee – for some more recent data, 1.36 million hours of new content was added to the platform in 2019. *That equates to 169 years' worth of material.* To put that in perspective: 'If you started watching 2019's new videos in 1850 you would still be watching them today'.[115] But it is not just sexualised, naked bodies that populate the internet. Non-pornographic bod-ies are absolutely everywhere too: in photo albums on Facebook, in Twitter feeds, on Instagram, TikTok and YouTube, on Google Images, university websites, Wikipedia, as mentioned already.[116] Furthermore, the fact that we do not protest to this state of affairs – the fact that we are not trying to eradi-cate bodies from the internet[117] – suggests that *the internet we want is not a disembodied one*, one that is scrubbed clean of material selves. It is high time we recognised the internet as a place where bodies live.

There is also another sense in which the internet is embodied. Our identi-ties travel with us when we go online. We do not 'leave them behind' in the 'real world'. We cannot check them at the landing page or log-in screen.[118] *We are not AIUs*, we are men, women, people of other genders, queers, straight, white, black, Asian and other people of colour, we are differently abled, we are younger and older, *we have identities*. And our identities don't disappear when we go online; 'our lived bodies can and do enter online space'.[119] Sometimes we consciously bring our material selves into online social spaces (e.g. because the platform enable us to self-represent with particular gender pronouns);[120] we put our material selves online via our photos, our usernames, emoji (e.g. the way people use the rainbow flag on Twitter to signal that they are queer, or the Oxford cap to signal that they have a PhD), profile picture frames (which can signal anything from political leanings to moral values to identity traits), and through who we choose to friend, follow, block, Like, not to mention the groups we choose to join (e.g. such as 'tag groups' on Facebook). But even when we are presenting anonymously or pseudonymously on social media, our conduct has certain 'tells' that reveal aspects of who we are. Several theorists have noted that people exhibit group-based identity traits, such as their gender, in the way they communicate online, through the communication itself.[121]

This is because human *being* is really just experiencing all aspects of the world as an embodied consciousness, as a corporeal subject. Subjects are not 'minds concealed by flesh and skull'.[122] The human experience of *being* is inescapably an embodied one. We are 'first and foremost embodied percipient sentient beings'.[123] That is to say, we are all embodied subjects, and embodied subjects are 'beings whose capacity for thought and feeling are intimately bound up with the kinds of bodies we have and the things these bodies do'.[124] Importantly, everyone experiences the world through the particularities of their own body, which is significant because there is no *one* type of human body. This means we should be wary of any imaginary which proffers only a singular imagined subject as its inhabitant: AIUs in the digital imaginary, the ethico-political Individual, or the legal Person. And, in addition to being corporeal, every person's sense of self is necessarily mediated through social mores, too. That's because we are born into social contexts full of shared meanings, including meanings attached to bits of bodies.[125] Immersed in some context – already structured by dominant social imaginings – 'individuals incorporate social ideas in their bodily expressions'.[126] Social ideas about what is normal, or right, or common, or expected for differently embodied people (e.g. masculine things for males; feminine things for females) receive uptake in the body. (Or, if they are rejected, they are rejected through the embodied uptake of 'improper' expressions, for example, masculine dispositions in females; feminine dispositions in males.) Because of this, we end up communicating aspects of ourselves through bodily expressions, even when we are not trying to. And note, crucially, that commenting and conversing online is literally an expression of a specific body: 'the other's texts, as speech, can be part of the other's lived body', and 'we can perceive some-one's expressive, lived body while not being in the same physical place as their objective body'.[127]

What I am getting at here, then, is that this image of a disembodied internet has 'rogue metaphysical commitments',[128] which obfuscate that, in fact, any time we enter online spaces we do not check our bodies (and the social lessons we have learned from, through, and with those bodies) at the log-in screen or landing page. Just because one's self is expressive at a screen does not mean that aspects of one's identity are not conveyed in cyberspace. In a deeper sense, then, we can recognise that *cyberspaces are embodied, gendered spaces*. If 'individuals incorporate social ideas in their bodily expressions',[129] then they can (and will) communicate things about their identity (like femininity and masculinity) without necessar-ily doing so deliberately. The implication stemming from this ontological reimaging of how we inhabit cyberspaces is that 'our raced, classed, and gendered bodies are encoded into our online behaviours, even when we're pretending to be something above or beyond or below what we "really" are IRL [in real life]'.[130] Even behind a screen, a pseudonym, a stock image, we still communicate aspects our identity. From this, we should conclude that all cyberspaces are (at least) *gendered* spaces in the same way that all terrestrial spaces are gendered spaces. What's more, it is *important* to see cyberspaces as such because 'users continue to make judgements about the sex of others in cyberspace, and respond to them on the basis of these gen-dered assumptions', even when they profess adherence to difference-blind liberal equalism.[131]

CULTURAL REVOLUTION

This book has argued that hate speech is a type of group-directed violence that is systemic, and I have offered evidence that women, as a group, are systemically targeted with discriminatory speech that constitutes, for them, a hostile environment (i.e. I have offered evidence that they suffer from hate speech). Here, I want to turn to an observation made by Iris Marion Young:

> To the degree that institutions [e.g., social media platforms, Governments] and social practices [e.g., the practice of public debate] encourage, tolerate, or enable the perpetration of violence against members of specific groups, those institutions and practices are unjust and should be reformed. Such reform may require the redistribution of resources or positions [e.g., hiring more content moderators], but *in large part can come only through a change in cultural*

images, stereotypes, and the mundane reproduction of dominance and aversion
in the gestures of everyday life.[132]

The question thus becomes, *how* can we change our cultural images and stereotypes? *How* do we stop the mundane reproduction of social identity power? And this question is difficult to answer because the problem of hate speech against women online is as complex as the activity itself is common. Again, to Young:

> The behaviour, comportments, images, and stereotypes that contribute to the oppression of bodily marked groups are pervasive, systemic, mutually generating, and mutually reinforcing. They are elements of dominant cultural practices that lie as the normal background of our liberal democratic society. *Only changing the cultural habits themselves will change the oppressions they produce and reinforce*, but change in cultural habits can occur only if individuals become aware of and change their individual habits. This is cultural revolution.[133]

I have argued that members of my milieu are habituated to a patriarchal status quo, and that hate speaking against women is, for some, a habituated disposition; that is, hate speech against women is an immediate response that is unthinking and nearby for a great many more of us than we'd all like to think – hence why there is so much of it online (and offline too, for that matter). Thus, the project of ending the social practice of hate speaking against women online is vast, for we must collectively become aware of and then challenge the tacit disposition of misogyny in us all – for it is this which tends some to hate speaking. So, where to from here? As La Caze reminds us, images can work to close off certain questions but new images can play a constructive role in developing new ideas, of making our world meaningful in new ways, of sedimenting in our habituated behaviours, and so are the seeds of social change – of cultural revolution.[134] But where to find these images and how to make them stick? I address this question in the conclusion to this book.

NOTES

1. James Curran, 'The Internet of Dreams: Reinterpreting the Internet', in *Misunderstanding the Internet*, 2nd ed., ed. James Curran, Natalie Fenton, and Des Freedman (London Routledge, 2016), 11.
    2. For a recent explicit contribution to this project, see: Millicent Churcher and Moira Gatens, 'Reframing Honour in Heterosexual Imaginaries', *Angelaki* 24 (2019): 151–164.

3. Marguerite La Caze, *The Analytic Imaginary* (Ithaca: Cornell University Press, 2002), 29.

4. La Caze, *Analytic Imaginary*, 29.

5. José Medina demonstrates this with respect to racial oppression, for example. See: José Medina, 'Racial Violence, Emotional Friction, and Epistemic Activism', *Angelaki: Journal of the Theoretical Humanities* 24 (2019): 22–37.

6. See: Emma Jane, *Misogyny Online: A Short (and Brutish) History* (Los Angeles: Sage Swifts, 2017), 55; Sarah T. Roberts, *Behind The Screen: Content Moderation in the Shadows of Social Media* (New Haven: Yale University Press, 2019), 8; Katharine Gelber and Susan Brison, 'Digital Dualism and the "Speech as Thought" Paradox', in *Free Speech In The Digital Age* (New York: Oxford University Press, 2019), 12; Susan J. Brison and Katharine Gelber, 'Introduction', in *Free Speech In The Digital Age* (New York: Oxford University Press, 2019), 4.

7. See Anastasia Powell and Nicola Henry, *Sexual Violence in a Digital Age* (London: Palgrave Macmillan, 2017), chap. 5 for more examples.

8. See: Alexandra James, Jennifer Power, and Andrea Waling, 'Conceptualising the Continuum of Female Genital Fashioning Practices', *Health Sociology Review* (2020): 1–18, https://doi.org/10.1080/14461242.2020.1811749; Kaylee Skoda and Cory L. Pedersen, 'Size Matters After All: Experimental Evidence that SEM Consumption Influences Genital and Body Esteem in Men', *SAGE Open* 9 (2019): 1–11.

9. Debby Herbenick, Tsung-Chieh Fu, Paul Wright, Bryant Paul, Ronna Gradus, Jill Bauer, and Rashida Jones, 'Diverse Sexual Behaviors and Pornography Use: Findings From a Nationally Representative Probability Survey of Americans Aged 18 to 60 Years', *The Journal of Sexual Medicine* 17 (2020): 623–633.

10. Jacob Bernstein, 'How OnlyFans Changed Sex Work Forever', *The New York Times*, February 9, 2019, accessed September 16, 2020, https://www.nytimes.com/2019/02/09/style/onlyfans-porn-stars.html.

11. La Caze, *Analytic Imaginary*, 19.

12. Lucy Osler, 'Taking Empathy Online', *Inquiry* (2021): 2, https://doi.org/10.1080/0020174X.2021.1899045.

13. These are not the only images that are central in the digital imaginary – for example, we have *waves* and *floods* of information, filter *bubbles*, *viral* content, site *traffic*, a *marketplace* of ideas, echo *chambers*, *intoxicating* and *addictive* sites, and so on – but these are the most important images given the topic of this book.

14. La Caze, *Analytic Imaginary*, 41.

15. Jessica Megarry, 'Online Incivility or Sexual Harassment? Conceptualising Women's Experiences in the Digital Age', *Women's Studies International Forum* 47 (2014): 46, 48.

16. Megarry, 'Online Incivility', 48.

17. Jürgen Habermas, 'The Public Sphere: An Encyclopedia Article (1964)', *New German Critique* 3 (1974): 49.

18. Charles Taylor, *Modern Social Imaginaries* (Durham: Duke University Press, 2004), 90.

19. Taylor, *Modern Social Imaginaries*, 91, my emphasis.

20. Taylor, *Modern Social Imaginaries*, 90, original emphasis.

21. They are too numerous to list here, but see for example: Armando Salvatore, 'New Media, the "Arab Spring," and the Metamorphosis of the Public Sphere: Beyond Western Assumptions on Collective Agency and Democratic Politics', *Constellations* 2013 (20): 217–228; Bianca Fileborn, 'Justice 2.0: Street Harassment Victims' Use of Social Media and Online Activism as Sites of Informal Justice', *British Journal of Criminology* 57 (2017): 1482–1501; Brian McNair, Terry Flew, Stephen Harrington, and Adam Swift, *Politics, Media, and Democracy in Australia: Public and Producer Perceptions of the Political Public Sphere* (New York: Routledge, 2017); Jamie Stoops, 'Just Like Heroin: Science, Pornography, and Heteronormativity in the Virtual Public Sphere', *Porn Studies* 4 (2017): 364–380; Patrick Weber, 'Discussions in the Comments Section: Factors Influencing Participation and Interactivity in Online Newspapers' Reader Comments', *New Media and Society* 16 (2013): 941–957; Robert Post, 'Privacy, Speech, and the Digital Imagination', in *Free Speech in the Digital Age*, ed. Susan Brison and Katharine Gelber (Oxford: Oxford University Press, 2019), 104–121.

22. As Taylor explains, 'Although the media are multiple, as are the exchanges, that take place in them, they are deemed to be in principle intercommunicating. The discussion we're having on television now takes account of what was said in the newspaper this morning, which, in turn, reports on the radio debate yesterday, and so on' (*Modern Social Imaginaries*, 83).

23. Taylor, *Modern Social Imaginaries*, 86.

24. Taylor, *Modern Social Imaginaries*, 69.

25. Post, 'Digital Imagination', 104; see also: James Weinstein, 'Cyber Harassment and Free Speech: Drawing the Line Online', in *Free Speech in the Digital Age*, ed. Susan Brison and Katharine Gelber (Oxford: Oxford University Press, 2019), 69. However, as Ashutosh Bhagwat points out, this statement fails to highlight that major social media platforms (like Twitter and Facebook) are privately owned. See: Ashutosh Bhagwat, 'Free Speech Categories in the Digital Age', in *Free Speech in the Digital Age*, ed. Susan Brison and Katharine Gelber (Oxford: Oxford University Press, 2019), 92.

26. McNair et al., *Politics*, 4; Roberts, *Behind The Screen*, 56.

27. Tarleton Gillespie, *Custodians of the Internet: Platforms, Content Moderation, and the Hidden Decisions that Shape Social Media* (New Haven: Yale University Press, 2018), 32.

28. Triple J Hack, 'What is Going On with Facebook's News Ban?' *ABC News*, February 18, 2021, accessed February 20, 2021, https://www.abc.net.au/triplej/prog rams/hack/facebook-news-ban-explained/13168152.

29. James Purtill, 'Facebook Thinks it Won the Battle of the Media Bargaining Code – But So Does the Government', *ABC News*, February 26, 2021, accessed March 15, 2021, https://www.abc.net.au/news/science/2021-02-26/facebook-google -who-won-battle-news-media-bargaining-code/13193106.

30. Amanda Meade, 'Facebook Threatens to Block Australians From Sharing News in Battle over Landmark Media Law', *The Guardian*, September 1, 2020, accessed February 20, 2021, https://www.theguardian.com/media/2020/sep/01

/facebook-instagram-threatens-block-australians-sharing-news-landmark-accc-media-law.

31. Q+A, 'Bargaining with Big Tech', hosted by Hamish Macdonald, aired February 18, 2021, on ABC, https://www.abc.net.au/qanda/2021-18-02/13141040.

32. Dissatisfied with the panel's response, the same commentator later remarks 'So, the issue I have is the news was free before. The news . . . We didn't . . . You know, they didn't charge for news, and then now the government wants to ask them, you know, to pay for it. It doesn't make sense. What was free doesn't become monetised overnight just because of legislation'. This is just further evidence that Facebook is *not* tacitly imagined as a for-profit business in a capitalist neoliberal world, even though that's exactly what it is. Again, the state is (illegitimately) exercising power over the people through its (implicitly, unjust) financial motives, interfering with our public sphere in the process.

33. Brison and Gelber, 'Introduction', 5, my emphasis.

34. Packingham v. North Carolina, 137 S Ct. 1730 (2017), cited in Post, 'Digital Imagination', 104.

35. Danielle Keats Citron, 'Restricting Speech To Protect It', in *Free Speech in the Digital Age*, ed. Susan Brison and Katharine Gelber (Oxford: Oxford University Press, 2019), 129.

36. Gelber and Brison, 'Digital Dualism', 13.

37. Bhagwat, 'Free Speech Categories', 88–103.

38. Gelber and Brison, 'Digital Dualism', 13.

39. Gelber and Brison, 'Digital Dualism', 13.

40. Post, 'Digital Imagination', 104.

41. Gelber and Brison, 'Digital Dualism', 14.

42. Brison and Gelber, 'Introduction', 7.

43. Gérard Bouchard, *Social Myths and Collective Imaginaries*, trans. Howard Scott (Toronto: University of Toronto Press, 2017), 3.

44. Though, for the sceptical among us, one might think that this 'rights talk' is ultimately 'more about not wanting to be told what to do, particularly by individuals whose perspective one doesn't respect'. See: Whitney Phillips, *This Is Why We Can't Have Nice Things: Mapping The Relationship Between Online Trolling and Mainstream Culture* (Cambridge: MIT Press, 2015), 133.

45. Misha Ketchell, 'Australia Doesn't Protect Free Speech, But It Could', *The Conversation*, June 7, 2019, accessed May 22, 2020, https://theconversation.com/au stralia-doesnt-protect-free-speech-but-it-could-118448.

46. Mary Anne Franks, 'Not Where Bodies Live: The Abstraction of Internet Expression', in *Free Speech in the Digital Age*, ed. Susan Brison and Katharine Gelber (Oxford: Oxford University Press, 2019), 139.

47. Frederik Stjernfelt and Anne Mette Lauritzen, *Your Post Has Been Removed: Tech Giants and Freedom of Speech* (Cham: Springer Open, 2020), 145.

48. Michael P. Lynch, *The Internet of Us: Knowing More and Understanding Less in the Age of Big Data* (New York: Liveright Publishing Corporation, 2016).

49. Jane, *Misogyny Online*, 44.

50. Franks, 'Not Where Bodies Live', 139.

51. Franks, 'Not Where Bodies Live', 140.

52. The Editors of Encyclopaedia Britannica, 'Troll', *Encyclopaedia Britannica*, 20 July 1998, accessed May 7, 2020, https://www.britannica.com/topic/troll.

53. Powell and Henry, *Sexual Violence*, 62.

54. Phillips, *Nice Things*, 15.

55. Phillips, *Nice Things*, 15.

56. Paulie Socash (subcultural troll), cited in Phillips, *Nice Things*, 153.

57. Phillips, *Nice Things*, 24, 153, 9.

58. Phillips, *Nice Things*, 57, 21, my emphasis. Lulz is a corruption of LOL – laugh out loud – and refers to 'acute amusement in the face of someone else's distress, embarrassment, or rage' (Ibid.).

59. Phillips, *Nice Things*, 8.

60. Gillespie, *Custodians*, 29.

61. Jane, *Misogyny Online*, 44.

62. Weinstein, 'Cyber Harassment', 52, my emphasis. Indeed, it allows people to 'engage in behaviours they would never replicate in professional or otherwise public settings' (Phillips, *Nice Things*, 25).

63. Franks, 'Not Where Bodies Live', 140.

64. David J. Gunkel, 'Editorial: Introduction to Hacking and Hacktivism', *New Media and Society* 7 (2005): 595–597.

65. Diana L. Ascher and Sufiya Umoja Noble, 'Unmasking Hate on Twitter: Disrupting Anonymity by Tracking Trolls', in *Free Speech in the Digital Age*, ed. Susan Brison and Katharine Gelber (Oxford: Oxford University Press, 2019), 176, 183.

66. Matthew Costello and James Hawdon, 'Hate Speech in Online Spaces', in *The Palgrave Handbook of Cybercrime and Cyberdeviance*, ed. Thomas Holt and Adam Bossler (Cham: Springer Nature, 2020), 1411.

67. Costello and Hawdon, 'Hate Speech', 1411.

68. Jane, *Misogyny Online*, 5.

69. Once again, there are too many instances of this image to comprehensively list them, but see, for example: Ascher and Noble, 'Unmasking Hate', 170–188; Manuela Caiani and Linda Parenti, 'The Dark Side of the Web: Italian Right-Wing Extremist Groups and the Internet', *South European Society and Politics* 14 (2009): 273–294; Raphael Cohen-Almagor, *Confronting the Internet's Dark Side: Moral and Social Responsibility on the Free Highway* (New York: Cambridge University press, 2015); Won Kim, Ok-Ran Jeong, Chulyun Kim, and Jungmin So, 'The Dark Side of the Internet: Attacks, Costs and Responses', *Information Systems* 36 (2011): 675–705; Christoph Lutz and Christian Pieter Hoffmann, 'The Dark Side of Online Participation: Exploring Non-, Passive and Negative Participation', *Information, Communication & Society* 20 (2017): 876–897; David A. Makin and Amber L. Morczek, 'The Dark Side of Internet Searches: A Macro Level Assessment of Rape Culture', *International Journal of Cyber Criminology* 9 (2015): 1–23; Powell and Henry, *Sexual Violence*, 63; Roland Heickerö, *The Dark Sides of the Internet: On Cyber Threats and Information Warfare* (Frankfurt: Peter Lang, 2013). Karla Mantilla, *Gendertrolling: How Misogyny Went Viral* (Santa Barbara: Praeger, 2015)

describes the internet as the 'wild West', which has the same connotation of danger and lawlessness.

70. Costello and Hawdon, 'Hate Speech', 1409.

71. Stjernfelt and Lauritzen, *Your Post*, 145.

72. Costello and Hawdon, 'Hate Speech', 1408.

73. Citron, 'Restricting Speech', 122.

74. Roberts, *Behind the Screen*, 153, 168.

75. Facebook, cited in Gillespie, *Custodians*, 62.

76. Ascher and Noble, 'Unmasking Hate', 172.

77. Sarah Sobieraj, 'Bitch, Slut, Skank, Cunt: Patterned Resistance to Women's Visibility in Digital Publics', *Information, Communication and Society* 21 (2018): 1711.

78. Sobieraj, 'Bitch', 1711.

79. Lucy Osler, 'Feeling Togetherness Online: A Phenomenological Sketch of Online Communal Experiences', *Phenomenology and the Cognitive Sciences* 19 (2020): 573.

80. Alexander Brown notes, 'today the police have powers to track down and seize digital evidence, along with other forms of evidence', and this is common knowledge. See: Alexander Brown, 'What Is So Special About Online (As Compared To Offline) Hate Speech', *Ethnicities* 18 (2017): 299.

81. Niall McCarthy, 'Facebook Deleted More Than 2 Billion Fake Accounts In The First Quarter Of The Year', *Forbes*, May 24, 2019, accessed May 7, 2020, https ://www.forbes.com/sites/niallmccarthy/2019/05/24/facebook-deleted-more-than-2-bi llion-fake-accounts-in-the-first-quarter-of-the-year-infographic/#f8bab9167e30.

82. Phillips, *Nice Things*, 152; Jane, *Misogyny Online*, 35.

83. Australian Government, 'Fact Sheet – Online Safety Bill', *Consultation on a Bill for a new Online Safety Act*, 2020, accessed February 4, 2021, https://www.com munications.gov.au/have-your-say/consultation-bill-new-online-safety-act.

84. The Australian Federal Police (AFP) chair the Virtual Global Taskforce, 'an alliance of international law enforcement agencies and private sector partners work-ing together to combat online child sexual abuse', which provides users with a site to report suspicious content, and which works with internet service providers and inter-net content hosts that have become aware of child exploitation or child abuse material on their server(s). The AFP's 2018-19 Annual Report indicates 112 overseas children rescued from potential sexual abuse, which is interconnected with online child por-nography (e.g. Operation Bayldon). See: Australian Federal Police, 'Online Child Sex Exploitation', *Australian Centre to Counter Child Exploitation*, 2018, accessed July 14, 2020, https://www.afp.gov.au/what-we-do/services/child-protection/online-child -sex-exploitation; and 'Annual Report 2018-19', *Annual Reports*, October 11, 2019, accessed July 14, 2020, https://www.afp.gov.au/about-us/publications-and-reports/ annual-reports, 6, 74.

85. Mantilla, *Gendertrolling*, 183.

86. Taylor, *Modern Social Imaginaries*, 90, my emphasis.

87. Iris Marion Young, *Justice and the Politics of Difference* (Princeton: Princeton University Press, 1990), 100.

88. Taylor, *Modern Social Imaginaries*, 90.

89. Young, *Justice*, 100.

90. John Perry Barlow, 'A Declaration of the Independence of Cyberspace', *Electronic Frontier Foundation*, February 8, 1996, accessed May 11, 2020, https://www.eff.org/cyberspace-independence.

91. Phillips discusses this contrast with respect to AIUs and subcultural trolls: 'we – average Internet users – are reasonable, civil, and fair, while they – the ruthless trolls – are aggressive, misanthropic, and cruel', a self-perception she argues is fundamentally false. See Phillips, *Nice Things*, 134.

92. Mari Matsuda, 'Public Response to Racist Speech: Considering the Victim's Story', in *Words that Wound: Critical Race Theory, Assaultive Speech, and the First Amendment*, ed. Mari Matsuda, Charles R. Lawrence III, Richard Delgado, and Kimberlè Williams Crenshaw (Boulder: Westview Press, 1993), 22.

93. Megarry, 'Online Incivility', 49.

94. Danielle Celermajer, Millicent Churcher, Moira Gatens and Anna Hush, 'Institutional Transformations: Imagination, Embodiment, and Affect', *Angelaki* 24 (2019): 4; see also Megarry, 'Online Incivility', 48.

95. Megarry, 'Online Incivility', 48. See also: Sobieraj, 'Bitch', 1703.

96. Megarry, 'Online Incivility', 49.

97. Sobieraj, 'Bitch', 1700. See also Lucy Nicholas and Christine Agius, *The Persistence of Global Masculinism Discourse, Gender and Neo-Colonial Re-Articulations of Violence* (Cham: Palgrave Macmillan, 2017), 50.

98. Sobieraj, 'Bitch', 1710.

99. Tanya D'Souza, Laura Griffin, Nicole Shackleton, and Danielle Walt, 'Harming Women with Words: The Failure of Australian Law to Prohibit Gendered Hate Speech', *UNSW Law Journal* 41 (2018): 970.

100. Young, *Justice*, 123; Franks, 'Not Where Bodies Live', 140; Soraya Chemaly, 'Demographics, Design, and Free Speech: How Demographics Have Produced Social Media Optimized for Abuse and The Silencing of Marginalized Voices', in *Free Speech in the Digital Age*, ed. Susan Brison and Katharine Gelber (Oxford: Oxford University Press, 2019), 152.

101. Phillips, *Nice Things*, 131.

102. Millicent Churcher, *Reimagining Sympathy, Recognizing Difference: Insights from Adam Smith* (London: Rowman and Littlefield International, 2019), 165.

103. Anya Daly, 'The Declaration of Interdependence! Feminism, Grounding, and Enactivism', *Human Studies* 44 (2021): 48.

104. Powell and Henry, *Sexual Violence*, 52–59.

105. Elizabeth Grosz, *Volatile Bodies: Toward A Corporeal Feminism* (St Leonards: Allen & Unwin, 1994), 5–10.

106. Gelber and Brison, 'Digital Dualism', 21. See also: Susan Brison, 'Speech, Harm, and the Mind Body Problem in First Amendment Jurisprudence', *Legal Theory* 4 (1998): 53.

107. Brison, 'Mind Body Problem', 53. See also Daly, 'Declaration', 53.

108. Moira Gatens, *Imaginary Bodies: Ethics, Power, and Corporeality* (London: Routledge, 1996), 109.

109. John Locke, Chap. xxvii. Of Identity and Diversity, in *Great Books of the Western World*, ed. Mortimer J. Adler, vol. 33 (Chicago: Encyclopædia Britannica Inc.: 1994), 218–228.

110. Lucy Osler, 'See You Online', *The Philosopher's Magazine* 90 (2020): 77. Jacqueline Broad, 'The Early Modern Period: Dignity and the Foundation of Women's Rights', *The Wollstonecraftian Mind*, eds. Sandrine Bergès, Eileen Hunt Botting, Alan Coffee (Abingdon: Routledge, 2019), 29.

111. Broad, 'Early Modern Period', 29.

112. Osler, 'See You Online', 79, original emphasis.

113. Des Freedman, 'The Internet of Rules', in *Misunderstanding the Internet*, ed. James Curran, Natalie Fenton and Des Freedman, 2nd edition (London, Routledge, 2016), 117.

114. Susanna Paasonen, *Carnal Resonance: Affect and Online Pornography* (Cambridge: The MIT Press, 2011), 43.

115. PornHub, 'The 2019 Year In Review', PornHub Insights, December 11, 2019, accessed July 14, 2020, https://www.pornhub.com/insights/2019-year-in -review.

116. Megarry, 'Online Incivility', 49, writes, 'Social networks such as Facebook, Twitter and MySpace encourage users to construct their personal identities through online profiles, which commonly contain real names and photographs, and conform to traditional norms of masculinity and femininity'.

117. I am dubious that those who would oppose internet pornography would like-wise oppose the other bodily displays I have mentioned online.

118. Osler, 'Feeling Togetherness Online', 575.

119. Osler, 'Taking Empathy Online', 3.

120. Ascher and Noble, 'Unmasking Hate', 174.

121. Ascher and Noble, 'Unmasking Hate', 173; Jane, *Misogyny Online*, 65–66; Megarry, 'Online Incivility', 49; Phillips, *Nice Things*, 1124–128; Powell and Henry, *Sexual Violence*, 59 – 65; Roberts, *Behind The Screen*, 159.

122. Lucy Osler, 'See You Online', *The Philosopher's Magazine* 90 (2020): 77.

123. Daly, 'Declaration', 56; see also Osler, 'Taking Empathy Online', 4.

124. Osler, 'See You Online', 77.

125. Elizabeth Grosz (*Volatile Bodies*, XI) makes this point. For her, the body has an 'organic openness to cultural completion'. That cultural completion *is* the develop-ment of a self. She believes there is no '"real", material body on one hand and its vari-ous cultural and historical representations on the other'; rather, 'these representations and cultural inscriptions quite literally constitute bodies and help to produce them as such' (ibid., X.).

126. Powell and Henry, *Sexual Violence*, 63.

127. Osler, 'Taking Empathy Online', 24, 8. Osler adds, 'we need to understand how words as speech, while not a part of our physical body, are incorporated into the field of expression of our lived body', because words are *tools*. Tools, she says, 'can be incorporated into our lived body when they are used in a way that they become transparent, come to shape and mould our experiences . . . Language and words are also part of our equipment which we incorporate into our lived body' (ibid., 17, 18).

128. Daly, 'Declaration', 53.

129. Powell and Henry, *Sexual Violence*, 63.

130. Phillips, *Nice Things*, 41.

131. Megarry, 'Online Incivility', 49; See also: Nicholas and Agius, *Global Masculinism Discourse*, 37.

132. Young, *Justice*, 63, my emphasis.

133. Young, *Justice*, 152, my emphasis.

134. La Caze, *Analytic Imaginary*, 29.

Conclusion
Imaginal (R)Evolution

Imagination is the faculty of transforming the experience of what is into a projection of what could be . . .

—Iris Marion Young[1]

As Jessica Megarry sums it up, 'equality online is dependent not only on the ability to occupy a space, but to be able to influence it and speak without fear of threat or harassment'.[2] The aim is to facilitate cyberspaces where women do not need to go through the constant bodywork to ensure their own cyber-safety, for women to have the tacit assurance they will not only be respected as an individual user, but also the confidence that one will not run up against disparaging comments made of one's identity-based group, and even subsets of this group (i.e. Bad Women as they are variously figured). This, in turn, requires challenges to normative, habituated behaviour, and *that* requires new models through which we can understand (aspects of) our worlds and our place within them as specific kinds of subjects. When we find it is 'impera-tive to shift deeply ingrained habits of perception and feeling',[3] the way we meet this imperative is by developing and testing out new or borrowed images. There is much that needs to change to bring about the ultimate aim, which is an aim of gender equality. To that end, I have highlighted several images that need to be challenged: that women are (men's) service workers; that cyberspace is inevitably dangerous; that an ideal internet is disembod-ied; that 'hate speech' is bound normatively by the principle of neutrality; that hate speech is harmful like a pollutant; that singular models of imagined subjectivity – the average internet user (AIU), the Individual, the Person and so on – can adequately represent facets of human *being*. And certainly there are many more. The difficulty with cultural revolution, which entails imaginal (r)evolution, is that some images sediment into our central imaginaries more easily than others.

Is there any strategy one could undertake to shift problematic sedimented images that is likely to be successful? As Susan James has written 'in many cases, the task of modifying the way we understand ourselves and others, together with the way we feel, will be long and unpredictable, and will be achieved by imaginative techniques over which we have at best imperfect control'.[4] Indeed, I think this is true. However, this is not to say that there are *no* techniques to employ, nor that we can have *no* control whatsoever over the shape our imaginaries take. To that end, I draw the reader's attention to six elements I take to be necessary (*but not sufficient*) for imaginal (r)evolution which may guide us in our creative pursuit.[5] These six elements are: contradiction within or across imaginaries, collective desire for change, awareness of social power relations, critique of the harmful image and/or practice, resonance of the new image and/or practice and time. While these necessities can be theoretically separated, in practice they typically run together.

CONTRADICTION, OR EPISTEMIC-AFFECTIVE FRICTION

When Facebook suddenly wiped the content from Australian news organisations' pages and prevented users from sharing Australian news, there was a dramatic affective and epistemic rupture in at least my own user-experience. Certain capacities had been curtailed. My newsfeed looked (and felt) different. I had to find new avenues of accessing information relevant to me (by, for example, downloading local news apps). I could not see people's opinions on current events, and nor could I contribute to them. Such epistemic-affective frictions[6] – which are sometimes *ruptures* – result in a general awareness that one's shared images, norms and practices no longer 'make sense' in the way that they used to. They become inadequate for the world of experience. The contradiction in this scenario was between how Facebook was thought about, felt and used – as medium and media of the public sphere – and the actions of the company which represented it as something other, namely, its being a kind of media monopoly, powerful enough to challenge the state, and caring only about its bottom line, not the Australian user. Facebook has no obligation to be a news platform to us, and the user was forced – through experience – to reckon with this fact. You might say that this event interrupted the taken-for-granted role social media plays in our day-to-day lives.

Some epistemic and affective frictions occur without warning, like the above, but others arise because incoherent expectations are placed on an imagined subject, and actual people who embody that identity find themselves in an impossible double-bind, unable to do or be all of the things that this type of subject is expected to be. For example, in the central sexual imaginary, a Woman is not supposed to be a 'slut' but she also shouldn't be 'frigid'.[7] What exactly is the right amount of sex she should have so as to find herself unblemished by either label? This contradiction is felt in that one's lived experiences 'run up against and exert pressure on dominant social narratives'.[8] These kinds of contradictions make it such that one may no longer experience a coherent *gestalt* (if they ever really did in the first place).[9] Because individuals always dwell across multiple social imaginaries, and because dominant imaginaries tend to reflect a *gestalt* that reflects the interests and experiences in the interest of privileged rather than oppressed collectives, moments of epistemic-affective friction – these contradictions, tensions, paradoxes or ruptures to the superficially coherent gestalt – are the cracks through which the light of alternative, presently marginal imag(in)ings can enter.[10]

Of course, one must acknowledge that the mere emergence of an epistemic-affective friction does not necessarily lead a person to reckon with the inconsistency it reveals. For example, the return of Facebook's user and page functions within a week of the initial de-platforming has meant that a friction which could have become a wide, gaping rupture ready for the entry of new images has instead become a minor 'blip', a 'glitch', something to be ignored rather than reflected upon. Using Facebook now *feels* just the same as it did before. Additionally, when the epistemic-affective frictions one encounters relate to imagined subjectivity and one's own (or another's) place in the world, it is not surprising to find that this sometimes generates cognitive dissonance, insensitivity or closed-mindedness and wilful ignorance instead of reflection and revaluation.[11] These vices can be difficult to ward off precisely because they are not merely cognitive. They are affective too, such as when one's interlocutors not only exhibit endorsement of false beliefs, but, when challenged, they respond with affective resistance (e.g. superbia, apathy, disinterest, irritation), and/or cognitive resistance (e.g. prejudice, stigma, misrecognition), and/or embodied resistance (becoming agitated or red in the face, or suddenly switching to frenzied 'ALL CAPS' communication), and/or defence mechanisms (e.g. shifting the burden of proof, or changing the subject).[12] It is important to remember that certain sorts of people benefit from unjust hierarchical imaginaries at work in a specific time and place. They have a vested interest in maintaining their central imag(in)ings (though they may not consciously realise this). Hence, 'attempts to implement social reforms cannot afford to overlook the *embodied investments* that people have in established arrangements, values and customs', for it is *these* that drive resistance to change.[13]

DESIRE

What I mean by 'desire' is a collective fellow-feeling that yearns for a change in the structure of one's society, specifically aiming at the just treatment of social groups.[14] Such a desire may be expressed 'negatively' (e.g. through anger at the current structure) or 'positively' (e.g. through hope for a better future), so we should not expect a particular (or singular) direction of affect in efforts for social revolution. It is to be expected that the seeds of this desire will first spring from the oppressed collective themselves though; after all, 'there is nothing but what is, the given, the situated interest in justice, from which to start'.[15] Those who are more likely to be attuned to injustice are those who are experiencing it. Most crucially, though, it is in the *collective* desire for change wherein the possibility of successful social transformation lies. As Millicent Churcher explains, 'having others acknowledge and echo our feelings constitutes a mode of social recognition that is crucial to our happiness and self-esteem'.[16] What's more, as Danielle Celermajer and others have argued, 'the expression of the experience of injustice from people who have historically been silenced and marginalised can provoke *shame*, that can in turn be mobilized to motivate significant transformations in how those groups are positioned, regarded and treated in the social imaginary'.[17] Shame is not the only provocative and productive emotion that leads to a desire for social change, just a particularly strong one (others are anger, love, compassion, indignation, hope, etc.). What is important is eliciting a desire for change among both dominant and subordinate groups. If 'the people' don't see a certain issue (e.g. hate speech against women online) as a particularly serious problem that needs to be addressed, there will only be apathy. Hence, the cultivation of *fellow-feeling* beyond the affected group is necessary.[18]

How is this cultivation of fellow-feeling possible? First, by developing one's sympathetic imagination. (Note: 'sympathy', following Churcher's take on Adam Smith, entails that 'I consider what I should suffer *if I was really you*, and I not only change circumstances with you, but *I change persons and characters*'.[19]) In other words, individuals must (be helped to) empathise with the situation of the other as if one was themselves that other, rather than the same self in a different situation. One must not presume that the other's situation is simply the inverse of one's own — one needs to hold open a space into which others' images of themselves can enter. Thus, second, and necessary to the first, one must cultivate a capacity to recognise the other's difference. With recognition comes new images, and with new images come new affects, and with new affects come differential (ideally, *better*) normative practices. If we do not understand how to be sensitive to and recognitive of *difference as such*, then we cannot utilise the sympathetic imagination.[20] The other's difference must no longer be imagined as their 'deviance in relation to a norm', but rather 'names relations of similarity and dissimilarity that can be reduced neither to coextensive identity nor nonoverlapping otherness'.[21] Difference is alterity, specificity, variation. Finally, one must always remember 'to account for the continuing presence of the past'.[22] With respect to the act of hate speech, one must remember that 'violence starts with the act, but lives on after the act has ceased'.[23] For those who are ignorant of past acts of violence targeting some group, or who assume that the effects of a specific instance of violence cease when the act ceases fail to see how 'it is logical to link together several-thousand real-life stories into one tale of caution', and thus to fail to realise the continuing impact of past group-directed violence and other forms of oppression in the present.[24] Context and history must always be actively held in mind to achieve adequate fellow-feeling.

POWER

For imaginal revolution to take place, 'we need to understand the positionality and relationality of social agents in networks of power relations'.[25] Indeed, Moira Gatens reminds us to ask: 'whose stories, whose imaginings, carry the force to bestow efficacious meaning on human action and social behaviour'?[26] The answer to this question depends on the central social imaginaries at stake. Every social imaginary has imagined subjects, and all imagined subjects are the product of everyday habits and normative practices enacted upon and applied to bodies, permitting certain actors to undertake certain tasks and roles but not others and structuring how they should engage with other imagined subjects in the same milieu.

In chapter 2 we saw that, in the ethico-political realm, the imaginings and stories proliferated by real flesh-and-blood, white European property-owning cisgender heterosexual 'rational' adult Men figured the political subject (the Individual), and it is the image of his rights and interests that have most sedimented into the normative and formal structures of our institutions and interpersonal dynamics in the Anglosphere today.[27] This is not only true of our central ethico-political imaginary, but also of our central sexual imag(in)ings. Our sedimented images of Men, Women and their proper relation to one another have, by and large, come from men. Without rehashing too much of what has gone before, I will just say that the pattern I am trying to elucidate here is that, whichever subject is the most 'at home' in that imaginary is usually the same subject whose imaginings and stories carry the force to bestow efficacious meaning on human action and social behaviour. In the central ethico-political imaginary, men (as Men) more closely embody the image of the Individual than do women. Men's imaginings have been, and continue to be, central. In the central sexual imaginary, Men have been figured as the superior sex, both physically and mentally. And it is certainly the case that the images of Woman in this imaginary revere only the mythical Good Woman.[28]

However, this is not to say that women are *powerless* to contest these images.[29] We can put meta-awareness of social identity power to work in favour of the oppressed. First, people can be brought to recognise that they belong to a group with social identity power, and if one so recognises oneself, then one can 'sympathetically apprentice' oneself to members of the subjugated group.[30] Apprenticeship, crucially, involves the cultivation of skills and virtues, of learning how to listen to and adequately comprehend claims of structural injustice.[31] It also requires the meta-awareness that privileged groups *have* prejudicial habits so as to *survey* our prejudicial habits that can always affect our judgement.[32] This is a way of dealing with *insensitivity* to social identity power, but it requires 'a preparedness to adjust (perhaps significantly) how one imagines the world and others in it'.[33] (But this is not yet possible if an agent is stubbornly insensitive to their insensitivities — that is, if they are *meta-insensitive* to social identity power.[34]) Second, for those allies who have become sensitive to the weight of their social identity power, we should continue to allow them to speak *with* us to our cause. This works at the level of credibility attribution. If there is 'a prejudice against taking seriously the experienced world outside of white men' or 'a refusal to enter into truly cooperative interdependence with knowers situated outside dominant social positions' among the meta-insensitive, then they may be more receptive to alternative imag(in)ings when delivered by members of their own ingroup.[35] (But, proceed with caution: it is important allies do not speak *for*, only *with* subjugated peoples with their epistemic resources as they have developed them.[36])

What is more, social identity power is not the only type of structural power that exists. Specifically, as several theorists argue,[37] it is imperative that *institutions* – both formal and informal – function, or are reformed to function, to rectify the effects of stigma tending to oppressive practices. This essentially tracks with what de Silva, Gelber, Molnar and Lepoutre are arguing for in their reimagining of 'counterspeech' (see chapter 5). Wherein power imbalances exist, the argument goes, it is reasonable to enlist the support of stronger parties to rectify forms of systemic discrimination, including patterns of violence. The state is the most obvious source of such an extensive power, but it is not the only body that can 'compete' with deeply entrenched systems of identity power by reimagining those very same identities. There are activist groups who can, for instance, organise and promote the cognitive-affective interventions described above on a large scale through mainstream media (e.g. consider GetUp!'s advert *It's Time* which supported same-gender marriage and which went viral[38]); individuals can congregate to collectively demonstrate via marching, chanting and the use of placards to convey an alternate image or impression to the wider public. This can also be done more informally on a potentially much grander scale through hash-tag activism and even meme-circulation online.[39] This demonstrates 'the potential of online space to be claimed by women and other diverse groups as a counter-cultural space', that is, as a site of and for counterpublics.[40] Michael Warner further explains, 'Counterpublics are spaces of circulation in which it is hoped the poesis of scene making [i.e., imagining] will be transformative'.[41] Hence, feminists constitute a counterpublic insofar as they offer alternative imaginings of how the world might be for women, men and others, in their commitment to gender justice. We might even think of such counterpublics as informal institutions, whose collective acts 'can act as crucial sites for moulding and remoulding individual sentiments, habits of behaviour and imaginaries that shape agency and motivation'.[42] However, the internet is not just a home for justice-oriented counterpublics; there also exist counterpublics who want to assert extreme forms of gender subjugation against women,[43] and we cannot but recognise that internet platforms are crucial sites where 'a battle of the imaginations' is being waged.[44]

CRITIQUE

Critique is a hugely important part of imaginal (r)evolution. While there is no guaranteed method for eliciting an epistemic and affective friction which leads to critique or vice versa – though many agree that *art* does this particularly well[45] – we all can work on developing more critical and curious stances to the worlds in which we find ourselves thrown. We may be inclined to think of some people as 'naturally' inquisitive. But curiosity can be encouraged, and one of the key ways of achieving this is through educating for good questioning. Lani Watson explains that questioning 'guides and shapes inquiry', and good questioning 'enables us to effectively navigate our informational environment',[46] here understood as one's *gestalt*. The aim of questioning is to elicit information, however 'successfully eliciting information is not a requirement for *good* questioning'.[47] This matters because a great many questions are very difficult to answer with much certainty, as philosophy shows us. For, once we begin to philosophise, as Bertrand Russell reminds us, we find

that even the most everyday things lead to problems to which only very incomplete answers can be given. Philosophy, though unable to tell us with certainty what is the true answer to the doubts which it raises, is able to suggest many possibilities which enlarge our thoughts and free them from the tyranny of custom.

Thus, while diminishing our feeling of certainty as to what things are, it greatly increases our knowledge as to what they may be; it removes the somewhat arrogant dogmatism of those who have never travelled into the region of liberating doubt, and it keeps alive our sense of wonder by showing familiar things in an unfamiliar aspect.[48]

From this it is clear to see how asking questions, making the familiar wholly strange (and vice versa) can spawn further questioning, new imaginings and creative solutions to problem which seem to be without answers. The role of philosophy here is not just to separate the true from the false (if this can be known). Rather, philosophy is to be deployed to help us recognise what images we are invested in and whether they fit coherently together; it is also to suggest alternatives to smooth out epistemic and affective frictions. Learning to challenge our assumptions and taken-for-granted attitudes is never a completed process, of course, but cultivating curiousness can encourage a cognitive-affective disposition of openness to alternative images. Learning how to question, to elicit information (even if incomplete), from an early age may just be the kind of training we need to motivate our imagination. These are also skills that can be institutionally supported.

RESONANCE

Because imagination is the faculty involved in perception, and because we rely on pre-established socially shared images as heuristics for understanding while we are in the ongoing process of perception, the implication is that images, including those which oppress (or contribute to oppression), can only ever be replaced with new images. If we critique our central images without offering resonant alternatives, we may trigger meaning-vertigo, the result of which may be a doubling-down on the status quo.[49] We need to do this work at the imaginal level because if conscious, rational, endorsed belief were enough to eliminate the residues of oppressive images, then we would find ourselves in a situation where *only* individual bigots actively harm members of certain socially salient groups, but this is not the case. Oppression is also sustained by the 'unconscious assumptions and reactions of well-meaning people in ordinary interactions, media and cultural stereotypes, and structural features of bureaucratic hierarchies and market mechanisms – in short, the normal processes of everyday life'.[50] Clinging to the belief that human rationality has such power is to deny 'the importance of the affective and imaginative dimensions of human collective life', and indeed the very mechanism through which the world appears as it does for us at all.[51] This is not to say that there is no place for reasoning in the fight to challenge oppressive social imaginaries; indeed, it is imperative for change that problematic images are identified and critiqued – and reasoning is just the right tool for this process. But we must also provide alternatives.[52] In providing an alternative, resonant image, one hopes those who encounter it will 'become sensitive to cruelty and to develop affective capacities to feel empathy, grief, and anger, as well as the cognitive-affective capacities to understand the grief and anger of others'.[53] This is what may lead to a just society.

Now, if an alternative image is to receive dominant uptake, something about that new image must resonate with the communities that are being asked to adopt it. The reason for this is simple: if the new image has no resonance whatsoever, it will be simply incoherent. That said, alternative images can be more or less resonant, or resonate with *other* problematic images. So we must note that while our 'conscious, deliberate images [are] generally designed to fulfil a particular purpose . . . they can still contain presuppositions and have implications which their authors and readers are unaware', such as the problematic ontologies Anya Daly warns us of (see chapter 6).[54] What is important, then, is not to latch onto any single image just because it resonates strongly with the target community, but to also be critical towards the new images one puts forward too in the hopes of minimising the unintended implications of adopting new images as must as possible, and always seeking new modes and models of understanding.

TIME

Finally, we must allow that the process of effecting 'constructive and enduring social change . . . will necessarily be a slow, gradual, and incremental task'.[55] New images take time to sediment into centrally shared imaginaries. This, however, does not mean that we just passively wait in hope that the alternate imag(in)ings offered will become sedimented. Rather, as José Medina makes explicit, we need to engage in 'sustained cultivation of activist interventions over time until they leave a mark'.[56] This is entrenched through acts of remembrance and honour, for example.[57] The act(ivism) of shifting dominant images is ongoing. Cementing the point, Medina continues: 'It is important that we think of activism as aiming not simply at provoking emotional reactions in a public but rather at triggering a complex process of emotional restructuration that needs to unfold over time'.[58] Churcher agrees, writing: 'Reformist strategies that critically engage and negotiate the particular "habits" and "prejudices" of a people in a peaceable yet deep manner pave the way for the development of more robust and enduring attachments of pride and esteem to new standards of practice'.[59] Put differently, the place of duration in this process is inescapable. Just as the effects of past acts of oppression *endure* in one's society, so too can counteractions and counter-imaginings come to endure. The more resonant an image, the quicker its sedimentation may be, but one must think of the 'long game' – not all new imag(in)ings are equally good.

It is plain to see why these elements are necessary in efforts to shift (parts of) the dominant Western social imaginary. Without duration, meaning cannot cement itself; without noticing a contradiction within or across imaginaries, current conditions will pertain; without a desire to change our imaginaries, there is no impetus driving us to deal with the contradictions we encounter; without critique, there is no clear sense of what precisely must change and what might be better; without resonance, there is no 'sense' or communicability of idea or affect; and without understanding how power is manifest in one's milieu, it is not clear how to target our efforts for change or how we may get these efforts to endure. It remains to be seen whether the alternative images I have proposed around hate speech and harm in this book will be found to exhibit each of these six elements. But as for those images still to be imagined, these criteria offer a handy evaluative guide to determine whether we should put such new, borrowed, or repurposed images into circulation.

While this book has been about the problem of hate speech against women online, fundamentally its concern is with the fact that women remain an oppressed group in the Anglosphere today, and that hate speaking against women online is both (a) cause and (one) symptom of this fact. Really, this book is about challenging inequality, about the ways in which our dominant social imaginary can be host to discordant images, including paradoxical figurings of subjects across its constitutive central imaginaries – especially the images of Man, (Good/Bad) Woman, AIUs, and the Individual. I want to see an end to hate speech against women online, but my analysis here is not limited to this desire for a certain sort of well-being. I have sought to explore the ways in which we can change *my* (but really, *any*) milieu such that women will no longer *expect* to, and, in fact, *will not* encounter the discursive violence that is presently meted out to us whenever we venture into public (cyber-)spaces. I also believe tactics for instigating and then cementing imaginal (r)evolution can have far-reaching effects because these criteria for imaginal (r)evolution are adaptable to other contexts where change is needed. That is not to say that solutions will come easy. But I do hope what I have proposed herein functions as a reasonably reliable methodology for the pursuit of imaginal change, one that eventually leads to an alternative egalitarian gestalt.

NOTES

1. Iris Marion Young, *Justice and the Politics of Difference* (Princeton: Princeton University Press, 1990), 6.

2. Jessica Megarry, 'Online Incivility or Sexual Harassment? Conceptualising Women's Experiences in the Digital Age', *Women's Studies International Forum* 47 (2014): 47.

3. Millicent Churcher, *Reimagining Sympathy, Recognizing Difference: Insights from Adam Smith* (London: Rowman and Littlefield International, 2019), 152.

4. Susan James, 'Freedom and the Imaginary', in *Visible Women: Essays on Feminist Legal Theory and Political Philosophy*, ed. Susan James and Stephanie Palmer (Oxford: Hart Publishing, 2002), 187.

5. I have mentioned these in previous research but have not given them a lengthy treatment. See Louise Richardson-Self, 'Same-Sex Marriage and the "No" Campaign', *Humanities Australia* 9 (2018): 32–39, and *Justifying Same-Sex Marriage: A Philosophical Investigation* (London: Rowman and Littlefield International, 2015), chap. 6.

6. Medina calls these forms of 'negative emotional friction' which underpins insensitivity to the plight of the other, versus 'positive emotional friction' which generates support for the new way of seeing one's world. See José Medina, 'Racial Violence, Emotional Friction, and Epistemic Activism', *Angelaki: Journal of the Theoretical Humanities* 24 (2019): 31.

7. Marilyn Frye, *The Politics of Reality: Essays in Feminist Theory* (Freedom: The Crossing Press, 1983) 3.

8. Churcher, *Reimagining Sympathy*, 18.

9. Those groups whose cultural horizon is fundamentally distinct from the group whose world is presented as *the* world, those groups who are – to use Iris Marion Young's (*Justice*, 123) terminology – suffering from cultural imperialism, come to constitute *counterpublics*.

10. Celermajer Danielle Celermajer, Millicent Churcher, Moira Gatens and Anna Hush, 'Institutional Transformations: Imagination, Embodiment, and Affect', *Angelaki* 24 (2019): 8.

11. See Churcher, *Reimagining Sympathy*, 101; José Medina, *The Epistemology of Resistance: Gender and Racial Oppression, Epistemic Injustice, and Resistant Imaginations* (Oxford: Oxford University Press, 2013); Gaile Pohlhaus Jr., 'Relational Knowing and Epistemic Injustice: Toward a Theory of *Willful Hermeneutical Ignorance*', *Hypatia* 27 (2012): 715–735.

12. José Medina, 'On Refusing to Believe: Insensitivity and Self-Ignorance', in *Rationality Reconsidered: Ortega y Gasset and Wittgenstein on Knowledge, Belief, and Practice*, ed. Astrid Wagner and José María Ariso (Berlin: De Gruyter, 2016): 191.

13. Churcher, *Reimagining Sympathy*, 140.

14. Such desire for change must always *centre* the oppressed group, otherwise fellow-feeling can go disastrously wrong. Millicent Churcher discusses how this played out through the paternalistic 'care' shown for Indigenous Australians (who deserved a chance at a 'civilised' life) by 'sympathetic' whites removing children from their families, resulting in what is now known as the Stolen Generations. See Churcher, *Reimagining Sympathy*, 70–75. Rachel McKinnon raises the same concern with respect to trans allies gaslighting the community. See Rachel McKinnon, 'Allies

Behaving Badly: Gaslighting as Epistemic Injustice', in *The Routledge Handbook of Epistemic Injustice*, ed. Ian James Kidd, José Medina, and Gaile, Jr. Pohlhaus (London: Routledge, 2017), 167–174.

15. Young, *Justice*, 5.

16. Churcher, *Reimagining Sympathy*, 40.

17. Celermajer et al., 'Institutional Transformations', 9, my emphasis.

18. Churcher, *Reimagining Sympathy*, chap. 2.

19. As quoted in Churcher, *Reimagining Sympathy*, 50, original emphasis.

20. As Carol Gilligan puts it, 'it is difficult to say "different" without saying "better" or "worse"' (cited in Lucy Nicholas and Christine Agius, *The Persistence of Global Masculinism Discourse, Gender and Neo-Colonial Re-Articulations of Violence* (Cham: Palgrave Macmillan, 2017), 13). What we must seek is 'equal regard' of the Other. See: Richardson-Self, *Same-Sex Marriage*, chap. 3.

21. Young, *Justice*, 171.

22. Moira Gatens, 'The Politics of "Presence" and "Difference": Working through Spinoza and Eliot', in *Visible Women: Essays on Feminist Legal Theory and Political Philosophy*, ed. Susan James and Stephanie Palmer (Oregon: Hart Publishing, 2002), 162.

23. Vittorio Bufacchi and Jools Gilson, 'The Ripples of Violence', *Feminist Review* 112 (2016): 34.

24. Mari Matsuda, 'Public Response to Racist Speech: Considering the Victim's Story', in *Words that Wound: Critical Race Theory, Assaultive Speech, and the First Amendment*, ed. Mari Matsuda, Charles Lawrence III, Richard Delgado, and Kimberlè Crenshaw (Boulder: Westview Press, 1993), 22.

25. Medina, *Epistemology of Resistance*, 15.

26. Moira Gatens, 'Can Human Rights Accommodate Women's Rights? Towards an Embodied Account of Social Norms, Social Meaning, and Cultural Change', *Contemporary Political Theory* 3 (2004): 282.

27. In Iris Marion Young's (*Justice*, 147) words, 'the form of cultural imperialism in the modern West provides and insists on only one subject position, that of the unified, disembodied reason identified with white bourgeois men'.

28. Andrea Dworkin, *Right-Wing Women* (New York: Perigee Books, 1983), 204–208.

29. Amy Allen, 'Rethinking Power', *Hypatia* 13 (1998): 32.

30. Churcher, *Reimagining Sympathy*, 147–148.

31. E.g. eradicating 'embodied habits of inattention, denial and defensiveness' which often strike the subjugated in their efforts to communicate. Celermajer et al., 'Institutional Transformations', 14. See also: Millicent Churcher, 'Reimagining the Northern Territory Intervention: Institutional and cultural interventions into the Anglo-Australian imaginary', *Australian Journal of Social Issues* 53 (2018): 64.

32. Churcher, *Reimagining Sympathy*, XIII.

33. Churcher, *Reimagining Sympathy*, 89.

34. Medina, *Epistemology of Resistance*, 24.

35. Karen Frost-Arnold argues, in cases of online abuse, and in critiques of privileged normative society, subordinated people have, online, offered the image of 'role model' to members of privileged groups via the image of the 'good ally'. The good ally models appropriate behaviour to other privileged people. See: Karen Frost-Arnold, 'Social Media, Trust, and the Epistemology of Prejudice', *Social Epistemology* 30 (2016): 525.

36. Pohlhaus, 'Relational Knowing', 729–731, McKinnon, 'Allies', 167–174.

37. Celermajer et al., 'Institutional Transformations', 3–21.

38. Richardson-Self, *Same-Sex Marriage*, 37.

39. See, for an example of this: Verity Trott, 'Connected Feminists: Foregrounding the Interpersonal in Connective Action', *Australian Journal of Political Science* 53 (2018): 116–129.

40. Bianca Fileborn, 'Justice 2.0: Street Harassment Victims' Use of Social Media and Online Activism as Sites of Informal Justice', *British Journal of Criminology* 57 (2017): 1493.

41. Michael Warner, 'Publics and Counterpublics', *Public Culture* 14 (2002): 88.

42. Celermajer et al., 'Institutional Transformations', 4.

43. Nicholas and Agius, *Global Masculinism*, chap. 2.

44. Millicent Churcher and Moira Gatens, 'Reframing Honour in Heterosexual Imaginaries', *Angelaki* 24 (2019): 158.

45. In addition to those mentioned in chapter 6, see, for example, Churcher, *Reimagining Sympathy*, 167; Katharine Gelber, *Speech Matters: Getting Free Speech Right* (St Lucia: University of Queensland Press, 2011); bell hooks, *Art on My Mind: Visual Politics* (New York: New Press, 1995) and *Outlaw Culture: Resisting Representations* (New York: Routledge, 2008 (1994)); Audre Lorde, *Sister Outsider* (Berkeley: Crossing Press, 2007 [1984]), 36–39.

46. Lani Watson, 'Educating for Good Questioning: A Tool for Intellectual Virtues Education', *Acta Analytica* 33 (2018): 360, 358.

47. Watson, 'Educating', 358, my emphasis. Acting competently involves making "appropriate judgements about who, when, where, and how to elicit information: the good questioner asks the right questions, of the right information source(s), at the right time and place" (ibid.).

48. Bertrand Russell, *The Problems of Philosophy* (Oxford: Oxford University Press, 2001 [1912]), 91.

49. Filipa Melo Lopes, 'Perpetuating the Patriarchy: Misogyny and (Post-) Feminist Backlash', *Philosophical Studies* 176 (2019): 2531.

50. Young, *Justice*, 41.

51. Moira Gatens, 'Conflicting Imaginaries in Australian Multiculturalism: Women's Rights, Group Rights, and Aboriginal Customary Law', in *Political Theory and Australian Multiculturalism*, ed. Geoffrey Brahm Levey (New York: Berghahn Books, 2008), 161.

52. Frost-Arnold, 'Social Media', 525.

53. Medina, 'Racial Violence', 33.

54. Marguerite La Caze, *The Analytic Imaginary* (Ithaca: Cornell University Press, 2002), 13.

55. Churcher, *Reimagining Sympathy*, 141.
56. Medina, 'Racial Violence', 28–29.
57. Medina, 'Racial Violence', 33.
58. Medina, 'Racial Violence', 28–29.
59. Churcher, *Reimagining Sympathy*, 142.

Bibliography

Ahmed, Sara. *The Cultural Politics of Emotion*. 2nd ed. Edinburgh: Edinburgh University Press, 2014.

———. 'Introduction: Sexism—A Problem With A Name'. *New Formations: A Journal of Culture/Theory/Politics* 86 (2015): 5–13.

———. 'The Skin of the Community: Affect and Boundary Formation'. In *Revolt, Affect, Collectivity: The Unstable Boundaries of Kristeva's Polis*, edited by Tina Chanter and Ewa Ziarek. Albany: State University of New York Press, 2005, 95–112.

Alkiviadou, Natalie. 'The Legal Regulation of Hate Speech: The International and European Frameworks'. *Croatian Political Science Review* 55 (2018): 203–229.

Allen, Amy. 'Rethinking Power'. *Hypatia* 13 (1998): 21–40.

Ascher, Diana L. and Sufiya Umoja Noble. 'Unmasking Hate on Twitter: Disrupting Anonymity by Tracking Trolls'. In *Free Speech in the Digital Age*, edited by Susan Brison and Katharine Gelber. Oxford: Oxford University Press, 2019, 170–188.

Ashwell, Lauren. 'Gendered Slurs'. *Social Theory and Practice* 42 (2016): 228–239.

Australian Federal Police. 'Annual Report 2018–19'. *Annual Reports*, 6, 74, 11. October 2019. Accessed 14 July 2020. https://www.afp.gov.au/about-us/publicat ions-and-reports/annual-reports.

———. 'Online Child Sex Exploitation'. *Australian Centre to Counter Child Exploitation*, 2018. Accessed 14 July 2020. https://www.afp.gov.au/what-we-do/s ervices/child-protection/online-child-sex-exploitation.

Australian Government. 'Exposure Draft—Online Safety Bill 2020'. *Consultation on a Bill for a New Online Safety Act*. Accessed 20 February 2021. https://www.com munications.gov.au/have-your-say/consultation-bill-new-online-safety-act.

———. 'Fact Sheet—Online Safety Bill'. *Consultation on a Bill for a New Online Safety Act*. Accessed 20 February 2021. https://www.communications.gov.au/have -your-say/consultation-bill-new-online-safety-act.

———. 'Online Safety Bill—Reading Guide'. *Consultation on a Bill for a New Online Safety Act*. Accessed 20 February 2021. https://www.communications.gov .au/have-your-say/consultation-bill-new-online-safety-act.

Barker, Kim and Olga Jurasz. *Online Misogyny as a Hate Crime: A Challenge for Legal Regulation?* London: Routledge, 2019.

Barlow, John Perry. 'A Declaration of the Independence of Cyberspace'. *Electronic Frontier Foundation*. 8 February 1996. Accessed 11 May 2020. https://www.eff .org/cyberspace-independence.

Beauvoir, Simone de. *The Second Sex*. Translated by Constance Borde and Sheila Malovany-Chevallier. London: Vintage Books, 2010 [1949].

Benhabib, Seyla. *Another Cosmopolitanism*. Oxford: Oxford University Press, 2006.

Bernstein, Jacob. 'How OnlyFans Changed Sex Work Forever'. *The New York Times*. 9 February 2019. Accessed 16 September 2020. https://www.nytimes.com/2019/02 /09/style/onlyfans-porn-stars.html.

Bhagwat, Ashutosh. 'Free Speech Categories in the Digital Age'. In *Free Speech in the Digital Age*, edited by Susan Brison and Katharine Gelber. Oxford: Oxford University Press, 2019, 88–103.

Bottici, Chiara. *Imaginal Politics: Images Beyond Imagination and the Imaginary*. New York: Columbia University Press, 2014.

Bouchard, Gérard. *Social Myths and Collective Imaginaries*. Translated by Howard Scott. Toronto: University of Toronto Press, 2017.

Brecher, Bob. 'Andrea Dworkin's *Pornography: Men Possessing Women*—A Reassessment'. In *Women and Violence: The Agency of Victims and Perpetrators*, edited by Herjeet Marway and Heather Widdows. Basingstoke: Palgrave Macmillan, 2015, 145–161.

Brison, Susan. 'Speech, Harm, and the Mind Body Problem in First Amendment Jurisprudence'. *Legal Theory* 4 (1998): 39–61.

———. '"We Must Find Words or Burn": Speaking Out Against Disciplinary Silencing'. *Feminist Philosophy Quarterly* 3 (2017): 1–10.

Brison, Susan and Katharine Gelber. 'Introduction'. In *Free Speech In The Digital Age*, edited by Susan Brison and Katharine Gelber. Oxford: Oxford University Press, 2019, 1–11.

Broad, Jacqueline. 'The Early Modern Period: Dignity and the Foundation of Women's Rights'. In *The Wollstonecraftian Mind*, edited by Sandrine Bergès, Eileen Hunt Botting and Alan Coffee. London: Routledge, 2019, 25–35.

Brown, Alexander. *Hate Speech Law: A Philosophical Examination*. New York: Routledge, 2015.

———. 'What is Hate Speech? Part 1: The Myth of Hate'. *Law and Philosophy* 35 (2017): 419–468.

———. 'What is Hate Speech? Part 2: Family Resemblances'. *Law and Philosophy* 36 (2017): 561–613.

———. 'What is So Special About Online (As Compared To Offline) Hate Speech'. *Ethnicities* 18 (2017): 297–326.

Bufacchi, Vittorio and Jools Gilson. 'The Ripples of Violence'. *Feminist Review* 112 (2016): 27–40.

Caiani, Manuela and Linda Parenti. 'The Dark Side of the Web: Italian Right-Wing Extremist Groups and the Internet'. *South European Society and Politics* 14 (2009): 273–294.

Calhoun, Cheshire. *Feminism, the Family, and the Politics of the Closet: Lesbian and Gay Displacement*. Oxford: Oxford University Press, 2000.

Card, Claudia. 'Rape as a Terrorist Institution'. In *Violence, Terrorism, and Justice*, edited by R. G. Frey and Christopher W. Morris. Cambridge: Cambridge University Press, 1991, 296–319.

Celermajer, Danielle, Millicent Churcher, Moira Gatens and Anna Hush. 'Institutional Transformations: Imagination, Embodiment, and Affect'. *Angelaki* 24 (2019): 3–21.

Chalmers, Max '"Internet Troll" Zane Alchin Who Mocked Women Threatening Legal Action Enters Guilty Plea'. *New Matilda*. 20 June 2016. Accessed 5 February 2021. https://newmatilda.com/2016/06/20/internet-troll-zane-alchin-who-mocked -women-threatening-to-take-him-to-court-enters-guilty-plea/.

Chambers, Claire. 'Feminism'. In *The Oxford Handbook of Political Ideologies*, edited by Michael Freeden, Lyman Tower Sargent and Marc Stears. Oxford: Oxford University Press, 562–582.

Chemaly, Soraya. 'Demographics, Design, and Free Speech: How Demographics Have Produced Social Media Optimized for Abuse and The Silencing of Marginalized Voices'. In *Free Speech In The Digital Age*, edited by Susan Brison and Katharine Gelber. Oxford: Oxford University Press, 2019, 150–169.

Chen, Gina Masullo, Ashley Muddiman, Tamar Wilner, Eli Pariser and Natalie Jomini Stroud. 'We Should Note Get Rid Of Incivility Online'. *Social Media and Society* 5 (2019): 1–5.

Churcher, Millicent. 'Reimagining the Northern Territory Intervention: Institutional and Cultural Interventions into the Anglo-Australian Imaginary'. *Australian Journal of Social Issues* 53 (2018): 56–70.

———. *Reimagining Sympathy, Recognizing Difference: Insights from Adam Smith*. London: Rowman and Littlefield International, 2019.

Churcher, Millicent and Moira Gatens. 'Reframing Honour in Heterosexual Imaginaries'. *Angelaki* 24 (2019): 151–164.

Citron, Danielle Keats. *Hate Crimes in Cyberspace*. Cambridge: Harvard University Press, 2014.

———. 'Restricting Speech to Protect It'. In *Free Speech In The Digital Age*, edited by Susan Brison and Katharine Gelber. Oxford: Oxford University Press, 2019, 122–136.

Code, Lorraine. 'Patriarchy'. In *Encyclopedia of Feminist Theories*, edited by Lorraine Code. New York: Routledge, 2000, 378–379.

———. 'Sexism'. In *Encyclopedia of Feminist Theories*, edited by Lorraine Code. New York: Routledge, 2000, 441.

Cohen-Almagor, Raphael. *Confronting the Internet's Dark Side: Moral and Social Responsibility on the Free Highway*. New York: Cambridge University press, 2015.

Costello, Matthew and James Hawdon. 'Hate Speech in Online Spaces'. In *The Palgrave Handbook of Cybercrime and Cyberdeviance*, edited by Thomas Holt and Adam Bossler. Cham: Springer Nature, 2020, 1397–1416.

Creed, Barbara. *The Monstrous-Feminine: Film, Feminism, Psychoanalysis*. London: Routledge, 1993.

Curran, James. 'The Internet of Dreams: Reinterpreting the Internet'. In *Misunderstanding the Internet*, edited by James Curran, Natalie Fenton and Des Freedman. 2nd ed. London Routledge, 2016, 1–47.

D'Souza, Tanya, Laura Griffin, Nicole Shackleton and Danielle Walt. 'Harming Women with Words: The Failure of Australian Law to Prohibit Gendered Hate Speech'. *UNSW Law Journal* 41 (2018): 939–976.

Daly, Anya. 'The Declaration of Interdependence! Feminism, Grounding, and Enactivism'. *Human Studies* 44 (2021): 43–62.

Dolkart, Jane. 'Hostile Environment Harassment: Equality, Objectivity, and the Shaping of Legal Standards'. *Emory Law Journal* 43 (1994): 151–244.

Drescher, Jack. 'Queer Diagnoses Revisited: The Past and Future of Homosexuality and Gender'. *International Review of Psychiatry* 27 (2015): 386–395.

Dworkin, Andrea. *Right-Wing Women*. New York: Perigee Books, 1983.

Editors of Encyclopaedia Britannica. 'Troll'. *Encyclopaedia Britannica*. 20 July 1998. Accessed 7 May 2020. https://www.britannica.com/topic/troll.

Electronic Frontiers Foundation. *The Santa Clara Principles: On Transparency and Accountability in Content Moderation*. Accessed 18 February 2021. https://santacl araprinciples.org/.

Facebook. 'Hate Speech'. In *Facebook Community Standards*. Accessed 9 February 2021. https://www.facebook.com/communitystandards/hate_speech.

———. 'Oversight Board'. In *Facebook Community Standards*. Accessed 9 February 2021. https://www.facebook.com/communitystandards/oversight_b oard.

Facebook for Business. 'Admin's Guide to Moderating Your Page'. *Facebook*. Accessed 25 August 2020. https://www.facebook.com/business/a/page-moderatio n-tips.

———. 'Aussies on Facebook: Mobile is the First Screen and Video is Exploding'. *Facebook News*. 9 July 2015. Accessed 12 April 2021. https://www.facebook.com/ business/news/Key-Trends-Australians-on-Facebook.

Facebook Newsroom. 'Stats'. *Facebook Company Info*. Accessed 14 August 2019. https://newsroom.fb.com/company-info/.

Fahs, Breanne. 'Perilous Patches and Pitstaches: Imagined Versus Lived Experiences of Women's Body Hair Growth'. *Psychology of Women Quarterly* 38 (2014): 167–180.

Fattal, Alex. 'Counterpublic'. In *The International Encyclopedia of Anthropology*, edited by Hilary Callan. London: John Wiley & Sons, 2018, 1–2.

Fausto-Sterling, Anne. *Sexing the Body: Gender Politics and the Construction of Sexuality*. New York: Basic Books, 2020.

Felmlee, Diane, Paulina Inara Rodis and Amy Zhang. 'Sexist Slurs: Reinforcing Feminine Stereotypes Online'. *Sex Roles* 83 (2019): 16–28.

Fileborn, Bianca. 'Justice 2.0: Street Harassment Victims' Use of Social Media and Online Activism as Sites of Informal Justice'. *British Journal of Criminology* 57 (2017): 1482–1501.

Fileborn Bianca and Rachel Loney-Howes, eds. *#MeToo and the Politics of Social Change*. Cham: Palgrave Macmillan, 2019.

Ford, Clementine. *Fight Like A Girl*. Sydney: Allen & Unwin, 2016.

Franks, Mary Anne. 'Not Where Bodies Live: The Abstraction of Internet Expression'. In *Free Speech In The Digital Age*, edited by Susan Brison and Katharine Gelber. Oxford: Oxford University Press, 2019, 137–149.

Fraser, Nancy. 'Rethinking the Public Sphere: A Contribution to the Critique of Actually Existing Democracy'. In *Habermas and the Public Sphere*, edited by Craig Calhoun. Cambridge: MIT Press, 1992, 109–142.

Freedman, Des. 'The Internet of Rules'. In *Misunderstanding the Internet*, edited by James Curran, Natalie Fenton and Des Freedman. 2nd ed. London Routledge, 2016, 117–114.

Fricker, Miranda. *Epistemic Injustice: Power and the Ethics of Knowing*. Oxford: Oxford University Press, 2007.

Frost-Arnold, Karen. 'Social Media, Trust, and the Epistemology of Prejudice'. *Social Epistemology* 30 (2016): 513–531.

Frye, Marilyn. *The Politics of Reality: Essays in Feminist Theory*. Freedom: The Crossing Press, 1983.

Gatens, Moira. 'Can Human Rights Accommodate Women's Rights? Towards an Embodied Account of Social Norms, Social Meaning, and Cultural Change'. *Contemporary Political Theory* 3 (2004): 275–299.

———. 'Conflicting Imaginaries in Australian Multiculturalism: Women's Rights, Group Rights, and Aboriginal Customary Law'. In *Political Theory and Australian Multiculturalism*, edited by Geoffrey Brahm Levey. New York: Berghahn Books, 2008, 151–170.

———. *Feminism and Philosophy: Perspectives on Difference and Equality*. Cambridge: Polity Press, 1991.

———. *Imaginary Bodies: Ethics, Power, and Corporeality*. London: Routledge, 1996.

———. 'The Politics of "Presence" and "Difference": Working through Spinoza and Eliot'. In *Visible Women: Essays on Feminist Legal Theory and Political Philosophy*, edited by Susan James and Stephanie Palmer. Oxford: Hart Publishing, 2002, 159–174.

———. 'Polysemy, Atopia, and Feminist Thought'. In *Michèle Le Dœuff: Operative Philosophy and Imaginary Practice*, edited by Max Deutscher. Amherst: Humanity Books, 2000, 45–59.

Gatens, Moira and Genevieve Lloyd. *Collective Imaginings: Spinoza, Past and Present*. London: Routledge, 1999.

Gelber, Katharine. 'Differentiating Hate Speech: A Systemic Discrimination Approach'. *Critical Review of International Social and Political Philosophy* (2019): 1–22. https://doi.org/10.1080/13698230.2019.1576006.

———. 'Reconceptualizing Counterspeech in Hate Speech Policy (with a Focus on Australia)'. In *The Context and Content of Hate Speech: Rethinking Regulation and Response*, edited by Michael Herz and Peter Molnar. New York: Cambridge University Press, 2012, 198–216.

———. *Speech Matters: Getting Free Speech Right*. St Lucia: University of Queensland Press, 2011.

Gelber, Katharine and Susan Brison. 'Digital Dualism and the "Speech as Thought" Paradox'. In *Free Speech In The Digital Age*, edited by Susan Brison and Katharine Gelber. Oxford: Oxford University Press, 2019, 12–32.

Gelber, Katharine and Luke McNamara. 'Anti-vilification Laws and Public Racism in Australia: Mapping the Gaps Between the Harms Occasioned and the Remedies Provided'. *UNSW Law Journal* 39 (2016): 488–511.

Gilbert, Ben. 'How Facebook Makes Money From Your Data, in Mark Zuckerberg's Words'. *Business Insider Australia*. 12 April 2018. Accessed 4 June 2020. https://www.businessinsider.com.au/how-facebook-makes-money-according-to-mark-zuckerberg-2018-4?r=US&IR=T.

Gillespie, Tarleton. *Custodians of the Internet: Platforms, Content Moderation, and the Hidden Decisions that Shape Social Media*. New Haven: Yale University Press, 2018.

Ging, Debbie and Eugenia Siapera, eds. *Gender Hate Online: Understanding the New Anti-Feminism*. Cham: Palgrave Macmillan, 2019.

Gorman, Ginger. *Troll Hunting: Inside the World of Online Hate and Its Human Fallout*. Melbourne: Hardie Grant Books, 2019.

Grosz, Elizabeth. *Volatile Bodies: Toward A Corporeal Feminism*. St Leonards: Allen and Unwin, 1994.

Gunkel, David J. 'Editorial: Introduction to Hacking and Hacktivism'. *New Media and Society* 7 (2005): 595–597.

Habermas, Jürgen. 'The Public Sphere: An Encyclopedia Article (1964)'. *New German Critique* 3 (1974): 49.

Haraszti, Miklos. 'Foreword: Hate Speech and the Coming Death of the International Standard before It Was Born'. In *The Context and Content of Hate Speech: Rethinking Regulation and Response*, edited by Michael Herz and Peter Molnar. New York: Cambridge University Press, 2012, xiii–xviii.

Harjunen, Hannele. *Neoliberal Bodies and the Gendered Fat Body*. London: Routledge, 2016.

Harmer, Emily and Sarah Lewis. 'Disbelief and Counter-Voices: A Thematic Analysis of Online Reader Comments About Sexual Harassment and Sexual Violence Against Women'. *Information, Communication and Society* (2020). https://doi.org/10.1080/1369118X.2020.1770832.

Herbenick, Debby, Tsung-Chieh Fu, Paul Wright, Bryant Paul, Ronna Gradus, Jill Bauer and Rashida Jones. 'Diverse Sexual Behaviors and Pornography Use: Findings From a Nationally Representative Probability Survey of Americans Aged 18 to 60 Years'. *The Journal of Sexual Medicine* 17 (2020): 623–633.

hooks, bell. *Ain't I a Woman: Black Women and Feminism*. London: Pluto Press, 1982.

———. *Art on My Mind: Visual Politics*. New York: New Press, 1995.

———. *Outlaw Culture: Resisting Representations*. New York: Routledge, 2008.

Horvath, Miranda A. H., Llian Alys, Kristina Massey, Afroditi Pina, Mia Scally and Joanna R. Adler. '"Basically...Porn is Everywhere": A Rapid Evidence Assessment on the Effects that Access and Exposure to Pornography has on Children and Young People'. *The Office of the Children's Commissioner (England).* 2013. Accessed 15 September 2020. https://www.mdx.ac.uk/__data/assets/pdf_file/0026/48545/BasicallyporniseverywhereReport.pdf.

Inspiring the Future. 'Redraw the Balance'. *YouTube.com.* 15 March 2016. Accessed January 20, 2020. https://www.youtube.com/watch?v=qv8VZVP5csA.

James, Alexandra, Jennifer Power and Andrea Waling. 'Conceptualising the Continuum of Female Genital Fashioning Practices'. *Health Sociology Review* (2020): 1–18. https://doi.org/10.1080/14461242.2020.1811749.

James, Susan. 'Freedom and the Imaginary'. In *Visible Women: Essays on Feminist Legal Theory and Political Philosophy*, edited by Susan James and Stephanie Palmer. Oxford: Hart Publishing, 2002, 175–195.

Jane, Emma. 'Feminist Digilante Responses to a Slut-Shaming on Facebook'. *Social Media and Society* 3 (2017): 1–10.

———. 'Gendered Cyberhate as Workplace Harassment and Economic Vandalism'. *Feminist Media Studies* 18 (2018): 575–591.

———. *Misogyny Online: A Short (and Brutish) History.* Los Angeles: Sage Swifts, 2017.

Janzen, Caitlin, Susan Strega, Leslie Brown, Jeannie Morgan and Jeannine Carrière. '"Nothing Short of a Horror Show": Triggering Abjection of Street Workers in Western Canadian Newspapers'. *Hypatia* 28 (2013): 142–162.

Ketchell, Misha. 'Australia Doesn't Protect Free Speech, But It Could'. *The Conversation.* 7 June 2019. Accessed 22 May 2020. https://theconversation.com/australia-doesnt-protect-free-speech-but-it-could-118448.

Kim, Won, Ok-Ran Jeong, Chulyun Kim and Jungmin So. 'The Dark Side of the Internet: Attacks, Costs and Responses'. *Information Systems* 36 (2011): 675–705.

Kristeva, Julia. *Powers of Horror: An Essay on Abjection.* New York: Columbia University Press, 1982.

Krueger, Joel and Lucy Osler. 'Engineering Affect: Emotion Regulation, the Internet, and the Techno-Social Niche'. *Philosophical Topics* 47 (2019): 205–232.

Kukla, Quill. 'Slurs, Interpellation, and Ideology'. *The Southern Journal of Philosophy* 56 (2018): 7–32.

La Caze, Marguerite. *The Analytic Imaginary.* Ithaca: Cornell University Press, 2002.

Langton, Rae. *Sexual Solipsism: Philosophical Essays on Pornography and Objectification.* Oxford: Oxford University Press, 2009.

Lawrence, Charles, Mari Matsuda, Richard Delgado and Kimberlè Williams Crenshaw. 'Introduction'. In *Words that Wound: Critical Race Theory, Assaultive Speech, and the First Amendment*, edited by Mari Matsuda, Charles R. Lawrence III, Richard Delgado and Kimberlè Williams Crenshaw. Boulder: Westview Press, 1993, 1–16.

Lennon, Kathleen. 'Imaginary Bodies and World'. *Inquiry* 47 (2004): 107–122.

———. *Imagination and the Imaginary.* London: Routledge, 2015.

Lepoutre, Maxime. 'Hate Speech Laws: Expressive Power Is Not The Answer'. *Legal Theory* 25 (2020): 272–296.

Lillian, Donna. 'A Thorn by Any Other Name: Sexist Discourse as Hate Speech'. *Discourse and Society* 18 (2007): 719–740.

Lloyd, Genevieve. *The Man of Reason: Male and Female in Western Philosophy.* New Yorkshire: Methuen, 1984.

Locke, John. 'Chap. xxvii. Of Identity and Diversity'. In *Great Books of the Western World*, edited by Mortimer J. Adler. vol. 33. Chicago: Encyclopædia Britannica Inc., 1994, 218–228.

Lopes, Filipa Melo. 'Perpetuating the Patriarchy: Misogyny and (Post-)Feminist Backlash'. *Philosophical Studies* 176 (2019): 2517–2538.

Lord, Beth. 'Spinoza on Thinking Substance and the Non-Substantial Mind'. In *Philosophy of Mind in the Early Modern and Modern Ages: The History of The Philosophy of Mind*, edited by Rebecca Copenhaver. Vol. 4. London: Routledge, 2018, 174–194.

Lorde, Audre. *Sister Outsider.* Berkeley: Crossing Press, 2007.

Lu, Alexander and Y. Joel Wong. 'Stressful Experiences of Masculinity Among U.S.-Born and Immigrant Asian American Men'. *Gender and Society* 27 (2013): 345–371.

Lutz, Christoph and Christian Pieter Hoffmann. 'The Dark Side of Online Participation: Exploring Non-, Passive and Negative Participation'. *Information, Communication & Society* 20 (2017): 876–897.

Lynch, Michael P. *The Internet of Us: Knowing More and Understanding Less in the Age of Big Data.* New York: Liveright Publishing Corporation, 2016.

MacKinnon, Catharine. *Only Words.* Cambridge: Harvard University Press, 1993.

———. 'Sexuality, Pornography, and Method: Pleasure Under Patriarchy'. *Ethics* 99 (1989): 314–316.

Maitra, Ishani. 'Subordinating Speech'. In *Speech and Harm: Controversies Over Free Speech*, edited by Ishani Maitra and Mary Kate McGowan. Oxford: Oxford University Press, 2012, 94–120.

Maitra, Ishani and Mary Kate McGowan. 'Introduction and Overview'. In *Speech and Harm: Controversies Over Free Speech*, edited by Ishani Maitra and Mary Kate McGowan. Oxford: Oxford University Press, 2012, 1–23.

Makin David A. and Amber L. Morczek. 'The Dark Side of Internet Searches: A Macro Level Assessment of Rape Culture'. *International Journal of Cyber Criminology* 9 (2015): 1–23.

Manne, Kate. *Down Girl: The Logic of Misogyny.* Oxford: Oxford University Press, 2018.

———. *Entitled.* New York: Crown, 2020.

Mantilla, Karla. *Gendertrolling: How Misogyny Went Viral.* Santa Barbara: Praeger, 2015.

Matsuda, Mari. 'Public Response to Racist Speech: Considering the Victim's Story'. In *Words that Wound: Critical Race Theory, Assaultive Speech, and the First Amendment*, edited by Mari Matsuda, Charles R. Lawrence III, Richard Delgado, and Kimberlè Williams Crenshaw. Boulder: Westview Press, 1993, 17–53.

McCarthy, Niall. 'Facebook Deleted More Than 2 Billion Fake Accounts In The First Quarter of the Year'. *Forbes.* 24 May 2019. Accessed 7 May 2020. https

://www.forbes.com/sites/niallmccarthy/2019/05/24/facebook-deleted-more-than
-2-billion-fake-accounts-in-the-first-quarter-of-the-year-infographic/#f8bab9167
e30.

McGowan, Mary Kate. 'Oppressive Speech'. *Australasian Journal of Philosophy* 87 (2009): 389–407.

———. *Just Words: On Speech and Hidden Harm*. Oxford: Oxford University Press, 2019.

McKinnell, Jamie. 'Former Detainee Dylan Voller Gets Court Win Against Media Giants Over Facebook Comments'. *ABC News*. 24 June 2019. Accessed 10 February 2021. https://www.abc.net.au/news/2019-06-24/court-finds-media-liable
-for-facebook-comments-by-public/11240826.

McKinnon, Rachel. 'Allies Behaving Badly: Gaslighting as Epistemic Injustice'. In *The Routledge Handbook of Epistemic Injustice*, edited by Ian James Kidd, José Medina and Gaile, Jr. Pohlhaus. London: Routledge, 2017, 167–174.

McNair, Brian, Terry Flew, Stephen Harrington and Adam Swift. *Politics, Media, and Democracy in Australia: Public and Producer Perceptions of the Political Public Sphere*. New York: Routledge, 2017.

McNamara, Luke. 'Explainer: What is Section 18C and Why Do Some Politicians Want It Changed?' *The Conversation*. 1 September 2016. Accessed 9 February 2021. https://theconversation.com/explainer-what-is-section-18c-and-why-do-s
ome-politicians-want-it-changed-64660.

McWeeny, Jennifer. 'Operative Intentionality'. In *50 Key Concepts for a Critical Phenomenology*, edited by Gail Weiss, Ann V. Murphy and Gayle Salamon. Evanston: Northwestern University Press, 2020, 255–261.

Meade, Amanda. 'Facebook Threatens to Block Australians from Sharing News in Battle Over Landmark Media Law'. *The Guardian*. 1 September 2020. Accessed 20 February 2021. https://www.theguardian.com/media/2020/sep/01/facebook-
instagram-threatens-block-australians-sharing-news-landmark-accc-media-law.

Medina, José. *The Epistemology of Resistance: Gender and Racial Oppression, Epistemic Injustice, and Resistant Imaginations*. Oxford: Oxford University Press, 2013.

———. 'On Refusing to Believe: Insensitivity and Self-Ignorance'. In *Rationality Reconsidered: Ortega y Gasset and Wittgenstein on Knowledge, Belief, and Practice*, edited by Astrid Wagner and José María Ariso. Berlin: De Gruyter, 2016, 187–199.

———. 'Racial Violence, Emotional Friction, and Epistemic Activism'. *Angelaki: Journal of the Theoretical Humanities* 24 (2019): 22–37.

———. 'The Relevance of Credibility Excess in a Proportional View of Epistemic Injustice: Differential Epistemic Authority and the Social Imaginary'. *Social Epistemology* 25 (2011): 15–35.

Megarry, Jessica. 'Online Incivility or Sexual Harassment? Conceptualising Women's Experiences in the Digital Age'. *Women's Studies International Forum* 47 (2014): 46–55.

Molnar, Peter. 'Responding to "Hate Speech" with Art, Education, and the Imminent Danger Test'. In *The Context and Content of Hate Speech: Rethinking Regulation and Response*, edited by Michael Herz and Peter Molnar. New York: Cambridge University Press, 2012, 183–197.

Morag, Talia. 'Comparison or Seeing-As? The Holocaust and Factory Farming'. In *Morality in a Realistic Spirit: Essays for Cora Diamond*, edited by Andrew Gleeson and Craig Taylor. New York: Routledge, 2019, 194–214.

Naffine, Ngaire. 'Can Women Be Legal Persons?' In *Visible Women: Essays on Feminist Legal Theory and Political Philosophy,* edited by Susan James and Stephanie Palmer. Oxford: Hart Publishing, 2002, 69–90.

Ngo, Helen. *The Habits of Racism: A Phenomenology of Racism and Racialized Embodiment*. Lanham: Lexington Books, 2017.

Nicholas, Lucy and Christine Agius, *The Persistence of Global Masculinism Discourse, Gender and Neo-Colonial Re-Articulations of Violence*. Cham: Palgrave Macmillan, 2017.

Nussbaum, Martha. 'Objectification'. *Philosophy and Public Affairs* 24 (1995): 249–291.

———. 'Objectification and Internet Misogyny'. In *The Offensive Internet*, edited by Saul Levmore and Martha Nussbaum. Cambridge: Harvard University Press, 2010, 68–87.

O'Brien, Connor. 'A Look Back at Most Controversial Tony Abbott Moments, after Prime Minister Apologises for Winking'. *News.com.au.* 23 May 2014. Accessed 15 April 2020. https://www.news.com.au/national/a-look-back-at-most-controv ersial-tony-abbott-moments-after-prime-minister-apologises-for-winking/news-sto ry/8cf978d61184346161ff48ec0099cb02.

Osler, Lucy. 'Feeling Togetherness Online: A Phenomenological Sketch of Online Communal Experiences'. *Phenomenology and the Cognitive Sciences* 19 (2020): 569–588.

———. 'See You Online'. *The Philosopher's Magazine* 90 (2020): 80–86.

———. 'Taking Empathy Online'. *Inquiry* (2021): 18. https://doi.org/10.1080/0 020174X.2021.1899045.

Paasonen, Susanna. *Carnal Resonance: Affect and Online Pornography*. Cambridge: The MIT Press, 2011.

Pateman, Carole. *The Sexual Contract*. Stanford: Stanford University Press, 1988.

Perry, Imani. *Vexy Thing: On Gender and Liberation*. Durham: Duke University Press, 2018.

Phillips, Anne. 'Defending Equality of Outcome'. *The Journal of Political Philosophy* 12 (2004): 1–19.

Phillips, Whitney. *This Is Why We Can't Have Nice Things: Mapping The Relationship Between Online Trolling and Mainstream Culture*. Cambridge: MIT Press, 2015.

Pohlhaus Jr., Gaile. 'Relational Knowing and Epistemic Injustice: Toward a Theory of *Willful Hermeneutical Ignorance*'. *Hypatia* 27 (2012): 715–735.

PornHub. 'The 2019 Year In Review'. *PornHub Insights*. 11 December 2019. Accessed 14 July 2020. https://www.pornhub.com/insights/2019-year-in-review.

Post, Robert. 'Privacy, Speech, and the Digital Imagination'. In *Free Speech In The Digital Age*, edited by Susan Brison and Katharine Gelber. Oxford: Oxford University Press, 2019, 104–121.

Powell, Anastasia. 'Seeking Rape Justice: Formal and Informal Responses to Sexual Violence Through Technosocial Counter-Publics'. *Theoretical Criminology* 19 (2015): 571–88.

Powell, Anastasia and Nicola Henry. *Sexual Violence in a Digital Age*. London: Palgrave Macmillan, 2017.

Purtill, James. 'Facebook Thinks It Won the Battle of the Media Bargaining Code—But So Does the Government'. *ABC News*. 26 February 2021. Accessed 15 March 2021. https://www.abc.net.au/news/science/2021-02-26/facebook-google-who -won-battle-news-media-bargaining-code/13193106.

Q+A. 'Bargaining with Big Tech'. Hosted by Hamish Macdonald. Aired 18 February 2021 on ABC. https://www.abc.net.au/qanda/2021-18-02/13141040.

Rich, Adrienne. 'Compulsory Heterosexuality and Lesbian Existence (1980)'. *Journal of Women's History* 16 (2003): 11–48.

Richardson-Self, Louise. 'Cis-Hetero-Misogyny Online'. *Ethical Theory and Moral Practice* 22 (2019): 573–587.

———. *Justifying Same-Sex Marriage: A Philosophical Investigation*. London: Rowman and Littlefield International, 2015.

———. 'Offending White Men: Racial Vilification, Misrecognition, and Epistemic Injustice'. *Feminist Philosophy Quarterly* 4 (2018): 1–25.

———. 'Same-Sex Marriage and the "No" Campaign'. *Humanities Australia* 9 (2018): 32–39.

———. '"There are Only Two Genders—Male and Female..." An Analysis of Online Responses to Tasmania Removing "Gender" from Birth Certificates'. *International Journal of Gender, Sexuality and Law* (2020): 295–322.

———. 'Woman-Hating: On Misogyny, Sexism, and Hate Speech'. *Hypatia* 33 (2018): 256–272.

Roberts, Sarah T. *Behind The Screen: Content Moderation in the Shadows of Social Media*. New Haven: Yale University Press, 2019.

Roberts, Steven, Signe Ravn, Marcus Maloney and Brittany Ralph. 'Navigating the Tensions of Normative Masculinity: Homosocial Dynamics in Australian Young Men's Discussions of Sexting Practices'. *Cultural Sociology* 15 (2020): 22–43.

Rosaldo, Michelle Zimbalist. 'Women, Culture, and Society: A Theoretical Overview'. In *Woman, Culture, and Society*, edited by Michelle Zimbalist Rosaldo and Louise Lamphere. Stanford: Stanford University Press, 1974, 17–42.

Russell, Bertrand. *The Problems of Philosophy*. Oxford: Oxford University Press, 2001.

Salvatore, Armando. 'New Media, the "Arab Spring", and the Metamorphosis of the Public Sphere: Beyond Western Assumptions on Collective Agency and Democratic Politics'. *Constellations* 20 (2013): 217–228.

Savigny, Heather. *Cultural Sexism: The Politics of Feminist Rage in the #MeToo Era*. Bristol: Bristol University Press, 2020.

Scharff, Christina. *Repudiating Feminism: Young Women in a Neoliberal World*. Surrey: Ashgate, 2012.

Schauer, Frederick. 'Recipes, Plans, Instructions, and the Free Speech Implications of Words That Are Tools'. In *Free Speech In The Digital Age*, edited by Susan Brison and Katharine Gelber. Oxford: Oxford University Press, 2019, 74–87.

Sills, Sophie, Chelsea Pickens, Karishma Beach, Lloyd Jones, Octavia Calder-Dawe, Paulette Benton-Greig and Nicola Gavey. 'Rape Culture and Social Media: Young Critics and a Feminist Counterpublic'. *Feminist Media Studies* 12 (2016): 1–17

Silva, Anjalee de. 'Addressing the Vilification of Women: A Functional Theory of Harm and Implications for Law'. *Melbourne University Law Review* 43 (2020): 1–46.

Sinclair, John. 'Political Economy and Discourse in Murdoch's Flagship Newspaper, *The Australian*'. *The Political Economy of Communication* 4 (2016): 3–17.

Skoda, Kaylee and Cory L. Pedersen. 'Size Matters after All: Experimental Evidence that SEM Consumption Influences Genital and Body Esteem in Men'. *SAGE Open* 9 (2019): 1–11.

Sobieraj, Sarah. 'Bitch, Slut, Skank, Cunt: Patterned Resistance to Women's Visibility in Digital Publics'. *Information, Communication and Society* 21 (2018): 1700–1714.

Sorial, Sarah. *Sedition and the Advocacy of Violence: Free Speech and Counter-Terrorism*. London: Routledge, 2013.

Stjernfelt, Frederik and Anne Mette Lauritzen. *Your Post Has Been Removed: Tech Giants and Freedom of Speech*. Cham: Springer Open, 2020.

Stoops, Jamie. 'Just Like Heroin: Science, Pornography, and Heteronormativity in the Virtual Public Sphere'. *Porn Studies* 4 (2017): 364–380.

Su, Leona Yi-Fan, Michael A Xenos, Kathleen M Rose, Christopher Wirz, Dietram A Scheufele and Dominique Brossard. 'Uncivil and Personal? Comparing Patterns of Incivility in Comments on the Facebook Pages of News Outlets'. *New Media and Society* 20 (2018): 3678–3699.

Summers, Anne. *Damned Whores and God's Police*, 2nd ed. Victoria: Penguin Books, 1994.

Tasmania Law Reform Institute. *Legal Recognition of Sex and Gender*. Final Report No. 31 (June 2020) 129. Accessed 11 April 2020. https://www.utas.edu.au/__data/assets/pdf_file/0018/1342080/tlri-legal-recognition-of-sex-final-report.pdf.

Taylor, Charles. *Modern Social Imaginaries*. Durham: Duke University Press, 2004.

Thornton, Margaret. 'Affirmative Action, Merit and the Liberal State'. *Australian Journal of Law and Society* 2 (1985): 28–40.

Tirrell, Lynne. 'Genocidal Language Games'. In *Speech and Harm: Controversies Over Free Speech*, edited by Ishani Maitra and Mary Kate McGowan. Oxford: Oxford University Press, 2012, 174–221.

———. 'Toxic Misogyny and the Limits of Counterspeech'. *Fordham Law Review* 87 (2019): 2433–2452.

Triple, J. Hack. 'What is Going on With Facebook's News Ban?' *ABC News*. 18 February 2021. Accessed 20 February 2021. https://www.abc.net.au/triplej/programs/hack/facebook-news-ban-explained/13168152.

Trott, Verity. 'Connected Feminists: Foregrounding the Interpersonal in Connective Action'. *Australian Journal of Political Science* 53 (2018): 116–129.

Vickery, Jacqueline Ryan and Tracy Everbach, eds., *Mediating Misogyny: Gender, Technology, and Harassment*. Cham: Palgrave Macmillan, 2018.

Wade, Lisa and Myra Marx Ferree. *Gender: Ideas, Interactions, Institutions.* 2nd ed. New York: W. W. Norton and Company, 2019.

Waldron, Jeremy. *The Harm in Hate Speech.* Cambridge: Harvard University Press, 2012.

Warner, Michael. 'Publics and Counterpublics'. *Public Culture* 14 (2002): 49–90.

Watson, Lani. 'Educating for Good Questioning: A Tool for Intellectual Virtues Education'. *Acta Analytica* 33 (2018): 353–370.

Weber, Patrick. 'Discussions in the Comments Section: Factors Influencing Participation and Interactivity in Online Newspapers' Reader Comments'. *New Media and Society* 16 (2013): 941–957.

Weinstein, James. 'Cyber Harassment and Free Speech: Drawing the Line Online'. In *Free Speech In The Digital Age*, edited by Susan Brison and Katharine Gelber. Oxford: Oxford University Press, 2019, 52–73.

Weston-Scheuber, Kylie. 'Gender and the Prohibition of Hate Speech'. *QUT Law and Justice Journal* 12 (2012): 132–150.

Whitbourn, Michaela. 'High Court to Hear Appeal over Controversial Facebook Defamation Ruling'. *Sydney Morning Herald.* 8 December 2020. Accessed 9 February 2021. https://www.smh.com.au/national/high-court-to-hear-appeal-over -controversial-facebook-defamation-ruling-20201208-p56lnz.html.

Y. F. and Lolrus. 'Rules of the Internet'. *Know Your Meme.* 2019. Accessed 13 July 2020. https://knowyourmeme.com/memes/rules-of-the-internet.

Young, Iris Marion. *Justice and the Politics of Difference.* Princeton: Princeton University Press, 1990.

———. *Throwing Like A Girl and Other Essays in Feminist Philosophy and Social Theory.* Bloomington: Indiana University Press, 1990.

Zuylen-Wood, Simon van. '"Men are Scum": Inside Facebook's War on Hate Speech'. *Vanity Fair.* 26 February 2019. Accessed 16 February 2021. https://www .vanityfair.com/news/2019/02/men-are-scum-inside-facebook-war-on-hate-speech.

Index

About the Author

Louise Richardson-Self is a feminist social philosopher and lecturer in philosophy and gender studies at the University of Tasmania. She was awarded her PhD in philosophy from the University of Sydney in 2014.

She is currently an Australian Research Council Discovery Early Research Career Awardee (DE190100719: Hate Speech Against Women Online: Concepts and Countermeasures) and an Australian Research Council Discovery Awardee (DP200100395: Religious Freedom, LGBT+ Employees, and the Right to Discriminate, led by Prof. Douglas Ezzy). Louise also held a visiting position with the Humanities Institute, University of Connecticut (2017), as part of the Humility & Conviction in Public Life Project.

She publishes on a wide range of issues spanning political philosophy, feminist philosophy, queer theory, ethics and social epistemology. Her first book, *Justifying Same-Sex Marriage: A Philosophical Investigation*, was published with Rowman & Littlefield International in 2015.

Louise's research has been commended through the awarding of the Australian Academy of the Humanities' 2016 Max Crawford Medal, the Australasian Association of Philosophy's (AAP) 2019 Annette Baier Prize, and the UTAS College of Arts, Law and Education's 2019 Early Career Researcher Award.

You can keep up to date with Louise's latest publications on Twitter: @ LVRSelf